Hijacking

the

Runway

Hijacking

the
Runway

HOW CELEBRITIES ARE STEALING
THE SPOTLIGHT FROM FASHION DESIGNERS

TERI AGINS

GOTHAM BOOKS

GOTHAM BOOKS
Published by the Penguin Group
Penguin Group (USA) LLC
375 Hudson Street
New York, New York 10014

USA | Canada | UK | Ireland | Australia | New Zealand | India | South Africa | China
penguin.com
A Penguin Random House Company

LIBRARY OF CONGRESS CATALOGING-IN-PUBLICATION DATA
Agins, Teri.
Hijacking the runway : how celebrities are stealing the spotlight from
fashion designers / Teri Agins.
pages cm
Includes bibliographical references and index.
ISBN 978-1-592-40814-6 (hardback)
1. Clothing trade.   2. Fashion designers.   3. Celebrities.   4. Fashion.   I. Title.
HD9940.A2A353 2014
338.4'774692—dc23   2014008407

Printed in the United States of America
1   3   5   7   9   10   8   6   4   2

Set in Sabon LT Std
Designed by Spring Hoteling

To Genie, with all my love

Contents

CONTENTS

PROLOGUE

Billion-Dollar Babe:
Jessica Simpson and the New Age of Celebrity

On a March 2012 episode of *Fashion Star*, the Tuesday-night NBC reality-show competition featuring unknown designers, celebrity judge Jessica Simpson asked a contestant named Nicholas why his designs had so many zippers. A smug Nicholas told Simpson that if she only *understood* fashion-forward menswear trends, she would get it, adding, "It's very hard to understand the girls giving advice about men's fashion."

But Simpson, whose fast-growing namesake fashion label was becoming the millennial generation's answer to Liz Claiborne, wasn't having it. She snapped back: "I'm a little bit offended. Not a little bit, *a lot of bit*. To talk down to a woman in this business? We're running the world right now, okay? I'm trying to help." She added, chuckling, "I really kind of want to hit you across the face right now."

Her smackdown drew cheers from the TV audience as Simpson, the face behind her billion-dollar fashion brand, kept smiling.

Who could ever have imagined fifteen years earlier that this former teen backup singer from the outskirts of Dallas would have grown up to become a mainstream force in American fashion, with a footprint in European countries like Greece and Spain as well?

The Virgin Bride

Simpson's odyssey as a tastemaker had begun in 1997, when the newly signed Sony Music artist met Rachel Zoe, perhaps the most important of the many newcomers who soon would begin entering Simpson's dramatically changing life. Zoe was one of a new breed of Hollywood image makers known as stylists, who were essentially well-paid fashion fixers, using good taste and designer connections to give their clients arresting, individual looks. In order to have a shot at pop stardom, Simpson would need such a makeover. So Tommy Mottola, the CEO of Sony Music, introduced Zoe and Jessica. "She was seventeen," Zoe remembered to me in 2012. "She came to me with peroxide long hair and long nails. She couldn't have been more adorable. She didn't take herself too seriously."

Simpson was coming of age as a child of MTV and VH1 videos in the fast-paced era when entertainers started to worry about their on-camera close-ups as much as their singing voices and acting talents. They were particularly attentive to style and to fashion detailing. They had little choice. In the final years of the twentieth century, a convergence of media, social, and marketing trends were evolving a celebrity-centric culture, producing a perpetual parade of famous and infamous characters—bona fide and contrived—that fed a willing public's burgeoning fixation on living vicariously.

The ubiquitous images of celebrities invaded our homes. They entered our personal spaces on the covers of every magazine and on all our screens: computer, cell phone, and wall-to-wall reality TV. The sheer volume of the exposure was punctuated by the Instagram immediacy of social media, which boosted celebrity scrutiny exponentially. An orgy of year-round celebrity self-celebration ensued. The Oscars, Grammys, Golden Globes, Emmys, Video Music Awards, Cannes and Sundance film festivals, and assorted red-carpet events fueled celebrity worship for an insatiable global audience. Paparazzi armed with 200-mm lenses stalked in the bushes, recording the most unguarded private moments of celebrity prey, spilling every indiscretion—whether they were closet smokers, who they dated, and how good or bad they looked at a gallery opening, coming from the gym, or on vacation at the beach.

Increasingly, the focus was on what celebrities wore. Of all the things we worshipped in our favorite celebrities—beauty, charm, wit, talent— by far the easiest thing to emulate was their clothes. No matter how much we wanted to "be like Mike," we weren't going to acquire a forty-eight-inch vertical leap. But we damn well could buy a pair of Air Jordan sneakers.

Jessica Simpson managed to insert herself at the forefront of such celebrity tastemaking right as the great wave was forming. Simpson was pretty to begin with. The nubile Texan had great legs, gleaming, TV-ready teeth, and big boobs. ("Natural double Ds," Joe Simpson, Jessica's father and manager and a former Baptist minister, shamelessly bragged to everybody.) That was enough to get her noticed. When her fledgling singing career flagged just as reality TV was taking off, MTV executives bought into Joe Simpson's initial proposal, that Jessica, twenty-three— just married to Nick Lachey, twenty-nine, a member of boy band 98 Degrees—could do a reality show modeled after *The Osbournes*, the MTV reality hit featuring the family of heavy metal rocker Ozzy Osbourne.

In 2003, *Newlyweds: Nick & Jessica* debuted on MTV, following the pop-singing couple at the start of their married life. The hook of the show was the positioning of Jessica as a virgin bride, playing the innocence of the preacher's daughter.

The first show took place inside the couple's new Los Angeles home, six months after their wedding. They were eating in front of the TV when Jessica posed a simple question that would forever typecast her as the proverbial dumb blonde.

Jessica stabbed her fork into a chunk in her salad bowl and asked, "Is this chicken, what I have, or is this fish? I know it's tuna, but it says 'Chicken by the Sea.' Ha-huh, is that stupid?"

An incredulous Nick explained, "Chicken *of* the Sea is the brand. You know, a lot of people eat tuna the way they like to eat chicken."

Jessica mumbled sheepishly, "Ohhhh. I understand now. I read it wrong."

TV watchers snickered at her ignorance—was she *for real*? Yet the plainspoken Jessica was getting over—as an unpretentious, likeable, and very hot-looking babe. *Newlyweds* thus evolved into one of those quirky hits—so watchable because, apart from how attractive they looked, Nick and Jessica were refreshingly *regular*. The mindless thirty-minute show went down easy; it was like peering through a keyhole into a Middle America fairy tale.

When they were *The Newlyweds*: Nick Lachey and Jessica Simpson circa 2005.

Newlyweds ran for forty episodes through 2005, building a cult MTV following, as young viewers tuned in to catch Jessica's latest antics— and watch her be scolded and swept into the arms of her romantic husband, like a blonde Lucy Ricardo. As the eye candy and comic relief of the show, Jessica soon had millions of eyeballs locked on her every move and every curve.

But unschooled beauty wouldn't be enough to hold up under that kind of scrutiny. This gospel-singing, churchgoing young woman lacked a cosmopolitan edge. That's why years before she was on TV, Jessica needed Zoe, and she needed fashion with a capital *F*. But no one could have guessed back then that over the next decade, fashion would *need* Jessica Simpson.

Rachel Zoe's simple transformation of Jessica from bumpkin to fashion icon mutated into a new reality, where the clotheshorse became the rider, a fashion authority every bit as respected as the stylist.

"I worked hard with Jessica," recalled Zoe. "She is the all-American girl. She was open to playing with her image. We fought hard to keep her fresh and pretty and modern and fashionable. She had a very classy image, a very beautiful image, and the fans worshipped her."

In the music world the standard formula was sexy—skintight, short minidresses. But Jessica didn't want that image. So Zoe took another approach. "We did a lot of peasant dresses, white eyelet tops, and really great denim shorts, and great jeans," says Zoe. "She looked so beautiful in a simple white top and jeans. She is the most beautiful in her natural state."

Rail-thin, with long, center-parted, wavy blonde hair, Zoe, born in 1971, had begun her career in the early 1990s after graduating from George Washington University, as a fashion assistant and editor at teen fashion bible *YM* magazine, where she styled models and celebrities like the Backstreet Boys for photo spreads. Zoe's own eclectic wardrobe—a mélange of furry vests, vintage trinkets, and the long, hippie day dresses—gave her a signature '70s vibe. She rolled around town with New York swagger—so self-possessed in her huge sunglasses, gesturing with an armload of bangle bracelets. Her clients included people like Nicole Richie, Mischa Barton, and Keira Knightley.

Zoe would become a fixture in Jessica's retinue. Indeed, professional fashion fixers like Zoe, Phillip Bloch, and Jessica Paster had suddenly found themselves in the vanguard of Hollywood's hottest profession—stylists—a career that hadn't even existed before the 1990s. They were among the most enterprising former magazine editors and design assistants who worked their connections to corral exquisite designer gowns and diamond baubles on loan— as well as procure the trendiest jeans, leather jackets, and all the fashion trimmings of everyday living. Initially they toiled behind the scenes; the savviest stylists

Hollywood stylist Rachel Zoe helped Jessica Simpson develop her signature style.

usually didn't "dress and tell." Their discretion permitted stars to claim credit for having such great taste, for looking so "hip, cool, and pulled together," as stylist Wayne Scot Lukas told me in 1998. For working their fashion magic on celebrities, the stylists back then began earning around $1,500 to—when movie studios footed the bill—$6,000 a day and up.

Meanwhile, as *Newlyweds* wound to a close in 2005, Jessica now had something more valuable than a good voice: a hot image to take to the big screen in a hurry. But the "dumb blonde" persona meant that she made her Hollywood debut in a C movie—*The Dukes of Hazzard*—as Daisy Duke, with some forgettable cameos dressed in butt-flashing short-shorts and a bikini. "She and her attire make equally brief appearances," the *Hollywood Reporter* smirked.

Yet a funny thing had happened during Simpson's *Newlyweds* run. All those intrepid photographers who made their living shooting famous people and their fashions hadn't been able to get enough of Jessica Simpson. And millions of fans gobbled her up.

When they saw her looking adorable in a midriff top or Daisy Duke cutoffs and boots, they didn't think of the stylist who might have put together that outfit or the designer who created it. To them, the look was pure Jessica Simpson.

This wasn't lost on Los Angeles fashion company CEO Gerard Guez of Tarrant Apparel Group. Guez was one of the owners of the 1970s designer jeans sensation Sasson Jeans (launched by his older brother Paul) with their "Oo la la" TV commercial slogan. Guez keenly sensed that the winds of fashion were blowing in a new direction: away from the runways in New York and Paris and Milan and straight toward Hollywood. He wasted no time, racing ahead of other apparel makers to sign Jessica Simpson to launch a new jeans collection, starting at $49, aimed at her fans.

Jessica was no fashion designer, but she didn't have to be. She wouldn't have to create the look or do the heavy lifting. In her licensing contract with Tarrant, she was basically responsible for being the public face of her namesake brand, for a minimum guaranteed royalty payment of $4 million in the first year, Guez told me.

While Guez was pivotal as Jessica's launchpad into fashion, she would soon leave Tarrant behind as she soared to unexpected heights.

By 2012, her cursive Jessica Simpson signature would become a coveted label at stores like Macy's, for the trendiest platform shoes and handbags, sporty dresses, off-the-shoulder tops, and denim cutoffs—twenty-two product categories and counting that pulled in $1 billion in retail revenue a year, according to the Camuto Group. Her estimated annual cut of the booty: probably more than $20 million. Not bad, reflecting how her brand had mushroomed into a well-oiled fashion machine like any other on Seventh Avenue, using design teams and marketing experts enlisted to interpret Jessica's trendy look.

Jessica's inventive take on the lace-trimmed tops, zip-front jumpsuits, bustier maxi-dresses, and her famous wardrobe of high-heeled boots, were the building blocks of the look that Rachel Zoe helped her hone over the years. When teen shoppers headed to the mall, they asked for "you know, those Jessica Simpson–style boots." As for the booty, well that was Jessica's. In 2005, in a *People* magazine survey of 80,000 readers, Jessica Simpson's shapely rear outpolled the most famous butts in the business: Jennifer Lopez's and Beyoncé's. She could WEAR those tight jeans—and her fans lusted for them too.

Riding the Wave of Blurred Lines

"Brands matter more than ever—the consumer perceives greater value, higher quality, and greater status—but the definition of brands has broadened immensely," said Richard Jaffe, an analyst who follows retail stocks for Stifel, Nicolaus & Company. He told me in 2012, "A brand can be a fashion designer who has been making high-quality merchandise for a long time, or it can also be Alex Rodriguez or Donald Trump." A celebrity's name on a label effectively fast-tracks a new fashion brand—shaving off as much as ten years to develop widespread recognition.

It's not just Jessica Simpson. Brands like The Row by Mary-Kate and Ashley Olsen, Victoria Beckham, Tory Burch, Donald Trump, Air Jordan by Michael Jordan, Sean John by Sean Combs, Selena Gomez, Carlos Santana, and Daisy Fuentes are increasingly outstripping those of traditional fashion designers.

This is the brave new world we find ourselves in, one where the lines between celebrity and fashion designer have become blurred. How we got here—and what this means for the future of fashion—will be the story that unfolds in this book.

We start where else but in Paris.

Chapter One

. . . .

THE EMPRESS'S NEW CLOTHES

Old Hollywood and the Roots of Fashion's Celebrity Obsessions

Fashion designers came into being in the nineteenth century, because the emperor of France wanted a trophy wife.

In 1858, Napoléon III hired an innovative English tailor, Charles Frederick Worth, to create a magnificent wardrobe suitable for the new age of mass media—for his beautiful young wife, Eugénie.

Thus, the blue-eyed redhead, Empress Eugénie, became the world's first supermodel. As she carried out her public duties, she became a celebrity icon—and a walking advertisement for Worth's exquisite creations, like his bustle gowns, which rendered all those cumbersome hoopskirts of the era obsolete. Worth painstakingly confected one hundred innovative new gowns for her to wear for the official opening of the Suez Canal in Egypt in 1869. Her appearances at "the great State balls, the more intimate receptions at the Tuileries, the races at Longchamp served the same function as today's runway fashion shows," wrote historian Olivier Corteaux. Drawings of Eugénie were displayed in shop windows across Europe and America, as legions of well-to-do women started wearing her signature "empress blue," and her "à l'Imperatrice" coiffure.

The talented Mr. Worth—who was said to have taught himself the art of dressmaking by studying portraits at the National Gallery in London—deftly parlayed his invaluable Eugénie connection into a lucrative branding opportunity. Worth attached his signature and the royal crest to his creations, inventing the first fashion label sewn in clothes. He would be heralded as the preferred dressmaker of the crowned heads of Austria, Italy, and Russia.

Empress Eugénie of France (1826–1920), by Franz Xaver Winterhalter, 1854.

"Worth was the father of fashion," observes Pamela Golbin, chief curator of the Musée de la Mode et du Textile at the Louvre in Paris. "He invented fashion shows; he invented seasonal collections and fashion models—and most importantly, he invented the persona of a designer as an artist," she says, as he posed in a jaunty beret and affected a "painterly pose" in his best-known portrait.

Worth's "Eugénie moment" begins the symbiosis between fashion designers and celebrities, which established the very foundation on which high fashion was built.

As for Napoléon III, his trophy wife (along with his mistresses, who Worth diplomatically outfitted at the same time) amounted to far more than arm candy, for the emperor shrewdly accomplished his foremost commercial motive: triggering the demand for all the homegrown silk textiles, embroideries, and finery that France would come to export throughout Europe, as fashion grew to become the second-largest industry in France.

Paris dazzled as the fashion capital of the world, where discerning rich women bought the best: expensive, one-of-a-kind, handmade ensembles created by the legendary haute couturiers, including Worth, Jeanne Lanvin, Paul Poiret, Jean Patou, Madeleine Vionnet, Elsa Schiaparelli, and Coco Chanel. Such fashion houses assiduously courted celebrity clients—European royalty and American socialites and stage actresses—whose photographs would circulate in the women's pages in newspapers and the leading fashion magazines, which were *Harper's Bazaar* and *Vogue*.

Hollywood Calling: A Fashion Extravaganza

Countesses and society hostesses were fine as far as they went, but there was a new kind of celebrity, a fast-lane, higher-wattage form flickering on an ever-increasing number of screens around the world. As motion pictures pulled in millions of starstruck fans from all levels of society, the beautiful people who appeared larger than life in those dark theaters (and looked better in their clothes than anyone sitting in the cheap seats) became a new kind of ideal.

A collision of old fashion icons and new was inevitable. The Hollywood movie studios and the Paris fashion establishment ultimately locked horns in 1929. The stock market suddenly dropped—and so did hemlines—leaving Hollywood movies set to be released featuring actresses in straight flapper dresses instead of the newest midcalf to ankle-length day dresses with fitted waistlines, just introduced in Paris by Chanel, Schiaparelli, and Lanvin.

The now-dated flapper fashions just wouldn't fly with discerning moviegoers who paid "twenty-five cents apiece to be entertained with 'the latest,'" wrote Edith Head and Paddy Calistro in *Edith Head's Hollywood*.

The imperious movie moguls weren't about to forgive and forget. Their solution: Establish Hollywood, not Paris, as the fashion capital of the world. They banned French couture from the movies, as the studio costume departments took over producing original designs for all actresses. Head and Calistro wrote: "The studios were determined never again to be at the mercy of a small group of fey French designers."

The movie publicists launched a full-court press, promoting every major picture as a "fashion extravaganza," while courting influential fashion editors and gossip columnists, "all to establish Hollywood's chic new image." Studio costume designers also whipped up offscreen wardrobes for actresses who were hot on the social circuit—ensuring they would always be photographed in fashions that conformed to what was shown in the movies. It worked. The exotic Dorothy Lamour was costumed by Edith Head in her movie roles as a South Sea island beauty. "The sarong dress became Dorothy Lamour's trademark and everybody talked about it," remembered costume designer Bob Mackie, who worked under Head at Paramount. "Edith used to come on Art Linkletter's radio program and tell the ladies what to wear."

Throughout the 1930s and well into the 1950s, dressmakers, furriers, milliners, and beauty salons displayed stacks of the latest movie magazines so that "customers could ask for a dress like Carole Lombard's or a fur like Joan Crawford's or a hairdo like Dietrich's," observed Head and Calistro. "Discussions of whether Hollywood was a more important style center than New York began to occur along with these comparing New York to Paris," wrote historian Caroline Rennolds Milbank in *New York Fashion*.

On the front line of Hollywood's fashion takeover was the famed Gilbert Adrian—listed in movie credits as "Gowns by Adrian"—the costume designer who studied at the New School of Fine and Applied Art and began his career in the 1920s and ran the MGM costume department for sixteen years. In more than two hundred movies, he dressed all the great leading ladies, such as Judy Garland, Greta Garbo, Katharine Hepburn, Gloria Swanson, Myrna Loy, Bette Davis, Barbara Stanwyck, as well as Janet Gaynor, whom he married.

Adrian's favorite movie-star muse—his own Empress Eugénie—was none other than the famous and fabulous Joan Crawford, whom Adrian outfitted in thirty-one movies from 1929 to 1941, during the peak of her movie career. It was Adrian who put her in shoulder pads—and who else but La Crawford, with her sultry, not-so-subtly sexual gaze, could have turned such an unlikely and mannish style innovation into a global trend that captivated millions of women through the 1940s?

In 1932, Macy's experienced a bull run, selling fifty thousand knockoffs of Adrian's ruffled white organdy dress that Joan Crawford wore like a fairy princess in *Letty Lynton*. Copies of the dress caught fire. *Vogue* reported how "every little girl, all over the country, within two weeks of the release of Joan Crawford's picture, felt she would die if she couldn't have a dress like that."

The significant distinction, whose full implications would not be appreciated for decades to come, was that the reason moviegoers worked up such a lather for the fashion was Joan Crawford, not the dress. But even then, the

Joan Crawford as Letty Lynton in 1932. More than 50,000 copies of her Adrian gown sold at Macy's.

Hollywood fashion coup reminded designers that actresses were the queens—the real movers of style and fashion.

Different Strokes: Rene Lacoste's Winning Design

For most celebrities, popularizing fashion trends was about as far as they could ever imagine going. Creating fashion themselves would have never occurred to them. But there were a few celebrities who had the chops and the ambition to design fashions that could attract attention in their own right. The first celebrity to do it was French, of course: Tennis champion René Lacoste, who won seven Grand Slam singles titles, was one of the Four Musketeers, the French Davis Cup team, which dominated men's tennis in the 1920s and 1930s.

René Lacoste, lanky and elegant—and known for stylish strokes—was the Roger Federer of his time. He was obsessed with promoting tennis as well as looking *magnifique*. In 1927, he wrote an acclaimed book, *Tennis*, full of technical tips. His patented inventions included the first metal tennis racquet (1963)—a breakthrough that turned tennis into a faster, power game (he sold it to Wilson Sporting Goods, where it became the T2000, made famous by Jimmy Connors)—as well as the first tennis-ball machine designed for practice.

Lacoste was nicknamed "Le Crocodile" after a bet he made with the Davis Cup team captain. If Lacoste won a certain match, the captain promised to buy him a beautiful crocodile suitcase the two had admired together at a fancy Boston shop. Alas, Lacoste lost that match, but a sportswriter for the *Boston Evening Transcript* heard about the wager and began calling Lacoste "The Crocodile"—and the nickname stuck.

1920s French tennis champ René Lacoste created his own crocodile logo, and a sport-shirt style was born.

Lacoste, who loved the attention, designed a natty white blazer that he had embroidered with a crocodile on the chest pocket and wore to all his matches. In 1927, Lacoste took up designing so he could finally stop playing in sweaty long-sleeved dress shirts—which to that point had been the uniform of all players. He created a series of attractive and comfortable short-sleeved knit shirts with a ribbed collar, in a breathable cotton waffle-knit fabric.

All that was left was for Lacoste to brand his practical shirts with his embroidered crocodile logo, which he did in 1927—fashion's very first logo. He teamed up with the largest French knitwear producer to make the shirts commercially in 1933. The Chemise Lacoste shirts caught on immediately with tennis players and by 1952 were imported to America and advertised as "the status symbol of the competent sportsman," says the Lacoste.com website.

Call it beginner's luck. Lacoste's Chemise Lacoste shirt revolutionized men's wardrobes, creating a staple for guys to wear for tennis, golf, polo, or just knocking around. The Chemise Lacoste became a status symbol—the uniform of Ivy League preppies—that spawned countless knockoffs, with and without their own logos.

Guys couldn't resist popping up the Lacoste's ribbed collar—it just looked cooler that way. All it took was a star athlete who combined good design with his natural flair for marketing himself to create Lacoste, distinguished as the longest-running, bestselling celebrity fashion brand in the history of clothing, reporting 2011 sales of about $2.1 billion.

Gloria Swanson, Forever Young

Another early celebrity-turned-designer also had something of a sporty angle to her clothing. After nailing the role of the unforgettable Norma Desmond in *Sunset Boulevard* in 1950, silent-film siren Gloria Swanson retired from the movies and pivoted into the rag trade, a natural direction for someone who had had a penchant for stylish clothes since she was a teenager. Still fetching in her fifties, Swanson promoted her own line of dresses, manufactured by Puritan Dress Company, a leading New York firm. How fortuitous that Swanson's own image dovetailed with her marketing angle: Gloria Swanson was renowned in Hollywood as a health nut, a longtime practitioner of yoga (she liked to stand on her head) who swore by a macrobiotic diet and lived until she was eighty-six.

In 1951, her dress collection debuted: "Gloria Swanson by Forever Young," a nod to both her own indestructible looks and to every woman's desire to look youthful. Who knew—or even cared—if Swanson had anything to do with designing her signature silk-blend dresses created for churchgoing and cocktail parties? It hardly mattered. Puritan Dress was on the ball, with its own skilled in-house designers. Swanson upheld her end of the bargain: narrating department-store fashion shows featuring Forever Young dresses. She didn't even have to shill for her own fashions.

Yet Hollywood leading ladies of the day like Rita Hayworth, Ginger Rogers, and Anne Baxter, who thought nothing of seeing their likenesses in print ads among the "nine out of ten movie stars" who use Lux toilet soap, would have considered it beneath themselves to hawk ordinary merchandise—especially when it came to doing TV commercials, "which were considered lower-class media, because it interrupted what you were watching," says Robert Thompson, professor of television and pop culture at Syracuse University. TV actors, however, could get away with doing commercials selling cigarettes, for example, because they were already considered second-class citizens in the acting profession. "All they wanted was to be discovered by Hollywood and be in movies."

Swanson did them all one better. She proved she had a second act: Her fashion label endured for thirty years, until 1981.

Audrey Hepburn and the Little Black Dress

The divine black sheath gown that Hubert de Givenchy designed for Audrey Hepburn as Holly Golightly, in the opening scene on Fifth Avenue in the 1961 movie *Breakfast at Tiffany's*, sold at auction for $923,187 in 2006, at Christie's in London. While it was often cited by fashion historians as perhaps the most famous little black dress of all time, it was the enchanting Audrey Hepburn—Hollywood's most recognized fashion plate—who cast a spell on the dress—and on most ensembles she wore.

She began her close, lifelong friendship with Givenchy after he dressed her in the 1954 Billy Wilder romantic comedy *Sabrina*. It was the fashion-savvy Hepburn who, at twenty-four, insisted that she be dressed by the tall and talented twenty-six-year-old French creative sensation, who had recently opened his couture salon after leaving his senior position at the house of Schiaparelli. For *Sabrina*, Givenchy created another stunner: a superb black cocktail frock featuring carved-out armholes and a severe horizontal boat neckline—formerly known as a *décolleté bateau*, which after Hepburn made it famous would be referred to as the *décolleté Sabrina*, becoming one of fashion's most timeless silhouettes.

After *Sabrina*, which won the 1954 Oscar for best costume design, Hepburn chose to wear Givenchy exclusively, including for many of her film roles. "In a very real sense, Audrey Hepburn was the muse that inspired the house of Givenchy. In return, he helped make her the trademark of everything young, elegant and rare," wrote her biographer Alexander Walker in *Audrey: Her Real Story*.

In 1957, Givenchy introduced his first perfume, L'Interdit, which he dedicated to Hepburn and used her picture to advertise. He made a special concentration of L'Interdit for her exclusive use. She never dreamed of exploiting what she still considered a personal relationship for commercial purposes, though clearly that largesse was not returned by Givenchy. "Hepburn never received any money for the way she promoted the house of Givenchy. She even bought the perfume and paid for it at retail price too!" wrote Walker, citing his source as Henry Rogers, Hepburn's publicist at the time.

Audrey Hepburn in the wedding gown for *Funny Face* with its creator, Hubert de Givenchy, in 1956. They conquered fashion and fragrance together—and she didn't demand a dime.

In fact, Hepburn's chic image was worth inestimable millions— far more than she ever collected as an actress. And over the years, their casual arrangement would change after Rogers convinced Givenchy's brother and business partner that "Audrey should derive some financial return for the close liaison that had developed over the years with the couturier and his creations and his products." According to Rogers, "it was all settled very cordially," Walker wrote.

Michael Jordan: Big Shoes to Fill

In the 1980s, the first inkling that the power of celebrity in fashion could transcend Hollywood turned up in the most unlikely of places: on the professional basketball court. Nike Inc. made an astoundingly prescient move when it signed up a skinny, six-foot-six African American college star from the University of North Carolina, the third NBA draft pick, who had just joined the Chicago Bulls. His name was Michael Jordan.

Founded in the 1970s, Nike was an elite running-shoe brand that had failed to make a footprint on the surging NBA circuit in its first decade, all but shut out by Converse sneakers, which were the rage among top players. So Nike did an end around on the NBA ranks by harnessing star college players through endorsement deals with college coaches. In 1984, Nike signed Jordan, who was headed to the Chicago Bulls. Nike's plans for the talented rookie were to create a signature basketball shoe around him—a first in sneaker marketing.

It was a risky strategy in early 1984, a time when there were no crossover black stars in America—the pivotal *Cosby Show* hadn't even come on TV yet. "The idea of having a young black man sell shoes to white America was absurd. Let alone a young black man no one had ever met," wrote sportswriter Dan Wetzel in a 2009 profile on Jordan.

But the powers at Nike trusted the revered sports marketing genius Sonny Vaccaro, who chose the low-key Jordan. Vaccaro, like most of the rest of the country, had never even met the young ballplayer. As Vaccaro told Wetzel when asked how he knew Jordan would succeed, "I wish I could give you something. I just knew he was the guy." (Vaccaro's sixth sense would deliver again: For Adidas basketball shoes, Vaccaro picked Kobe Bryant, straight out of high school, who would become an enduring superstar for the Los Angeles Lakers.)

Ironically, Jordan's celebrity stature rose—he became known for his style in his very first season—before he became famous as a great player. It was Nike's edgy design that did it. For the 1984–85 season, Nike's designers created a distinctive—if clunky—basketball shoe in the Bulls signature red and black for Jordan. But NBA commissioner David Stern banned the flashy shoes designed exclusively for Jordan for violating the league's "uniformity of uniform rule." Jordan was fined $5,000 for every game he wore the shoes—which Nike gladly paid, further stoking the controversy and garnering even more attention. The outlawed shoe now carried the ultimate cachet—and sales exploded. Before Jordan got anywhere near a championship ring, he had a full-fledged fashion trend to his credit. Nike turned the Jordan brand into its most lucrative franchise, starting with Air Jordan sneakers (twenty-six official models—not counting variations—as of 2013) and Jumpman logo sportswear. By 1997, as

Jordan was closing in on his fifth of six NBA titles, Nike's sales had multiplied tenfold to $9.19 billion, up from $900 million in 1984.

Jordan's original five-year deal with Nike was worth $500,000 plus royalties. The terms of his current deal are a closely guarded secret, but royalties now generate more than $60 million annually for Jordan according to sources, *Forbes* reported in February 2013.

In 2013 Jordan turned fifty. And in 2012—ten years after his last NBA game—Jordan earned an estimated $80 million from corporate partners, including Nike, Gatorade, and Hanes. He is the second-highest-paid athlete in the world. (Champion boxer Floyd Mayweather Jr. topped the *Forbes* 2012 list, with estimated earnings of $85 million.)

The Jordan brand is doing "exceptionally well," said Susquehanna financial analyst Christopher Svezia. He estimated to *Forbes* that the brand grew from 25 percent to 30 percent in 2012 over 2011. At the time, the Jordan brand, including apparel, generated more than $1.75 billion globally and controlled a commanding 58 percent of the US basketball shoe market.

But Jordan became about so much more than sneakers. He personified the influential celebrity who kept making his mark on men's style trends. Macho Hollywood actor Yul Brynner's shaved head in the 1960s was considered the exotic exception. But under Jordan, shaved heads became a sexy mainstream style that was first copied by young black men, and eventually won over white men, including corporate businessmen.

Jordan didn't need a Milan runway to introduce knee-length baggy shorts to the world. He started his NBA career wearing the shorts of his beloved University of North Carolina uniform underneath his Chicago Bulls shorts—which then had to be baggier and longer in order to fit properly. Jordan had also said that he preferred the longer shorts, which were comfortable, allowing him to move aggressively, especially bending at the waist. Other NBA players wanted to "be like Mike" and followed his fashion lead. And now vintage pictures of stars like "Dr. J" (Julius Erving) and Magic Johnson slam-dunking in uniforms with tight short-shorts look comical as well as retro. Today it's just a given—all men wear longer, looser shorts for sports and leisure.

So Jordan evolved, becoming ever more fashionable over the years, a transcendent athlete who ushered in the rise of basketball cool and urban cool, a mega-celebrity such as we had never seen before, one with enough star power and universal appeal to bridge what had been seen as incompatible realms of interest: sports and fashion.

"Athletes are the most stylish, in having the chutzpah to try new things," says Jim Moore, the longtime *GQ* creative director and men's fashion authority. Moore marvels at the rabid young "sneakerheads" who devotedly collect the latest Air Jordans every season—even though Jordan as a basketball player came and went long before their time. "I have all these stylish kids who work for me who will only wear Air Jordans, that are so back in style," Moore told me in November 2012. "The sneaker is more iconic than the man."

Moore flashed back to 1988, when he first styled Jordan in a broad-shouldered suit for the cover of *GQ*—and also noted the popularity of Pat Riley, the dapper NBA coach of the Los Angeles Lakers and the Miami Heat whom designer Giorgio Armani picked to be the billboard for his signature relaxed-look suits around the same time. "Jordan raised the bar," said Moore. "A more style-conscious generation of men have spawned from that moment."

Jordan didn't just change the way consumers thought of fashion, he changed the way fashion thought of celebrity. Yes, designers and manufacturers had long used celebrities as billboards and models, but with Jordan's supernova of crossover success, for the first time the fashion world truly began to glimpse the power—and as-yet-untapped selling potential—of celebrity in and of itself.

This realization was deliciously embodied by Giorgio Beverly Hills, the perfume that became a celebrity.

Chapter Two

. . . .

THE SMELL OF SUCCESS
L'Eau de Celebrity

Whether you know it or not, you're a part of my family—and I thank you for unleashing the family secret of Passion to every woman and every man you meet. I'm counting on you to unlock the beauty and emotion of our passion in women. . . . I would like to share with you the creation of Elizabeth Taylor's Passion.

—Elizabeth Taylor, in a 1987 TV commercial

Ever since the 1960s, when TV hillbilly Jed Clampett trucked his kinfolk to reside in Beverly Hills, the fabled enclave of "swimming pools, movie stars," the celebrity myth about the city adjacent to Hollywood has loomed large and luxurious in American pop culture, reeking of the riches and hedonism under the California sun.

Amid the roaring consumerism of the 1980s, the Beverly Hills mythology became glossier—and racier—stoked by the slick bestselling novel

Scruples by first-time novelist Judith Krantz. Her sophisticated tale focused on the lush lives of beautiful people who worked in an exclusive Beverly Hills boutique of the same name. *Scruples* was a sex-filled chick-lit sensation that sold more than thirty million copies in twenty-two languages and became a hit TV miniseries starring Lindsay Wagner.

The notoriety of *Scruples* beckoned out-of-town tourists to the tony Rodeo Drive, past Cartier, Gucci, and I. Magnin, in search of the striped yellow awning that marked Giorgio Beverly Hills, the clubby, avant-garde designer boutique where stars like Barbra Streisand and Ali MacGraw shopped. Krantz spent a lot of time studying Giorgio in order to accurately paint her fictitious Scruples boutique as a fabulous facsimile. So the gawkers marched into Giorgio for a souvenir that captured the Hollywood mystique of it all: a $35 bottle of Giorgio Beverly Hills fragrance. For five years running, Giorgio sold more than $100 million worth of those three-ounce bottles each year— a demand so steady that stores around America couldn't keep Giorgio in stock.

THE BEST-SELLING FRAGRANCE IN BEVERLY HILLS.

THE GIFT. THE EXTRAORDINARY GIFT.
Exclusively at Giorgio, Beverly Hills, New York and very few select stores. Or call our Fragrance Specialists at 1-800-GIORGIO anytime.

The movie-star lifestyle in a bottle: a Giorgio Beverly Hills 1982 advertisement.

The executives at fragrance giants like Estée Lauder, Coty, Revlon, and Elizabeth Arden were flummoxed. Other than Chanel No. 5, the action at the perfume counter had always been theirs— the New York establishment— until it shifted to Beverly Hills, where Giorgio owners Fred Hayman, a former hotel manager, and his fashion-stylist wife, Gale, exploited the reflected glory of their storied boutique. The Haymans were undercapitalized too—with reportedly only a $300,000 initial investment in the scent. But they wisely capitalized on the excitement and allure surrounding the Hollywood lifestyle, treating Giorgio the fragrance just like it was a celebrity. It seemed like a crazy idea. But it worked.

Giorgio was all swagger: a bodacious, original blend of florals, spiked with patchouli and musky vanilla, that lasted for hours and marked a woman as soon as she entered a room. It felt very 1980s: Stylish women were channeling actress Joan Collins on TV's *Dynasty* in wearing big hair, tight leather pants, and mink coats—and the scents they liked to spritz were heavy and cloying like Yves Saint Laurent's Opium and Poison by Christian Dior. But Giorgio—with no designer pedigree or celebrity mascot—was still the most coveted, garnering the most buzz.

Women everywhere swallowed the hype—and joined the cult. For Giorgio's rollout in Cleveland in 1984, a white stretch limousine whisked a gigantic perfume bottle from the airport to the Halle Brothers department store downtown, where crowds waited behind velvet ropes. Also that year, when shipments of the perfume finally arrived at Dayton's department store in downtown Minneapolis, a skywriting plane above the city replied, THANK YOU, GIORGIO.

More than a decade before designer Giorgio Armani began hosting his own star-studded parties, the other Giorgio—this one that existed solely in a bottle—had its own "very black-tie" coming-out party on November 22, 1981, hosted by the Haymans—held under a yellow circus tent, where their 1952 Rolls-Royce with a GIORGIO vanity license plate was parked. Champagne and caviar flowed as TV camera crews captured all the stars who were there, such as Charles Bronson, Jill Ireland, Mark Harmon, Loretta Swit, Stella Stevens, Hugh O'Brian, Hal Linden, and Lorne Green. Merv Griffin crooned "You Know Who Wears It," a new song created for Giorgio perfume.

Actress Pamela Mason assumed she'd be hobnobbing with stars and jet-setters, who already treated the Giorgio Beverly Hills boutique like their own private club. Imagine her amusement—to put it mildly—when she discovered the true nature of the Giorgio soiree. "It was a nightmare of a night, what we call a rat fuck," she told author Steve Ginsberg in *Reeking Havoc: The Unauthorized Story of Giorgio.* "By that, I mean it's just a crowd of so many people and the press. . . . [Fred Hayman] was exploiting that fragrance fantastically."

Giorgio succeeded by such a ridiculous degree that at some point an alarm went off. If fake celebrity could be so potent, what would happen if you did a perfume with a *real* celebrity? And not just "a" celebrity. *The* celebrity. The most famous, the most glamorous, the most outrageous star in the Hollywood firmament: Elizabeth Taylor.

Elizabeth Taylor: Diamonds and Passion

It happened one night in 1987 at Spago, the swank Wolfgang Puck Beverly Hills hangout. Stepping out of a stretch limousine was the glorious Elizabeth Taylor, tanned and magnificent, those dazzling violet eyes set off by her teased black coiffure and diamond teardrop earrings. Her plunging décolletage was set off by a gown of spangled lavender satin with puffed sleeves, designed by *Dynasty* costumer Nolan Miller. It was the black-tie launch party for Elizabeth Taylor's Passion, her first perfume, which came in a purple art deco bottle, packaged inside a lilac box.

Just what was a "celebrity perfume"? And why had the luminous Hollywood legend deigned to slap her name on some cheesy cologne, as if she needed to panhandle for dollars? Posing the question that was on everybody's minds that night, a newswoman ventured tactfully to Taylor on the red carpet: "Why are you taking such a risk?"

La Taylor cocked her head jauntily, then volleyed back, grinning: "I've always taken risks, and perfume is something I've always adored. . . . I don't know, it was just time to do something new. I had definite ideas about what I wanted—a floral, oriental—and I had all kinds of scents to play around with. I felt like a chemist gone mad, and it took about a year and a half and it was great fun."

Was the violet packaging created to match her famous eyes? No, no, she countered playfully: "Purple is my favorite color. I don't think I have purple eyes; I have red."

The two-time best actress Oscar winner, with seven of her eight marriages behind her, hadn't made a movie in years. She played the moment with grace and nonchalance. But Taylor was acting. Just like countless celebrities who would follow her in the future, she agreed to do a perfume with one objective: to make money. Unbeknownst to most people, the star who dripped in the world's finest diamonds needed cold cash.

The Liz of the 1980s was a Hollywood legend—a coveted TV talk-show guest who hobnobbed with moguls like Malcolm Forbes. But with her movie career behind her, she'd had no steady source of income for years. The former child actress, whose film career was largely controlled by the powerful Hollywood studios, never knew the $20-million-a-picture free-agent paydays of a Cameron Diaz or Julia Roberts.

In 1960, Taylor made headlines when she commanded a stunning $1 million ($7.6 million in today's dollars) to star in *Cleopatra*. But by the '80s, that was ancient history. Her main assets were a modest art collection that included a Matisse and all the diamond jewelry from her husbands and chums like Michael Jackson. Taylor lived large, with servants and employees enabling habits that burned through a lot of cash.

"Liz wasn't liquid; she had no cash flow," says Joe Spellman, a former executive vice president at cosmetics marketer Elizabeth Arden who directed the creative development of the Elizabeth Taylor fragrances and worked closely with Liz to develop White Diamonds. "She signed on because she needed the money." So when she was approached to earn a tidy sum from her own perfume, Liz was ready to learn her lines for TV commercials and to make personal appearances at stores like Macy's. In one TV spot for Passion, a luminous Liz cooed breathlessly: "Whether you know it or not, you're a part of my family—and I thank you for unleashing the family secret of Passion to every woman and every man you meet."

The terms of her deal—the first celebrity fragrance since Zsa Zsa Gabor's Zig Zag from 1969—weren't disclosed. But industry experts believe the terms today are in line with similar contracts for top celebrities, typically structured with a $3 million to $5 million initial payout, with royalty on sales, ranging from 1 to 5 percent. In any event, Passion came out of the gate as a bestseller, with estimated sales of more than $40 million at wholesale in its second year, when it was sold at fewer than two thousand retail locations, according to the fashion trade paper *WWD*.

What made Taylor so appealing to fragrance shoppers was the fact that she was larger than life, while still mired in the kinds of difficulties all women faced. "Elizabeth Taylor has had more problems—with men, with drugs and alcohol, with weight—that so many women can relate to," says Spellman. "It's like 'I crash, I have to pick myself up. I'm vulnerable, I make mistakes, but I'm still here and I'm doing the best I can.' That's what makes for the empathy toward her."

Elizabeth Taylor signing a poster for her first fragrance, Passion by Elizabeth Taylor, launched in 1987.

And because they felt empathy, even sympathy, for this preternaturally gorgeous, super-glam celebrity, it allowed women to be genuinely happy for her when she fought back through her myriad troubles and appeared to be ascendant again.

That's partially why her second fragrance, White Diamonds, the scent she introduced in 1991, had the promise to be far more lucrative even than Passion. The '90s dawned as the best of times for Taylor—a moment when her fans rallied around her like never before. She was happy, healthy, and svelte again. Taylor had just completed treatment for the second time at the Betty Ford Center for substance abuse in Rancho Mirage, California, where she met and fell in love with a fellow patient, a construction worker named Larry Fortensky. Handsome and rugged—and twenty years her junior—Fortensky was her seventh husband and eighth marriage (counting twice with Richard Burton). He provided another sequel to Taylor's storied life—one that the public cheered when the two recovering alcoholics got hitched in October 1991.

"She had lost weight, she was being attractive for him. It was the perfect storm, the sweet spot. What could be better than the wedding, Elizabeth Taylor and white diamonds?" says Spellman.

Arden executives were psyched about White Diamonds. "We really thought that it could be big," Spellman says. "With White Diamonds, we did some tricks with the juice. Just like Giorgio, we used a twenty-five-percent concentration of oil, instead of twelve percent. It was heavier, it smelled beautiful. It was the recognition of the power of fragrance. A woman will say 'I've gotten more compliments when I wear this fragrance,' and she goes back and buys it again."

The White Diamonds TV commercial, shot in grainy black-and-white like an art house film, would be referred to in-house by Arden executives as "Elizabeth Taylor's last movie."

Spellman says: "It was always important for us to treat this as a movie. We didn't think of it as a commercial. This was also important for Taylor—this sense of scope. We were selling the movie that you bought as a bottle of fragrance."

Filmed in Acapulco, the thirty-second spot was designed to look like a movie location on the beach—with snippets from scenes in front and behind the camera. It began with a private plane landing on a beach, paparazzi cameras aimed at Taylor, with fast cuts of handsome, tanned men in the middle of a card game. Taylor, splendid in off-the-shoulder white, ambles over, cooing, "Not so fast, comrade," as she snatches off a diamond drop earring, then tosses it onto a pile of money on the game table. "These have always brought me luck," she says. Then the announcer says, "White Diamonds, the intriguing fragrance from Elizabeth Taylor."

The commercial was a huge hit, including a longer version that played before the trailers at movie theaters until the end of the year. Sales of White Diamonds soared that Christmas and every year since, always with the backdrop of that same commercial. It so perfectly fit the fragrance and showed a mature Liz Taylor at her prettiest, Arden executives agreed.

The fragrance royalties provided Taylor with security for the rest of her life. Says Spellman: "Elizabeth Taylor made more money from White Diamonds than from any other movie she had ever made in Hollywood."

Elizabeth Taylor, who had moved audiences for generations, had moved a major market. She had conferred legitimacy and even prestige on a new category—celebrity fragrances—putting White Diamonds right up there in the big leagues with designer perfumes like Chanel No. 5.

After Liz, a number of celebrities tried to cash in at the fragrance counter, but they fizzled in a hurry, proving that Liz had something they lacked. But what was it?

What's That Smell? Herb Alpert, Cher, and
Joan Collins Storm the Perfume Counter

A good place to begin the search for an answer is the comical scramble of celebrities at the perfume counter, especially at Christmastime, back when fragrances were coveted holiday gifts that many women put near the top of their wish lists. Among the novelties were all those first-time fragrances by actresses, singers, athletes, and other celebrities that department stores promoted to the hilt. I spent a Saturday morning in November 1989 at Macy's Herald Square watching Leonard Clinton, a dapper and determined young man in a tuxedo, who was one of the many professional spritzers canvassing the fragrance counters. His perfume bottle was cocked, aimed, and ready to spray the first outstretched wrist. "Ladies," he recited his lines with brio, "stop and Listen." Mostly women averted their eyes and scurried past him. Unfazed, Clinton pressed on. "They were dazzled and entertained by the excitement before they even smelled it," he told me, staying heroically on message.

Somewhere in America, pop trumpeter Herb Alpert was hoping that spritzers like Clinton were connecting shoppers to Listen, his new fragrance, described as a "nose-tingling blend of grapefruit and eucalyptus," formulated by experts inspired—according to the PR release—by listening to the sounds of Alpert.

And the celebrity scents just kept coming: Uninhibited by Cher, Spectacular by Joan Collins, Undeniable by Billy Dee Williams, Misha by Mikhail Baryshnikov, as well as scents from French actress Catherine Deneuve, Princess Stéphanie of Monaco, Regine the international disco queen, Argentine tennis star Gabriela Sabatini, and Julio Iglesias. There was even Moments by Priscilla Presley—Elvis's wife. The maker of Moments told me in an interview: "She remains in the minds of women in America as a fourteen-year-old who was involved in a great romance."

But all too soon, these copycat celebrity fragrances began to stink up the joint—especially when the stars didn't show up for photo ops. How many people could a store expect to turn out when a life-size cardboard cutout of Jaclyn Smith served as her stand-in when the former Charlie's Angel couldn't appear in person to promote her signature scent? Likewise, Dionne Warwick's eponymous fragrance became famous only as the prize for the dancers on TV's *Soul Train*.

Now we know in hindsight that the celebrity fragrances of the early 1990s were ahead of their time. People were still fascinated by designer fragrances from Calvin Klein, Giorgio Armani, and Yves Saint Laurent, among others. Designer scents still made up more than 90 percent of the market, and that's what people still wanted. The allure of celebrity had proven itself powerful, but not quite powerful enough to turn the established world of fashion upside down.

Not yet.

Chapter Three

. . . .

BRAVELY INTO THE GAP

The Stars of Dress-Down Nation

There used to be a time when a white shirt went with your intelligence. But there's no reason to do this anymore.

—Ronald Hoffman, executive vice president of Alcoa Inc., the first US corporation to shift to everyday casual dress codes in 1992

By the early 1990s, winds of fashion had blown way past Paris and New York, all the way out to the West Coast. But it wasn't the costume designers in Hollywood setting fashion trends again. It was three big apparel brands out West. Gap, Dockers, and Nike—all headquartered on the West Coast—were among the leading companies cashing in on the casual togs that everybody had now shifted to wearing all the time. As was now the pattern: The more famous the people who were identified wearing those brands, the more golden those and other casual labels became to consumers.

Millions of shoppers looked up in 1988 when Gap introduced the edgy black-and-white portraits in its "Individuals of Style," an ongoing ad campaign whose early stars were actress Kim Basinger in a white Gap T-shirt and pearls and jazz legend Dizzy Gillespie in a black mock turtleneck. Those ads were unexpected, evocative, and very effective. Hundreds of famous people starred in Gap ads over the years, including Karl Lagerfeld, Willie Nelson, Diane Keaton, Madonna, Lenny Kravitz, Missy Elliott, and Sarah Jessica Parker. Gap even tapped into old Hollywood with its 1996 campaign to sell its $30 khaki pants, featuring vintage photos with the captions "Sammy Davis wore khakis" or "Gene Kelly wore khakis."

The simple styles on those celebrated bodies created a sense of hip élan that connected with a wide swath of people and made Gap the go-to casual label all through the 1990s—mushrooming into the $14-billion-a-year Gap Inc. empire, counting its Banana Republic and Old Navy divisions. Gap taught Americans the value of simple classic basics—those pocket tees looked as cool on us as they did on celebrities. Or at least we could fantasize that they did.

Serendipity struck at the 1996 Oscars when awards presenter Sharon Stone, who was "confirmed" to wear Valentino onstage, changed her mind at the last minute and strolled onstage with copresenter Quincy Jones in a $22 Gap turtleneck and black skirt—upstaging all those other actresses trussed in strapless gowns. Gap simplicity represented pure elegance that night. For months to come, Gap sold thousands of what became known in-house as the "Sharon Stone shirt." (And lest we forget the geek celebrity mogul who made Gap's black long-sleeved turtleneck look über-cool: Steve Jobs of Apple.)

Sharon Stone's Gap turtleneck moment with Quincy Jones, presenting onstage at the 1996 Oscars.

Also in San Francisco, a brand called Dockers debuted in 1986 with a new take on men's casual pants. Dockers pleated khakis—which came in a range of neutral shades and were no-iron and stain-resistant—became the new uniform for business casual offices. Dockers, a new division of jeans giant Levi Strauss & Co., benefited from its proximity to the burgeoning Silicon Valley and was early out of the gate to take ownership of the business casual office crowd.

Dockers didn't need to chase celebrity endorsers because the company's styles—followed by Haggar, Farah, and the other men's pants brands

Dress-down billionaire: Microsoft founder Bill Gates wore Dockers at the Consumer Electronics Show in Las Vegas in 2006.

chasing the trend—were already being worn by America's newest captains of industry, most notably Microsoft founder Bill Gates, the world's richest man. Gates favored pleated casual pants with button-down long-sleeved shirts.

Dockers became as generic as Kleenex, a familiar refrain among traveling businessmen, such as: "I'm just packing a couple of pairs of Dockers and a few shirts—and probably my golf clubs too." By 1994, the Dockers brand had grown into a $1-billion-a-year business, as studies revealed that eight out of ten American men owned at least one pair of Dockers.

Farther north in Beaverton, Oregon, Nike Inc. rode the Michael Jordan juggernaut, as the unstoppable Air Jordans would forever turn sneakers into a celebrity marketing play, spreading to other basketball legends, starting in the late '80s. "The NBA was flooded with superstars—all these guys who had their own shoes, like Larry Bird, Charles Barkley, Magic Johnson, Patrick Ewing, Karl Malone, and Scottie Pippen. . . . There were enough stars to go around for Nike, Reebok, and Adidas," says Jay Corbin, sneaker historian and journalist/founder of the Nicekicks.com blog.

The sneaker culture gained more traction by way of rappers in music videos and '90s TV sitcoms like *The Fresh Prince of Bel-Air*, starring the influential rapper Will Smith, who wore "a different pair of Nikes on the show every week," says Corbin. In 2003, Reebok became the first brand to branch out into sneakers by rappers—Jay Z (S. Carter Collection by RBK) and 50 Cent (G-Unit)—and racked up hundreds of millions of dollars in sales and hype, as connoisseur "sneakerheads" coveted all those celebrity shoes like fine art.

Stars from basketball and hip-hop had the juice to keep the athletic shoe category forever trendy—the height of casual fashion—galvanizing the position of sneakers as the everyday shoes worn by people around the world.

It was the icing on the upside-down cake. America had morphed into Dress-Down Nation—all casual all the time. In the office, in church, or even at weddings, leather oxfords along with suits and dressier clothes were fading away, replaced with the simple, the comfortable, and—most devastating for the fashion industry—the inexpensive.

Desperate Fashion Execs Meet Desperate Housewives

The end of dress codes became the seminal game changer in end-of-the-twentieth-century fashion. Let's take a moment to fathom just what a wrench Dress-Down Nation threw into the order of things. T-shirts, jeans, and khakis by their nature did not embody the design frills that could come and go and, as a consequence, didn't go out of style as quickly as other dresses and suits did. That meant that people weren't compelled to shop for new clothes so often, canceling out the built-in obsolescence that had kept fashion dynamic—and profitable—as millions of people moved in lockstep to update their wardrobes every few seasons.

Bill Gates, Steve Jobs, and the entrepreneurs at Google and Yahoo! weren't thinking of fashion when they worked in their garages in T-shirts and flip-flops to create new economic platforms. And that was the point: They created a vast new economy, succeeded beyond anyone's fantasies of success, dressed like schlubs. And now that they were world-famous multibillionaire moguls, these powerful men had no interest in dressing up in $5,000 Brioni tailored suits and $1,600 John Lobb shoes. Their indifference inadvertently rewrote modern fashion mores, dethroning the business suit as the symbol of financial success and corporate authority.

Ironically, the very nature of the new technologies they created would have every bit as large an unintended impact on the history of fashion as the clothes they wore—though it would take a decade or two to play out. The tech boom enabled and fed the new information vehicles: hundreds of TV channels on cable and satellite and eventually streaming online, the development of an infinite number of blogs and news and social media sites on the web, and ultimately the ability to carry it with us 24/7 on our smartphones. All this new virtual space for communications demanded a staggering amount of content.

How to fill that space? With the easiest go-to vehicle that guaranteed consumer interest, instant buzz, and acceptance: celebrities. It was a perfect and self-reinforcing solution as information about celebrities, no matter how banal or salacious, drove bigger audiences—and bigger audiences made even more, and bigger, celebrities.

In the 24/7 Internet age, the fire hose of exposure created an entirely new range of celebrities out of cooks, housewives, models, and pretty much anyone with a pretty face who got swept up in the frenzy of the inexpensive-to-produce reality shows. Faded celebrities and perpetual B-, C-, and D-listers could suddenly zoom out of obscurity to the covers and home pages of the dozens of new celebrity-obsessed print magazines and websites, blooming like algae in the warm waters of a nutrient-rich ocean. The demand and competition for celebrity news spawned growing legions of paparazzi and reporters, who voraciously followed the growing legions of celebrities—on the red carpet, on vacation, even to the supermarket. The images of what they wore—on TV, in movies, and in real life became a powerful new force in fashion.

This did not go unnoticed by apparel manufacturers and fashion marketers, who—starved by the stampede to casual wear—began dreaming up new revenue streams for TV shows that worked in concert with the Internet.

Take for example the hit ABC TV series *Desperate Housewives* (2004–2012), which featured an ensemble cast of affluent, trendy—and, it goes without saying, gorgeous—women of Wisteria Lane, who were like prime-time fashion billboards. ABC created a website so that viewers could search every outfit worn by every character on every episode of the series and then be linked to look-alike merchandise on the market, such as the $277 embroidered cashmere sweater sold at Neiman Marcus that resembled the one worn by the Bree Van de Kamp character on a certain episode. Neiman shared the profits from the sales of the merchandise with ABC.

"The entertainment industry (has been) figuring out how to completely, synergistically turn these hit television shows into entire lifestyles," observes Robert Thompson, Syracuse University professor of TV and popular culture.

In fact, prime time's *Desperate Housewives* was cashing in on the last hurrah of the genre. In 2001–02, sitcoms comprised 38.9 percent of the top broadcast prime-time TV shows, with reality shows making up about 22.4 percent, according to Nielsen. But now sitcoms don't even rank in the top ten prime-time shows anymore, with reality shows making up over half of the most popular shows in the prime-time slot.

Which was fine with fashion marketers. Why rely on sly product placements and elaborate tie-ins between fictional characters' wardrobes and look-alike knockoffs when you can put real people in real clothes and make it frankly all about fashion?

Taking Off on the Runway

Among the reality shows with a fashion slant, *Project Runway*, which began in 2004, has been the biggest ongoing hit on both Bravo and Lifetime TV, where the 2008 season finale had 4.3 million viewers and broke records to become the most watched reality program among women eighteen and over. Likewise, *Keeping Up with the Kardashians* and Bravo's *Housewives* franchise had no plot to get in the way of a virtual nonstop fashion show of rich women sporting long hair extensions, Spandex sheath dresses, and platform stiletto heels. Botox optional.

Even the more traditional reality shows—proliferating award shows like the Oscars, the Grammys, and the Golden Globes—became ever more about the clothes. The 2014 Oscars were TV's second-biggest US draw after the Super Bowl (which is why the Oscars are also known as the Super Bowl for women)—with a global audience of about one billion viewers. In 2014, the 86th Academy Awards, hosted by talk-show host Ellen DeGeneres, drew 43.7 million viewers overall—up 8 percent from 2013—making it the most watched Oscars since 2000, when 46.5 million viewers tuned in.

Most eyeballs were on the fashions the stars wore. Counting the social media activity that began live on the red carpet hours before the awards, there were more than six solid hours of Twitter chatter starting at five thirty P.M. on the East Coast—until shortly after midnight, when the stars headed to the after-parties. During that time window of the 2014 Oscars, there were more than nineteen million Oscar-related tweets, sent by more than five million people and viewed by more than thirty-seven million people—or nearly as many people as watched the awards show itself.

The person most tweeted about at the 2014 Oscars was a fashionista, of course: actress Lupita Nyong'o, the stunning Kenyan ingénue who became an overnight red-carpet fashion sensation a month earlier at the Golden Globe Awards, when she donned that red-caped gown by Ralph Lauren. Lupita came to the stage to accept her Oscar for Best Supporting Actress in her very first movie role, *12 Years a Slave*, resplendent in a sea-blue princess gown by Prada, the Milan fashion house that knowingly cast Lupita in its 2014 spring fashion ads. Runner-up in the Twitter rankings was Best Supporting Actress nominee Jennifer Lawrence, in a red strapless Dior gown—and in fifth place on Twitter was Cate Blanchett, who hauled off her Best Actress trophy for *Blue Jasmine* in a jeweled, flesh-toned Giorgio Armani gown.

The one-two punch of live TV and social media made the Oscar fashion buzz more potent than ever, with lasting influence and impact. As millions of viewers stared at the fashions live, millions more read the tweets and saw the links to the red-carpet gowns everywhere online or splashed across the pages of their favorite celebrity magazines.

Turning the Page on Celebrities and Style

Recognizing the driving interest in what celebrities wore, publisher Time Inc. took a page from its winning formula at *People* and came up with a fashionable hybrid—*InStyle*. Founded in 1994, the magazine focused squarely on fashionable celebrities in full-length shots at all the red-carpet premieres and inside their fabulous homes—as well as a mix of designer and affordable looks that readers who wanted to copy the celebrities could buy. *InStyle* turned a profit in just three fast years.

The fastest-growing celebrity fashion magazine is now Time Inc.'s *People StyleWatch*, where advertising pages grew by almost 25 percent in 2008, at a time when ad pages declined by more than 25 percent for most magazines, according to Publishers Information Bureau. Since 2008, the magazine's circulation has hovered around eight hundred thousand, editor in chief Susan Kaufman confirmed to me in 2012.

Says Kaufman: "It's all about the celebrities who readers really relate to, like Lauren Conrad, who is our top-selling cover person. . . . She is very girl-next-door and readers really like her a lot." But readers won't learn anything about Conrad's diet or what she likes about her family life. Instead, readers will see only her pictures in candid shots where everything she wears is talked about in captions.

People StyleWatch is also a new magazine business model: The magazine doesn't do costly celebrity photo shoots; it relies on paparazzi shots as cheap as $150 apiece. Nor does it run feature articles or celebrity interviews, except pithy sound bites that *StyleWatch* editors elicit from celebrity publicists on behalf of their celebrity clients.

A typical page from the August 2013 issue: "How to Create Julianne's Casual-Chic Mix!" A caption reads, "She styled this outfit herself." There's a full-page picture of *Dancing with the Stars* two-time champ and professional ballroom dancer Julianne Hough in skinny jeans, a leather cargo jacket, a white lace blouse, and flat boots.

Those mass-market Dress-Down Nation clothes are a big part of *People StyleWatch* coverage: Cheap 1990s basics morphed into cheap, contemporary fashion merchandise produced in the twenty-first century by fast-fashion specialists Zara, H&M, Forever 21, and Uniqlo, who use state-of-the art technology and global sourcing to inexpensively turn out trendy, embellished dresses, jumpsuit rompers, faux-leather skirts, and denim jackets—meant to be worn for a season and then thrown out. Just what the fashion industry loves.

The power of the celebrity-cum-models in the magazine's pages, plus offers of reader discounts (20 percent off or higher) for featured products, has driven huge sales for advertisers. For example, Revolve-Clothing.com sold $1.4 million worth of merchandise after a 2009 *Style-Watch* discount offer, according to Kaufman. The result is a lot of happy campers—readers, advertisers, and brands featured in the magazine.

But there is one bit of market demographics that says more than any other: Readers spend an average of ninety-three minutes reading *People StyleWatch*, a magazine that has no articles to read.

That's more than an hour and a half doing nothing but marinating in the potent elixir of celebrity and fashion, more proof, if anyone needed it, that the biggest force in fashion of the early twenty-first century is not designers or manufacturers or retailers.

It is, quite simply, fame.

Chapter Four

. . . .

GILT BY ASSOCIATION
Celebrities Move to the Front Row

In some seasons, the reality show "Housewives" have been blacklisted by some designers, while others are desperate to have them in the front row, to have any boldfaced name.

—Fern Mallis, credited as the creator of 7th on Sixth productions,
now known as New York Fashion Week

The 1990s was the decade when the top fashion designers really got hip to the power of celebrities—and started photographing them and associating with them like never before.

Celebrities had begun to loom large during the twice-yearly designer runway collections shown in New York, Paris, London, and Milan. Their presence transformed what was once a clubby ritual for fashion insiders— trade shows for invited retail buyers, fashion editors, and select socialite clients—into multiplatform extravaganzas, showcased in print, on TV, and everywhere on the Internet. Credentialed photographers and video crews from as far away as Tokyo and São Paulo joined the Americans and Europeans, all converging in Manhattan to cover dozens of fashion shows, after-parties, and retail openings staged twice a year during New York Fashion Week. The 1990s fashion gatherings were also the heydays of those gorgeous, $10,000-a-day playmakers, also known as the supermodels—headliners like Cindy Crawford, Linda Evangelista, and Naomi Campbell, who added a layer of gloss and über-celebrity to the proceedings.

It was no wonder that so many actresses, reality-show personalities, rappers, and sports figures jockeyed to hook up fashion-show invitations so they could be in the thick of the action, inside the velvet rope, to soak up the buzz and to get their picture taken—with the ultimate objective of getting paid somewhere down the line.

Beginning in 1994, New York Fashion Week finally had an official venue: Two huge deluxe tents were erected twice a year in Bryant Park, behind the stately New York Public Library on Fifth Avenue. They were equipped with stadium-style seating and a lobby, where a dozen corporate sponsors like Evian water, Olympus cameras, and Mercedes-Benz each season paid to advertise their wares—for a stylish taste of "gilt by association," as they sidled up to the glamorous, influential fashion crowd.

As the '90s wore on, the potent mix of celebrity and fashion built momentum, and New York's Fashion Week began to glow with a light all its own—no longer in the shadow of the Paris collections. The ascendance was solidified in 1998, when Calvin Klein and German designer Helmut Lang (defecting to media-rich Manhattan) together succeeded in flipping the established order so that the New York collections went first (instead of last) on the international fashion-show calendar, ahead of the Fashion Weeks in London, Milan, and, finally, Paris—nearly a month later. No longer could the French deride the Americans for copying what had already been shown on Paris runways.

Ladies, Uncross Your Legs

The balance of Fashion Week power had really begun to shift five years earlier, in 1993, with what at first seemed like a merely logistical tweak—all the fashion-show photographers were moved from the front, where they encircled the runway, to a huge rectangular pit at the end of the runway. The front row was now unobstructed—ready to be filled up with celebrities, giving photographers an even more alluring target than the clothes parading down the runway.

Years before then, designers held fashion shows all around Manhattan in empty downtown industrial lofts and in ballrooms at the Pierre or Plaza hotels, where the configuration was typically a long elevated runway flanked by rows of folding chairs at ground level, where the viewing was best from the third or fourth row. There were typically no more than thirty or so runway photographers present—right up front, crouched on the floor, enveloping the runway, bobbing up and down with their clunky cameras and strobes riveted on those stunning Cindy Crawford or Claudia Schiffer clones parading in the latest designer collections.

But the new Fashion Week's official tents came with staggered rows of seating—with the front row on ground level and the rest of the rows ascending upward and in full view. With the photographers out of the way, huddled together in their designated pit at the end of the runway, "the front row had become part of the content of the show—and the vehicle for celebrities," Fern Mallis, the former executive director of the Council of Fashion Designers of America, who is credited for creating 7th on Sixth productions in 1993, now known as New York Fashion Week, reminisced to me in 2013. The stilettoed women seated in the front row were now butting right up against the runway—so close inside the picture frame in fact, that a chorus line of crossed legs poked out and ruined the shot. It then became something of a ritual that before every show, a commanding male voice from the photographers' pit shouted: "Ladies in the front row, uncross your legs!"

The photographers' pit expanded to accommodate all the new media outlets covering fashion, lured by the celebrities it attracted. More than three hundred photographers tightly huddled together in the pit at most of the big shows during Fashion Week. Mallis estimated about 20 percent of the photographers had no interest in fashion, with their telephoto lenses trained directly on the front row: "They've come to take in the celebrities and the scene and not the collections." And that's not even counting all the fashion-show guests in every row who aimed their cell phone cameras at the front row, ready to Instagram and tweet images to all their friends and followers.

"The messaging has changed and become all about the celebrities—and not the clothes. What's a shame is that a fashion show without celebrities is considered blah," she says.

Now the designer collections could reasonably be rated based on the level of celebrities in the front row rather than the appeal of the clothes. A subtle calculus has taken hold, in which the star power of the designer determines the star power of the big guns they could assemble on the front row. And vice versa.

"In some seasons," Mallis says, "the reality show 'Housewives' have been blacklisted by some designers, while others are desperate to have them in the front row, to have any boldfaced name" that will guarantee the show gets its due press coverage.

Right up to the hours before every show, fashion-show publicists working what's known as "the front of the house" painstakingly rejigger their seating charts to create a photogenic tableau. At Michael Kors's 2013 show, there were his glamorous celebrity regulars—Catherine Zeta-Jones and Michael Douglas, who had been coming for years—along with stars of the moment, all dressed in Kors: Olivia Munn, Hilary Swank, Jada Pinkett Smith, and Zoe Saldana. Hence, guests got busy Instagramming images and chattering right before the lights went down, agreeing to one another: "This is a hot show."

BFA

Posing to be chosen on the front row at the Hervé Léger fashion show: Kristin Chenoweth, Tinsley Mortimer, Harley Viera-Newton, and Leigh Lezark, in 2012.

Owned by designer Max Azria, the Hervé Léger label, famous for its $2,000 second-skin rayon-and-Spandex "bandage" dresses, plays the front row for maximum impact—a chorus line of four to eight gorgeous gals, each in a Hervé Léger tight dress furnished by the fashion house. During Fashion Week on February 11, 2012, the featured lovelies at Hervé Léger struck a familiar pose, as if on cue—legs crossed in the same direction, all in killer stilettos: actress Kristin Chenoweth, socialite Tinsley Mortimer, DJ/model Harley Viera-Newton, and DJ/model Leigh Lezark.

Inquiring minds will never know for sure who may or may not get paid to sit there, since that's all strictly on the down-low, quietly negotiated in advance.

Designing Celebrity: Isaac Mizrahi and Giorgio Armani Embrace Fame

The Fashion Week celebrity scene first came sharply into focus in *Unzipped*, the acclaimed 1995 documentary that followed designer Isaac Mizrahi through the exhilarating fits and starts during the months he prepared his 1994 fall collection. The lively film, which won the audience award at the Sundance Film Festival, captured the razzle-dazzle of the witty Mizrahi, cavorting with Eartha Kitt and Sandra Bernhard, air-kissing Richard Gere and Liza Minnelli, and stage-managing his bevy of supermodels backstage before the show—namely, Cindy Crawford, Naomi Campbell, Linda Evangelista, Shalom Harlow, and Carla Bruni.

It was so typical of Mizrahi, who tended to his celebrity image as assiduously as he created his award-winning fashion collections. While he was a student at New York's High School of Performing Arts, he was an extra in the appropriately titled 1980 movie *Fame*. He loved to perform his piano cabaret act onstage and act in bit parts on TV and in the movies—playing a fashion designer, of course.

But Mizrahi always struggled in his quest to sell his clothes at retail—and his critics tsk-tsked that he was too caught up in his stardom. Alas, his notoriety simply magnified his misfortune when his curtain finally came down: The news that Mizrahi went out of business on October 2, 1998, made the front page of *The New York Times*. Yet the funny thing about fame is that you're never easily forgotten—as was the case with Mizrahi, who would soon be poised for a comeback, with his name back in lights.

Comeback, in fact, was on the agenda for the entire fashion world in the 1990s. Dress-Down Nation continued to engulf the clothes-buying public with a determined persistence throughout the decade and beyond, but the fashion establishment refused to give up, maintaining faith that human nature would always push people to want to look attractive and sexy—not to mention to one-up their peers. Fashion marketers had parallel priorities: 1) Create a new fashion idiom of casual-friendly clothing styles at affordable prices that would be exciting to a critical mass of people; and 2) Fortify their ties with the celebrities of the moment, understanding that millions of people idolized and trusted them more than ever.

It was the formidable Giorgio Armani who was the first designer who managed to do both. On the fashion front, the Milanese maestro was well ahead of the curve when he dreamed up, way back in 1975, his radically chic notion of unconstructed, unlined men's suits, whose slouchy jackets and sloping lapels hung like a sweater. As Armani refined his innovative suits over the years, the 1990s versions looked relaxed enough to thrive in Dress-Down Nation. Armani's signature fabrics were featherweight cashmere, silk, and linen blends—materials that draped and rumpled gracefully, giving men a comfortable, effortless sophistication.

In a feminist era, Armani went over big with executive women, who loved his draped pantsuits, which telegraphed a quiet, elegant power look that ran contrary to the uptight, figure-molding couture associated with Paris. In 1997, the legendary Italian knitwear designer Rosita Missoni told me succinctly: "Armani put women in men's clothes. He is a genius."

With fashions that struck the right chord of the times, Armani was in pole position to milk the celebrity connections he had been building since he dressed Richard Gere as a snappy Beverly Hills stud in *American Gigolo* in 1980. Armani had developed a sophisticated publicity machine to get his clothes on Hollywood's most influential and most visible list of actors, directors, producers, and agents—who would keep his trademark in lights. The centerpiece of his celebrity strategy was the Academy Awards, the biggest photo op of the year.

After Armani opened a Beverly Hills boutique in 1988—having hired Wanda McDaniel, a former society columnist at the Los Angeles *Herald Examiner*, and wife of Hollywood producer Al Ruddy, as his chief celebrity wrangler—he set out to be the designer of choice at the Oscars. The idea of designers courting celebrities was still novel back then—and the designers called the shots. Selected celebrities got discounts on everything they bought in the boutique and gowns on loan for red-carpet events. Only choice "friends of the house" received free clothes.

"It started out as 'Oh my God, Armani is going to let me wear something!' It was like a privilege coming into the inner sanctum, it had mystique," McDaniel told me in 1998. Armani was adamant: He wasn't interested in writing out big checks to buy the stars. He strategically wooed the best people—targeting the difficult ones, the stars who couldn't be bought—women like Jodie Foster and Glenn Close, who would most likely remain loyal to Armani because they already loved wearing his clothes.

That's what made Pat Riley, the nattiest coach in the NBA, so ideal—he had been wearing Armani for years before McDaniel orchestrated Riley's more formal relationship with the house. The Lakers won four NBA championships under Riley in the 1980s, who got so much TV time during the long season, with the playoffs and the finals, as the cameras followed him pacing back and forth courtside in his Armani suits. Sports commentators couldn't stop calling him "GQ"—and millions of star-struck basketball fans went shopping for Armani suits—many who wore them without a tie, with the sleeves pushed up. Riley was the perfect surrogate—low-key, handsome, and self-assured, the personification of a sharp, regular guy.

When I interviewed the natty six-foot-three coach in 1997, he emphasized that he wasn't on Armani's payroll and that his position was more like an "unofficial spokesman." Each year both Riley and his wife Chris received a free Armani wardrobe, and the coach was obliged to show up at Armani-sponsored charity events and store openings. Armani also flew Riley to Milan to sit on the front row of his fashion shows, which was hardly a chore. Riley told me he loved studying the clothes on the runway.

By 1991, *WWD* called the Oscars "The Armani Awards," by virtue of the fact that anybody who was anybody was wearing Armani, including the host, Billy Crystal. His roll call of regular "gets" during the 1990s was the crème of Hollywood: Jodie Foster, Annette Bening, Martin Scorsese, Robert De Niro, Glenn Close, Michelle Pfeiffer, Anjelica

Huston, Winona Ryder, Sigourney Weaver, Faye Dunaway, and Salma Hayek.

Since then, Armani has further honed his technique. In recent years, selected Oscar-nominated stars have been known to receive a wonderful treat and keepsake: beautiful gift boxes containing a customized sketch of a sample gown—complete with fabric swatches—with the nominated actress's actual face drawn in the signed sketch. (The likenesses are so detailed that the actresses were bowled over.) Along with the sketch comes a handwritten note from Giorgio Armani.

(In case you wondered: The actresses no longer keep the couture gowns customized for them—they are returned to most fashion houses' archives. The actresses are never going to wear the dresses again anyway, so they are worth more to designers as historical artifacts. The exception is two-time Oscar winner and couture connoisseur Cate Blanchett, who is known to painstakingly preserve and store her red-carpet frocks from key occasions.) Following Armani's '90s lead, every top designer in Europe and America, along with the most famous jewelers—Fred Leighton, Lorraine Schwartz, Chopard, Tiffany, Harry Winston, and the rest—began jockeying to replicate his stunning success with the stars. The basic dynamic of supply and demand meant it didn't take long for the script to flip, as the celebrities—not the designers—began calling the shots. Fashion houses would roll the dice, splurging tens of thousands to whip up custom couture gowns on spec—in the hopes that an actress might wear the dress to a big event. In 1997, actress Lauren Holly, who was married to comedian Jim Carrey at the time, received—unsolicited—fifty-six free gowns from thirteen different designers. Out of control! But not for long.

The Art of the Deal

As the years went by, the business of dressing celebrities became more aggressive and more opaque than ever. The real art now is not fashion, but deal making, all the stylists and publicists who dress celebrities told me under the condition of anonymity. The fact is that nobody can really open the kimono to brag about how clever they've bagged their famous targets, because there are contracts drawn up, hundreds of thousands of dollars being exchanged in many transactions—complete with confidentiality clauses designed to preserve the mystique that these deals are more "organic" than they look.

Organic is the buzzword that the publicists love to throw around. Its precise meaning is never stated, but the impression they want to leave is like a fairy tale: that the actresses are naturally drawn to fashion's avant-garde—to the most creative designers—rather than by contracts worth hundreds of thousands of dollars paid to the top stars. When the publicists stage photo ops at high-profile events, or when designers dress celebrities, it's always got to look so natural and "organic," even though most of their jaded fans have read enough tabloids to know the real deal—that fashion houses ply celebrities with lots of free clothes, trinkets, and serious cash. So it's all one big, elaborate game.

Still, there's a heightened concern about the optics of celebrity payola, as social media feeds on the details, sending them viral in the time it takes to click "send." One leading New York publicist explains: "Celebrities are very sensitive about their images—they really don't want their fans to know that they're getting paid sixty thousand dollars or one hundred thousand dollars or more to wear a dress for one night. It just looks bad to people."

However it looks, the fact is that millions of dollars are changing hands among the designers, the stars, and their stylists—and the publicists who act as the handlers. Everybody along this fashion food chain gets paid. "If you're one of the stars of the moment, you're not just going to get all kinds of free clothes—gowns and casual clothes—you're going to get paid to wear them," another Manhattan publicist told me.

And as the stars got spoiled, so used to being paid, some have become downright sloppy about following the contracts they agreed to.

Watch What Happens to Charlize Theron

Oscar-winning actress Charlize Theron is tall, blonde, alluring—and famous for being the face for Christian Dior's J'adore fragrance, appearing in a memorable TV commercial where she walks down a long runway corridor peeling off her clothes.

But in 2007, Swiss watchmaker Raymond Weil sued Theron after she was caught two-timing, having been photographed wearing two other watch brands—Dior and Montblanc—at different public events, in violation of her contract with Weil from 2005 to 2006, in which she was paid "substantial funds" to be the face of Weil's watch campaigns. In court papers, Raymond Weil sought $20 million in compensation.

In a thirty-two-page ruling, a New York federal district court judge found Theron guilty of repeatedly breaching the terms of her contract. The judgment was a rare public airing that revealed the exact sums that luxury firms are willing to pay top actresses, noting that Theron received $3 million to endorse Dior perfume in a series of advertisements. The ruling also itemized other payments to Theron: from jeweler Chopard, $50,000 to wear jewelry at a London awards ceremony and another $200,000 to wear two items of jewelry to the 2006 Oscars. Separately, Montblanc paid a charity $250,000 for Theron to model one of its silver necklaces.

Watch out! Charlize Theron wore this Christian Dior watch in 2006 while she was under contract and was paid millions to wear Raymond Weil watches exclusively. Weil sued her and won a settlement.

The ruling said that Theron responded that her decision to wear the Dior watch at a Texas film festival was "regrettable" and that her lawyers claimed she was guilty of a simple mistake rather than a deliberate fraud and that she hadn't understood the terms of her original contract. But the judge ruled that Theron "was not an unwary agent," noting that she had initialed every page of the original ten-page contract. The parties reached an out-of-court settlement in 2008 that wasn't publicly disclosed.

When All You Have to Do to Win Is Show Up

Fashion publicists know better than to go on the record about today's deals between designers and celebrities. However, I talked to enough people to get a pretty clear sense of how demanding celebrities have become. In addition to paying celebrities fees for wearing their clothes at a range of events, from charity benefits to awards shows, designers may shoulder all of the expenses of the night—including stylists for hair and makeup and a limousine. And designers who just have to pay for the chauffeured black Lincoln Town Car should count themselves lucky: "Helicopters are the new limousines," one New York publicist declared, explaining how a Hollywood actress who was in Connecticut demanded—and received—a helicopter ride into Manhattan in addition to her appearance fee to attend an event.

There are some exceptions to the pay-to-pose arrangements. Stars who are genuine friends or have long-standing relationships with designers (Renée Zellweger has sworn by Carolina Herrera for years) and fabulously wealthy celebs like Beyoncé, Jay Z, George Clooney, or Angelina Jolie, put on the fine threads without demanding a fee.

But perhaps their stylists are. Because stylists are the middlemen, brokering many of the arrangements between designers and celebrities, they often get cut in on the cash, which sometimes their celebrity clients aren't even aware of. (Indeed, the top stylists have come a long way from the per diem slog of the 1990s—led by the enterprising Rachel Zoe, who parlayed her styling gigs into a hit reality show, *The Rachel Zoe Project,* assorted fashion endorsement deals, and even her own Rachel Zoe women's fashion label.)

Today's deals represent more than greed—the fact is that many of the most visible celebrities just aren't making the money they would have in earlier times. Just look how the Internet has robbed them of revenue. Free music file sharing and streaming audio mean fewer gold and platinum albums for artists. Reality shows and cable TV shows, the source of so much of the work for actors nowadays, typically pay far lower than the scripted network programs of the past that used to pay top stars on long-running shows like *Friends* as much as $1 million an episode—more than a decade ago, in 2002. There are also more low-budget independent films today, like *Lee Daniels' The Butler* (2013), in which all the actors worked for free. That's fine if you are Oprah, Jane Fonda, and Robin Williams, who were among the cast members.

But even for a lot of famous musicians, actors, and athletes, the actual paychecks they collect don't begin to add up to the fabulous lifestyles expected of them. They have come to depend on the money they collect by wearing certain designer clothes, or appearance fees for attending events. "They've gotta monetize their fame somehow," as one publicist told me.

In September 2012, on the last evening of Fashion Week, I met the stylish New York Knicks player Amar'e Stoudemire, who dropped by during the cocktail hour at a private dinner hosted by menswear designer Michael Bastian. Stoudemire was decked out in a Calvin Klein suit and was on his way to the Calvin Klein dinner celebrating the end of Fashion Week, with his stylist, Rachel Johnson, and his personal chef, Max Hardy.

He is paid by the fashion house to be a brand ambassador for Calvin Klein menswear. He wears Calvin Klein suits exclusively—he got married in one, of course—and he attends Calvin Klein fashion shows, sitting in the front row. He also attends the dinners and after-parties the company asks him to attend. Stoudemire was keen about getting to the dinner—which I assured him would not start on time. But he said he needed to leave—and he was gone after maybe twenty minutes. Now I know why.

Such agreements are said to be restrictive. As a Calvin Klein brand ambassador, he must take care not to attend other fashion companies' events—and certainly not to pose for pictures if he's there. The publicists at other menswear brands such as Zegna or Gucci, for example, know that he won't be attending store openings or other events they invite him to. He isn't supposed to be flitting to other designers' shows during Fashion Week either.

For that matter, celebrities under lucrative contracts are advised by publicists that they should just stay home the night before the fashion event they were paid to attend, to avoid the risk that their pictures might be taken and circulated on blogs and Facebook pages, spoiling the next day's impact. It's all deemed justifiable because fashion designers now insist on managing the celebrities they have relationships with, to work to their best advantage in terms of images and messaging.

With so many outlets in need of celebrity photos, and so many promoters needing celebrities to make their events buzz-worthy, celebrities like Stoudemire are a valuable commodity. Celebrities have the power to make or break an event. Assignment editors at *Us Weekly, People, The Hollywood Reporter,* or *Entertainment Tonight* make their decisions on what to cover based on who is "confirmed" to be attending.

Athletes Victor Cruz, Henrik Lundqvist, and Amar'e Stoudemire at a Calvin Klein menswear show in Milan in 2012.

The reason why Kim Kardashian was always seen going out? That's her profession; going out is what she does for her living. In 2011, Kardashian commanded fees ranging from $100,000 to $1 million, plus travel and expenses, to attend any number of events. Her fee includes her appearance and tweeting a couple of times during the evening. She even got $25,000 just to tap out a tweet for Armani, generating forty thousand hits on Armani's website. Kim admitted to *Cosmopolitan* magazine: "Appearances were a good way to make money and a great way for me to connect with people in places like Oklahoma where I would never go otherwise. Those girls going to the clubs will be buying my perfume."

Not all event promoters have the budget for a Kardashian. But that doesn't mean they are out of luck. "If they only have, say, fifty thousand dollars to spend on celebrities, they have to decide, do you want two celebrities at twenty-five thousand dollars or five celebrities at ten thousand dollars," one publicist explained to me. If all else fails, party throwers will settle for B-list gadflies—who are said to show up for as little as $5,000 or $7,000 a pop. So there's a famous person for every budget.

Chapter Five

. . . .

STILETTOS AND THE CITY

Fashion Steps into Its Accessories
Moment with Carrie Bradshaw and SJP

Carrie Bradshaw was bursting with anticipation. TV's most rabid fashionista, played by Sarah Jessica Parker, had just entered the inner sanctum of *Vogue* magazine: the office storage room where all that delicious designer loot from past photo shoots was stored. Carrie whipped past the racks of couture dresses and went straight for the shoes. Hundreds of them—lined up in neat rows on shelves from floor to ceiling. "Oh my God!" she squealed. "Do you know what these are? Manolo Blahnik Mary Janes. I thought these were an urban shoe myth!" Ignoring the size, she stuffed her feet into the $685 black patent leather treasures. She said, "If they don't fit, so help me, I will wear them anyway."

This vignette from a 1999 episode of the hit HBO series *Sex and the City* was an iconic moment in TV fashion lore that clicked with millions of women. Everywhere, women were turning into Carrie Bradshaws—obsessed with designer shoes, as well as handbags, both being the key accessories that were now the focal point of their wardrobes.

Fashion's "accessories moment" would endure well through the first decade of 2000 and showed no signs of letting up in 2014 as watches—collectible and disposable—and $300 sunglasses played into the trend.

It's the moment that mushroomed into a paradigm shift. Accessories, which used to be the trimmings—in the shadows of all those trendy dresses and sportswear ensembles—were now the stars in fashion.

It was a flip of the switch, a game-changing development that was grounded in fashion economics. Fashion houses needed a new strategy that could effectively revive the industry's rule of planned obsolescence—the revolving door of trends that compels women to update their wardrobes and, not coincidentally, keeps the multibillion-dollar global apparel industry thriving. Dress-Down Nation had robbed fashion of the novelties it needed to keep introducing.

Accessories would thus become high fashion's lifeline—the antidote to Dress-Down Nation, which had democratized fashion, homogenizing it to the point that the receptionist, the office manager, and the managing partner of the advertising agency—everybody—was reduced to looking the same in their casual clothes.

If the Shoe Fits

Obviously, the fashion industry could not allow this egalitarian state of affairs to stand.

The solution? Take advantage of the human need to stand out by creating a new generation of highly recognizable luxury accessories, re-igniting the snob appeal of expensive fashion. There was nothing subtle about these pricey items—in fact, just like Carrie Bradshaw, you could spot them from across a clothes-crowded showroom. For example: the $1,850 Fendi Baguette textured leather shoulder bag emblazoned with a double FF rhinestone buckle, or a pair of burgundy patent $785 Christian Louboutin stilettos, with their trademark red lacquered soles—which, worn together, tarted up a woman's humdrum Capri pants and V-neck jersey, while satisfying her real desire to stand out and show off a bit. As more women wore variations of that look to the country club and fine restaurants, fashion's accessories moment prompted a reassessment of what it meant to dress up.

If you had been a professional woman living in places like New York, Chicago, San Francisco, or Washington, DC, in the 1990s, you might have been teasingly labeled an "Ann Taylor"—which is the name of a women's retail chain of classic clothes, as well as the nickname of a type of yuppie career woman in her thirties or forties. An Ann Taylor had visited London and Paris on business or on vacation enough times to cultivate a taste for European labels to jazz up her work ensembles of cashmere pullovers and pencil skirts—which was as about as formal as she ever needed to be in Dress-Down Nation.

But starting around 1997, even an Ann Taylor began to crave status symbols to distinguish herself from the hoi polloi. And that's where all the Ann Taylors across America and Carrie Bradshaw converged—with their lust for luxury accessories from labels like Fendi, Louis Vuitton, Prada, and Gucci. Each purchase was a splurge of at least $500 for a pair of shoes and usually more than $1,000 for a bag. Accessories gave every Ann Taylor a status totem that impressed her peers. "As [clothes] styles got cleaner and simpler, you couldn't tell what was a real Armani and what was a knockoff," Sherry Cassin, a retail consultant (now a furrier) explained to me for *The Wall Street Journal* in 1999. "You could wear Gap clothes, but you needed that Prada bag."

Because in the end, fashion among grown women was just like in high school. There had to be some way to distinguish the girls who had it from those who simply, and sadly, did not. If that status marker happened to cost the equivalent of a month's worth of groceries for a middle-class family of four, then hey, it was just another swipe of a Visa card.

Still, some women didn't just buy into the accessories moment so easily. First they had to get over the admonition their mothers had drummed into them for years: Allocate most of your clothing budget to suits and a cashmere coat—then spend no more than $150 or so each for a fine leather handbag or a good pair of pumps.

But in the roaring current of a fashion trend, resistance is futile. Women had no choice but to forget those rules or find themselves left behind. For the fashion industry, the accessories wave was a godsend, a tide that lifted all ships and kept the books in the black.

For once, every ordinary woman had a seat at the table. You could be fifty-three years old, plump and plus-size, and still be a raging fashionista, decked out in the latest shoes and handbags. No wonder fashion accessories exploded at retail, because they allowed every woman to look and feel sensational.

Much as French designer perfumes had in the early 1980s—when about half to two-thirds of the top twenty fragrances sold across the United States were French—accessories in the 2000s provided the French couture houses with an easy lifeline: a steady and highly lucrative profit driver to buttress their often anemic fashion collections. Unbeknownst to most women, Paris houses like Chanel, Nina Ricci, Christian Dior, and Yves Saint Laurent quietly transformed themselves into little dress businesses attached to big fragrance companies, as the runway collections served largely to window-dress their trademarks. "It's like making a movie to sell the popcorn," Colombe Nicholas, the former head of Christian Dior USA, told me in 1998.

Princess Di's Brand-New Bag

In the age of accessories, handbags and shoes had taken over the role of perfumes, which weren't so lucrative anymore. The venerable Italian footwear maker Gucci was typical of brands in its class. Gucci's handbags and leather accessories—not counting its shoes—accounted for about $555 million, or about 56 percent of Gucci's reported 1997 sales, while only 10 percent of Gucci's revenue came from its apparel collections.

Thus the culture of fashion—once grounded in designer clothes—was forced to adjust as fashion marketers found new ways to spotlight the accessories that became the locomotives of their empires. Suddenly all the models began carrying handbags on the runways. There was that curious moment in Milan during a Prada fashion show where a movie camera was planted down low along the runway, projecting live images of all the models at ankle level on-screen around the perimeter of the space, so that the live audience could gawk at the screen and concentrate on the stars of the show: the newest Prada shoes!

The best shills for designer accessories were fashion magazine editors and socialite clients who were buddies of designers, along with a few choice celebrities—all of whom were showered with free handbags to carry around town, especially during Fashion Week. In 1995, the former French First Lady Bernadette Chirac sent Princess Diana a model of a new Christian Dior bag as a gift. Dior immediately named this unreleased bag "Lady Dior," and Princess Diana became a walking billboard for that quilted leather satchel with a metal Dior logo dangling from its handles like a charm bracelet, as photos of her ran everywhere. Sales took off after that.

Then along came Fendi. In 1997, the Roman fashion house best known for its exotic furs by Karl Lagerfeld introduced the Fendi Ba-

guette, a compact, horizontal handbag that tucked under the arm like a loaf of French bread. With its oversize FF buckle, the Baguette was a show-offy trinket—a blockbuster that ignited women's interest in luxury handbags. Women paid a lot of bread (from $895 to $4,000) for their Baguettes—the wide price range reflecting the hundreds of materials that the limited editions of the Baguette came in, including snakeskin, crocodile, embellished velvets, textured leathers, and mirrored fabrics. That's what made the Baguette a stroke of marketing genius. Women could join the cult but still feel special and unique—as they didn't worry about seeing themselves coming and going.

Princess Diana, here in 1996, often carried her Dior quilted satchel, which became known as the "Lady Dior" handbag.

More than three hundred thousand Baguettes sold in the first couple of years—and then Fendi spawned the mini-size Croissant, which women liked to shoulder to black-tie events. As unit sales climbed well into the millions, the buzz enveloping the Baguette seduced luxury goods giant LVMH to engage in a corporate bidding war to take control of all of Fendi in 2001, which spiked the valuation of the house of Fendi to an astounding $950 million.

Meanwhile, design houses toiled at the drawing board to create seasonal handbags, which they hyped heavily in the quest to become the next "it bag" of the moment—resulting in hits like YSL's Mombasa bag, Prada's Bowling bag, and Louis Vuitton's Murakami bags—and Fendi's own encore, the Spy bag.

Leave a Message for Carrie's Shoes

It's no coincidence that fashion's enduring shoe-and-bag fetish soared in precisely the same years that *Sex and the City* captivated huge audiences of mostly women from 1998 to 2010. The show's run included two Hollywood movies and an endless afterlife in syndication—reruns on E! Entertainment.

The series, famous for its sophisticated, sex-filled plots and stylish Manhattan locations, was a veritable fashion show of the hottest designer labels, including Roberto Cavalli, Dior, YSL, Narciso Rodriguez, Calvin Klein, Marc Jacobs, Versace, Gucci, Prada—none of whom paid for plugs to be on camera. They owed their prominent placement to the eclectic taste of costume designer Patricia Field, who scoured showrooms, vintage shops, and flea markets for original pieces, showing her talent for dressing the show's four lead characters to make them appear authentic, trendy, and nuanced enough to be believable. *Sex and the City* was absolutely entertaining and—organic!

Loyal viewers tuned in to see the stylish wardrobes of their favorite characters: Charlotte (played by Kristin Davis), the earnest yuppie socialite; Samantha (Kim Cattrall), the man-chasing publicist; and Miranda (Cynthia Nixon), the cynical corporate lawyer. Sarah Jessica Parker's Carrie was the clotheshorse of the quartet, carrying the torch for all things avant-garde, starting with her shoes and handbags. True, the word *fashion* wasn't in the show's title, but if anyone had any doubt that sex should have had second billing instead of first, consider that even with Carrie's active love life, she only changed boyfriends four times in twelve years. In the second movie alone, Parker told me, she changed outfits sixty times in 146 minutes.

A veteran romantic/comedy actress, Parker's signature personal style came shining through—a bonus for a show created to evoke the scotch-

and-skyline glamour that is Manhattan. In one episode, Carrie attended a red-carpet theater premiere gingerly toting a small Prada satchel dripping with a yard of fringe—an awkward look that most women could never pull off. In her private life, Parker made no secret that she loved borrowing hundreds of dresses and gowns, from Oscar de la Renta, Narciso Rodriguez, Tom Ford, Alexander McQueen, and Michael Kors—all designers who loved dressing her—making her and Carrie Bradshaw a seamless extension in people's minds.

In June 2004, when the Council of Fashion Designers of America honored her as the style icon of the year, Isaac Mizrahi presented the award to her, gushing: "Just think. There are millions of women all around America, all these Carrie Bradshaw wannabes, who want to be *you*!"

Sex and the City was a running showcase for the hottest designer accessories. Carrie once stashed her bikini undies inside a Fendi Baguette as she headed for a sleepover at her boyfriend's ("Mr. Big's") apartment. In another episode, she was wearing a Dior saddlebag purse when she and Mr. Big stumbled into the Central Park lake, and she hit the water shrieking, "Oh my Dior!"

But stiletto pumps were always Carrie's thing—and millions of women kicked off their abbreviated "kitten" heels and copycatted her. Carrie programmed her answering machine to tell callers, "I'm not here, but my shoes are, so leave a message." Carrie's size-seven feet were made for Manolo Blahnik, a label she mentioned so much that she single-handedly positioned Blahniks into one of the most coveted labels in shoedom. In one *Sex and the City* story line, a common street mugger spotted luxury when he cornered Carrie in a back alley, grabbed her purse, and then pointed his gun at her feet. "Take off the damn Blahniks!" he shouted as she tearfully stepped out of her shoes.

Smart robber. Carrie had no money in her purse, or in the bank, but her friend Miranda once estimated that Carrie had invested a total of about $40,000 in shoes—that would be one hundred pairs averaging $400 apiece.

At the end of the first *Sex and the City* movie, Carrie married Mr. Big wearing blue satin Manolo Blahnik pumps with a jeweled buckle. Women still troop into Blahnik's New York boutique on West Fifty-

Fourth Street in search of "Carrie's wedding shoes," a $965 style that is a perennial bestseller. "We sell them like cakes," designer Manolo Blahnik told CNN in 2010. Parker even appeared at the Blahnik boutique for a charity promotion in 2011, where she autographed "SJP" on the bottoms of certain styles she codesigned with Blahnik, as starstruck crowds lined up on the block outside the store waiting their turn to meet her and buy the shoes. Her fashion persona seemed as strong as ever three years later, leading her to enter into a formal partnership with George Malkemus, the CEO of Manolo Blahnik, to market her own exclusive SJP-label shoes (priced from $195 to $395) for Nordstrom, for spring 2014.

It was Carrie Bradshaw déjà vu on *The Wendy Williams Show* in February 2014 when Parker came bouncing out from backstage, swinging her blonde-streaked hair, in a full gray dress and turquoise ankle-strapped heels as the studio audience of rapt young women gave her a loud and long standing ovation. The forty-eight-year-old actress giggled as she talked up her new SJP collection: her choice of sleek silhouettes in vibrant shades like geranium and purple, with every pair featuring her understated logo—a narrow strip of grosgrain ribbon seam up the back heel. YouTube viewers watching the segment on the

Sarah Jessica Parker signed the soles of Manolo Blahnik shoes she helped design, on Fashion's Night Out in New York on September 8, 2011.

show gushed like this: April Josey posted "Love love love her shoe line. I will be buying J." And from Nikki Nicole: "I love them all! Simple yet sexy. I already created a Pinterest board for the SJP collection."

Before the advent of YouTube, Facebook, Twitter, and Instagram, HBO's *Sex and the City* website spread much of the show's fashion chatter, as it meticulously listed designer wardrobe credits for every outfit the characters wore—just like in the back pages of *Vogue*. Not that shoppers could run out and buy the characters' outfits, which were from past retail seasons. But the popular series exposed millions of women to designer fashions that were fanciful and a lot dressier than the knockaround sportswear they were accustomed to wearing.

And that amounted to a full-on potent fashion education that affected the show's rabid TV fans, stimulating their interest to own the latest accessories, helping catapult the category to the forefront of fashion. Shoes and handbags—or fashion, for that matter—would never play bigger on prime-time TV than they did during the stylish and unforgettable reign of *Sex and the City*.

Chapter Six

. . . .

EXPLOITING AMERICA'S SHOE FETISH
Jessica Simpson and Vince Camuto Play Footsie

These young women don't know who Marc Jacobs or Karl Lagerfeld are,
but if you mention Jessica [Simpson] to our sales associates, they light up.

—Dorrit Bern, CEO of Charming Shoppes Inc., which operated one
thousand Fashion Bug stores in 2005

As the first decade of the twenty-first century neared a midpoint,
SJP's foray into the fashion business wasn't an idiosyncrasy; it was
the leading edge of a wave that would rock the industry. Another early
adapter was a TV celebrity with an image that was the opposite of SJP:
Jessica Simpson.

In 2004, propelled by the popularity of her reality show and the endless photos in style and celebrity magazines it had spawned, she made the
plunge. She began on the edge of fashion, with scent—but not a glamorous perfume like Elizabeth Taylor's White Diamonds. Her kickoff

fragrance was a cheesy drugstore brand, strictly for juveniles to play dress-up with. Dessert Beauty by Jessica Simpson featured edible lip glosses and scents such as "Creamy" (reeking of vanilla and caramel) and "Dreamy" (scented with milk chocolate and coconut). Dessert Beauty was a low-rent start for Simpson, reflecting a dismissive view of the audience she first attracted and the low expectations that marketers had of her as a fashion brand.

In fashion you're only as good as your licensing partner, no matter how big of a celebrity you are. Simpson had signed with Tarrant Apparel Group, a middling Los Angeles apparel manufacturer of private-label sportswear for The Limited, Kmart, Chico's, and American Rag (TV's *American Idol* fashion label of sporty togs sold exclusively at Macy's). For Gerard Guez, Tarrant's chief executive officer, signing Jessica Simpson was a major coup for his company, which had been treading water for years. Tarrant's sales had never exceeded $350 million, and had plunged in 2003 to $155 million—after the company posted huge losses from factory closings. Tarrant was desperate for a new gimmick to jumpstart its fortunes. When Jessica Simpson launched her jeans collection in 2005, it had the potential to be the biggest brand in his portfolio.

But Guez didn't think Jessica Simpson's appeal could sustain an upmarket "premium denim" label, like the trendy $150-and-up jeans that since 2001 had been consistently blowing off the shelves at Barneys New York and Fred Segal. Instead he came up with "JS," a $49 jeans collection at the one-thousand-store Fashion Bug chain in the strip malls. Jessica's top-tier line would be $69 jeans and coordinates called "Princy" (her childhood nickname), sold to six hundred department stores, including Macy's and Dillard's.

Jessica + jeans = an easy idea, a marketing cinch for women who were primed to believe in the pretty starlet, such as the five million women who trooped through Fashion Bug stores every week. "Their whole world of importance is celebrities—how they look and think and behave," Dorrit Bern, the CEO of Charming Shoppes Inc. (owner of Fashion Bug) told me in 2005 when I was reporting on Jessica Simpson's foray into fashion for *The Wall Street Journal*. "These young women don't know who Marc Jacobs or Karl Lagerfeld are, but if you mention Jessica to our sales associates, they light up."

In the fall of 2004, when I first approached Guez about the story, he was gung ho about the promise of a page-one story in *The Wall Street Journal* profiling Jessica Simpson and his own Tarrant. Guez needed some upbeat press to buttress what he had recently promised Wall Street analysts: that the Jessica Simpson business would help Tarrant return to profitability by boosting its sales to the $250 million range in the next year. (He also disclosed that Tarrant had guaranteed Jessica royalty payments of at least $4.5 million in that first year.)

So it was a win-win, as I was happy to get the first crack at the story of the reality star's inaugural moves as a fashion brand. Visiting Tarrant, I got a good sense of how Simpson's deal would work. Jessica would be the face of the brand and the image—with the designing done by Tomoko Jones, a forty-nine-year-old Tokyo native and one of Tarrant's top in-house creators, whose job it was to interpret Jessica's personal style for the distressed jeans, frilly tops, and hoodies that made up the collection. The two had met previously when Simpson had given her some tear sheets from magazines of her favorite clothes, especially $350 True Religion jeans. (But Jessica also claimed her role in the tweaking and styling, saying, "I'm totally involved with everything that has my name on it.")

When I met Jessica at Tarrant's offices in Los Angeles, I was struck by how fresh-faced and downright pretty she was, even with barely any makeup on. She looked captivating in high-heeled western boots, rolled-up jeans, and a plunging gauze top, her golden hair loose and bedroom-messy. She was poised as she recollected her own knack for clothes when she was growing up in Texas—ostensibly before Rachel Zoe got ahold of her. She said: "Even though we were poor, I grew up loving clothes. Now before we go out, all my friends come over so I can help them get dressed."

This meeting was her first look at the sample clothing styles Tarrant had prepared for her review and approval. There were more than a hundred garments hanging on metal grids around the room, the jeans and tops and bottoms with distressed holes and embroidered appliqués, as well as several cutoff Daisy Duke styles in stonewashed denim. Jessica and I walked around as she pointed at different items. One set of jeans featured titles from her hit songs stitched on the waistband. "I nixed that, it's cheesy," she told me, chuckling.

We stopped in front of a knit top with the slogan CHICKEN OR FISH?

embroidered on it. Crinkling her nose, Jessica piped up and suggested, "Instead of the words, maybe you could show a chicken and a fish with a question mark in between."

Jessica was good-humored about her infamous "Chicken of the Sea" moment, which was seared in MTV viewers' minds and immortalized on YouTube. But after Tarrant's design team edited the samples, the chicken-fish idea got dropped. "Jessica said she didn't want her collection to be limiting and aimed only at her TV fans," Jones told me. What did make the cut was Jessica's favorite image—a small yellow rose of Texas, to be used on certain jeans and tops.

I checked in with Bern of Charming Shoppes, which was among the first retailers to review the completed collection. She sounded excited when she told me: "We were impressed that the jeans fit as well as they looked."

But this celebrity deal—aimed right at her Middle American fans—would turn out to be the soufflé that didn't rise. When it came time for deliveries and advertising, Tarrant came up short—largely because it failed to raise the $25 million of working capital it had previously specified that it would need to take Simpson's jeans from manufacturing to marketing. So instead of the tasty spread that Tarrant had tempted buyers with in meetings, in actuality, only a disappointing trickle of Jessica Simpson merchandise was shipped into stores.

Things got ugly pretty quickly. Tarrant sued Jessica, alleging that she breached her contract to promote the collections. In court papers Tarrant charged that it did not obtain "meaningful support from Ms. Simpson," alleging "she would not pose for photos or provide photographs to promote the jeans collections." As a result, the suit said, Charming Shoppes canceled a $44 million retail order with Tarrant, which said: "Without celebrity marketing, the product went nowhere."

Simpson countersued, alleging that Tarrant had failed to live up to its promises, and was joined by Camuto Group, which, like Tarrant, had already signed on as a licensee. The court dismissed most of Tarrant's claims; Tarrant ended its deal with Simpson, and the case was closed. Camuto ended up spending $15 million to buy the master license of Jessica Simpson from Kids Headquarters, the apparel maker that shared the rights with Jessica.

The end of 2005 was full of bad news for poor Jessica. *Newlyweds* was already off the air and Nick and Jessica were heading for a divorce, while her Hollywood debut as Daisy Duke in *The Dukes of Hazzard* was universally panned. But Jessica was getting ready to ride again, this time under the auspices of Camuto.

Vince Camuto, the Shoe Guy

Celebrity fashion labels are probably the most opportunistic business gamble there is, and every savvy financial backer knows not to spend too much investing in what is likely to be a flash-in-the-pan fashion label. Today's celebrity can become a has-been in a hurry.

Shortly after she graduated from Princeton, actress Brooke Shields came out with her own line of jeans in 1987 by jeans manufacturer Eric Rothfeld, who said crowds of women turned up in department stores to meet the actress who once did Calvin Klein jeans commercials. Sales were respectable at the beginning but dissipated in a few months after the novelty wore off, and retailers didn't place reorders. "Women just didn't see her as a designer like Calvin Klein," Rothfeld told me. It was a classic case of a "one year you're in, the next year out of business" casualty. Now some people were reading Jessica Simpson's disappointing outing into jeans as a one-and-done effort.

But Camuto Group knew exactly what it was doing. Owner Vince Camuto was one of the most experienced shoe manufacturers in America. He had different ideas for utilizing Jessica—forget the clothes for the moment and zero in on the shoes. Fashion's accessories moment had played right into his strong suit. Shoes were something Camuto happened to know a whole lot about. "We knew we could build a shoe business, because that's what we do, regardless of the brand," Alex Del Cielo, chief operating officer of Camuto Group told me in 2013. And that's why Vince Camuto had been a shoe guy forever. In the 1960s, the Bronx-born teenager dropped out of high school to help his widowed mom cover their daily expenses. He gravitated to a sales job that offered good commissions and the promise of fast advancement: Young Vince became a shoe salesman in Midtown Manhattan at I. Miller, the toniest women's footwear retailer in the business. Back then—a half century before women's shoe obsession turned footwear into a fashion juggernaut—shoes nonetheless held a hallowed spot, the accessory that finished a well-dressed woman's ensemble. In the 1960s, women's footwear choices were a narrow selection limited mainly to leather—black and black patent, shades of brown and bone for Easter and summer—with matching handbags.

I. Miller was a lofty, intimidating retailer that catered to the Junior League set, who loved Italian imports and alligator pumps. Shoes were well crafted in precise sizes, from narrow AAA to B and C widths, as well as half sizes. Salesmen—always authoritative and dressed in suits back then—painstakingly measured a woman's foot with a metal contraption before she tried on shoes in order to achieve the perfect fit. Women weighed their shoe purchases carefully and confided to their favorite salesmen like a girlfriend or a shrink: Would the black *peau de soie* pumps be dressy enough for the chiffon cocktail dress I just bought for the country-club party? Do these shoes make my feet look big? (It seems women have long been fixated on having the smallest feet.)

Vince Camuto, a handsome fellow with a ready smile and patient demeanor—he and his mother talked about everything at home, so he was accustomed to listening to women—developed a real talent for selling shoes. He paid attention to women, their desires and insecurities. He listened while they fretted and kept changing their minds. He also took note about their ideas regarding straps, bows, and heel heights—design ideas that he could pass on to the shoe buyers.

Above all he sold—boxes and boxes of shoes to I. Miller patrons—as he quickly rose to top salesman in the store. "I really liked selling shoes to women, and I was good at it," he recalled to me in 2012.

With his experience of listening to the customers, he belonged in the merchandising and design end of the shoe business. He became a fashion merchandiser for a shoe manufacturer in Miami, where he took on the challenge of turning around a struggling shoe factory. In reviving the factory—revamping everything from logistics to design—he made it profitable. Many job offers followed, and he became the head of an import division for a footwear retailer. His next move was entrepreneurial when Bank of Sumitomo in New York asked him to start a business in Brazil importing private-label shoes.

For shoes, the label MADE IN BRAZIL was beginning to become

almost as revered as MADE IN ITALY. Brazilian shoes were well made—
with cheap labor. Brazil's footwear industry was based in its southern-
most region in a city called Novo Hamburgo. In the 1800s, the region
attracted German immigrants, including skilled craftsmen who developed Brazil's shoe industry with leather tanneries and shoemaking
machinery. By the 1960s, Novo Hamburgo was exporting low-cost footwear around the world. Bank Sumitomo decided Brazil and its shoes
were a good investment, and so was Camuto.

Camuto became a pioneer of sorts, shuttling between New York and
Novo Hamburgo, working for Sumitomo's Brazilian factories. He soon
met Jerome Fisher, another American in Brazil hired by Sumitomo. The
pair decided to go out on their own, creating Fisher Camuto, making
private-label women's shoes for department stores, using Brazilian con-
tractors. When they opened their New York office in a high-rise office
building at 9 West Fifty-Seventh Street, they began to start thinking of a
brand name they could use. Camuto wasn't keen on using his own name,
but when he looked out the window and saw the large red 9 sculpture in
front of the building, the red 9 struck him as catchy. "That's how we
came up with the name Nine West," he told me. Nine West became the
name of the midpriced shoes they sold to department stores, and they
started to roll out Nine West stores in 1983 in Stamford, Connecticut, the company's corporate
headquarters.

Before Nine West, there
was an elite layer of expensive fashion shoes—trendy
labels like Salvatore Ferragamo, David Evins, Charles
Jourdan, Susan Bennis/War-
ren Edwards, Joan & David,
and Maud Frizon, with
shoes that sold for between
$150 and about $400. Be-
low them were the private-

Nine West founders Jerome Fisher (far left) and
Vince Camuto (in white suit) at their headquarters,
9 West Fifty-Seventh Street, in the 1970s.

label department-store shoes that most women wore (and that Fisher
Camuto made starting in the 1970s)—fashionable style priced from

$19 up to $200—as well as the footwear marketed by independent boutiques. Nine West set a new fashion standard for working women's shoes by introducing real variety: trendy pumps, sandals, and boots in many shades and novelty styles, priced affordably, from $20 to about $100. Nine West designers traveled to Italy and France scouting for unusual boutique styles they could reinterpret for American customers. Fashion footwear was in huge demand after millions of American women entered the workforce in the 1980s and started buying wardrobes of shoes for their pantsuits, dresses, and casual clothes. By the late 1980s, footwear experts believed that every woman in America owned at least a couple of pairs of Nine West shoes.

Camuto became chief executive officer of Nine West in 1993 when the company went public on the New York Stock Exchange, with annual sales of $552 million, and Brazilian factories turning out 130,000 pairs of shoes a day. Sales climbed to more than $1 billion as the company added labels and acquired other brands such as Easy Spirit and Pappagallo. By the end of the decade, the two biggest apparel makers on Seventh Avenue—Liz Claiborne Inc. and Jones Apparel Group—were locked in a bidding war to acquire Nine West, which Jones eventually bought in 1999 for $1.5 billion.

Camuto was first a merchant and then a manufacturer—and he still loved the shoe business. But after Nine West was sold, he had to move on. He would have to wait two years before he could go back into the shoe business, as stipulated in his noncompete agreement. Camuto spent that time in Greenwich, Connecticut, enjoying his family and his second wife, Louise Drevenstam, a former Miss Sweden and first runner-up to Miss Universe in 1989, as well as thinking about his next professional moves.

A modern, low-rise Greenwich office building whose tenants included a hedge fund became the headquarters for Camuto Group, as he became an expert resource to footwear retailers along with a number of his former Nine West colleagues such as Del Cielo, whom he brought on. Camuto received a call from his retail executive friend Alex Dillard, who convinced him to start manufacturing again: private-label shoes for his family's Dillard's department stores, the three-hundred-store chain based in Little Rock, Arkansas. Camuto Group launched four new shoe brands for Dillard's, starting with Antonio Melani, a name he says he made up during a business dinner in Italy by combining the name of the wine, Melani, with their waiter's first name that night.

Camuto's footwear licensing deals grew over the years to include major retail chains such as Banana Republic, Ann Taylor, and BCBG Max Azria, a fast-growing fashion label with three hundred stores. Camuto Group had footwear showrooms around Manhattan, but Vince stayed mostly in Greenwich, where his design teams worked.

Discovering Jessica

It was in fact in his Greenwich home in 2003, on an ordinary evening hanging out in front of the TV with his thirteen-year-old son, John, that Camuto told me he first laid eyes on Jessica Simpson. "We were just flipping channels and we happened to stop on MTV when Jessica was on," recalled John in 2013, now twenty-three and manager of product and retail development for Camuto Group. "She's such a beautiful woman, so that got our attention. And she was this personality, really bubbly; she was awesome, so that just kept us on that channel."

Vince Camuto had a good hunch about the possibilities for Jessica as a brand, but first he did his research, which led to meeting with her for the first time over dinner with her mother, Tina, in Manhattan. They hit it off immediately, Vince reported back to his son. "My dad always liked Jessica," John remembered to me.

After Tarrant stumbled out of the gate launching Jessica Simpson jeans, Camuto picked up the pieces, taking over the master license agreement. He now had the power to determine the future of the Jessica Simpson brand. His first order of business was to sever Jessica's association with the failed jeans line, which had begun to tarnish her image. Being Camuto, he naturally redirected her into the business he knew best: shoes. It just so happened that footwear also was the fashion category with the buzz of the moment and the healthiest profit margins, so the timing was fortuitous.

Sex and the City had already created mass lust for stiletto pumps. But millions of women couldn't afford to wear Carrie Bradshaw's $600 pairs of Manolo Blahnik, Christian Louboutin, or Jimmy Choo high heels, which left a huge, slavering market for sexy high heels with a younger edge that cost less than $100.

Camuto turned them out en masse—with a label in the cursive signature of Jessica Simpson—and they were a runaway (not runway) hit. Camuto went with Jessica's trademark look—the one captured by paparazzi everywhere—those thick cork platforms that women used to playfully nickname "fuck me" pumps for their former association with hookers. Jessica's beauty and innocence had transformed that faded streetwalker stigma into respectable fashion that was hip and jazzy and gave short women (Jessica is just five foot two) real stature. In paparazzi shots, Jessica could be seen tooling around town in those heels, tossing her long blonde hair and wearing big sunglasses; a minidress, shorts, or tight leggings; and carrying a big designer satchel over her arm.

Jessica's fame now centered less around her Brigitte Bardot cuteness and more on her struggles with boyfriends and her steady weight gain that took her from voluptuous to zaftig. The tabloids couldn't get enough of her, especially for the two years she dated Dallas Cowboys quarterback Tony Romo, who she proclaimed "the love of my life" on the cover of *People* magazine. On the eve of Jessica's twenty-ninth birthday, Romo broke up with her. She was crestfallen, and so were women across America. It wasn't a collective snicker, as in "knock the bitch off the throne," but more of an "aw, shoot" sigh, as in *Poor Jessica. I've been there.*

Jessica's losing the affection of Romo, ironically, expanded and solidified America's affection for Jessica Simpson. Women liked not only her shoes, but also that they could relate to her pain, which made her so approachable. She was their celebrity mascot—blonde and bruised and struggling with her weight. Of course, the shoes happened to look pretty good. Camuto's design teams dreamed up many iterations of stilettos and platforms in a rainbow of shades and materials—priced to move at $69 to $89.

A secret to the popularity of Jessica Simpson platform shoes was that they were designed for comfortable walking. It was what Camuto's expert technicians had worked on for years—the perfect balance of form and foam: the more foam rubber, the more comfortable. And as fashion trends pushed the height of those platforms to five inches or so from 2009 onward, the pitch and balance of the shoes was even more important.

When it came to platform shoes that all the twentysomething gals loved wearing to clubs, the Jessica Simpson brand ruled, with estimated retail sales in the hundreds of millions. Women who bought the shoes also gravitated to Jessica Simpson handbags, which became popular too.

With his layered curly gray hair and year-round tan, the soft-spoken Camuto was a fashionable, elegant septuagenarian, with the Italian manner of wearing a loose scarf around his open-necked shirt and fitted sport jacket. The first time he showed me an array of Jessica Simpson pumps in 2007 in his New York showroom, I was amazed at the range of colors and variety of styling that his design teams turned out. He picked up shoe after shoe, reciting prices between $50 and $70. Unbelievable what you could do when you manufactured in China, with labor costs more than 50 percent lower than in Brazil.

When I first started researching this book in 2011, I was always asking women I ran into—women in their thirties or older around New York—if they wore Jessica Simpson shoes and clothes. My query was almost always met with an incredulous "No way!" or even, "I wouldn't be caught dead in Jessica Simpson."

But at one point, I encountered my sister's wealthy fiftyish friend, a New Yorker named Anne Cardone wearing some good-looking leather-and-suede tall boots—which my sister told her were fabulous. Cardone leaned in and whispered, "Don't tell anyone, but they are Jessica Simpson."

That sort of thing began to happen more and more often. A lot of women over forty still couldn't get past Jessica's dumb-blonde hick image—never forgetting her silly bit part in *The Dukes of Hazzard*. But as the years went by and the more distance she had from *Newlyweds* and her singing career, the more she flattened out into a generic famous person, a celebrity who hadn't made any hits, runs, or major errors. Chicken of the Sea may have gotten her noticed, but her fashion brand had become more about the intrinsic value of the merchandise.

In 2012, I met Parija Kavilanz, a *CNN Money* senior writer covering retail at a press briefing for a licensing convention. I posed my usual question to her, and I was surprised to hear that this woman not only owned a number of Jessica Simpson garments, but she had grown to love the brand so much that she actually went shopping looking for Jessica Simpson. A pretty, dark-haired woman in her thirties, Kavilanz looked very New York and cool—and I must say she looked well dressed.

She told me that she was a loyal Macy's shopper. And it was also clear that she was a sophisticated journalist, one who was skeptical of hype (she was covering retail, after all!) and one who loved intrinsic fashion—clothes that were trendy, well made, and in her price range. She didn't splurge on status labels she couldn't afford. Kavilanz fell into the Simpson brand quite accidentally. She bought a couple of sweaters and some shoes she liked, and when she read the label afterward, "I was shocked," she said, "because I had this impression—the Daisy Duke shorts, the cleavage tops—I don't really dress the way she does.

"I was pleasantly surprised, both with the shoe line and clothing. There is something there for everybody. It's not as out there as you would think; it's surprisingly toned down. It looks like her designers have made a decision to make her collection as mainstream as they can. And that makes sense. It's at Macy's."

Not all of her friends are impressed. "I thought that my friends would get a kick out of it, but women don't have a favorable opinion of her. I did have someone say, 'You actually bought Jessica Simpson shoes?' And I said, 'Yeah, why not?' The shoes were comfortable, they looked great. Then I asked her, 'I'm wearing them right now, what do you think? Aren't they great?'"

Kavilanz's friend looked at her feet and then admitted: "Actually they are."

This was just the goal that every serious fashion business has in mind: Create a label that attracts attention long enough for people to notice that they actually like the product—so they keep coming back. Simpson, though at first burdened with a bit of a low-rent image, had begun to outgrow that to become a pretty blonde celebrity, a sometime singer, who was affable enough and now would be largely unknown except for her beauty and visibility. This made her a fairly easy marketing hook—almost like a model. Her personal biography became pretty ordinary after *Newlyweds*, which was fortuitous for Camuto. Instead of getting caught carousing at night or snorting lines of cocaine like Lindsay Lohan, she's having babies, throwing baby showers, and being seen in public more as a mom. Thus new licensees to make Jessica Simpson maternity and infant's wear were introduced.

"We are lucky that we attached ourselves to a celebrity who stayed clean and had a normal life. She's down to earth," said Del Cielo.

Well, "normal" may be a stretch: Simpson's estimated net worth is about $100 million, according to CelebrityNetWorth.com. Given her success, there's a lot of quiet resentment toward Jessica Simpson among fashion insiders. As far as they are concerned, she doesn't count. When I first spoke to Harold Koda, the curator in charge of the Costume Institute at the Metropolitan Museum of Art in New York, he sighed and waved off any discussion of Jessica Simpson. "Teri, Jessica Simpson is not a fashion designer."

Nor does she pretend to be. Jessica Simpson, who has never posed as a designer, will never be invited to become a member of the elite Council of Fashion Designers of America trade group, though she did get a nod from the Accessories Council as the Fashion Icon award winner in 2005.

How much time she spends in the showroom with the design team isn't part of the story that the brand has tried to convey. Simpson is known around Camuto Group to personally be most interested in her shoes, and her taste is reflected in the in-store boutique at Macy's, for example, which features a big low-hanging crystal chandelier and curvy white furniture—which were said to be her idea. As with all licensing agreements, she and her team, led by her mother, Tina, are on hand to sign off on what's being created by Camuto Group's designers and the design teams at licensees.

But it's the designers who have managed to create items that appeal to such a broad and diverse group of consumers, and that's ultimately the brand's genius.

"Too many times we as fashion companies only look to the left coast or to the right coast, but Middle America loves Jessica Simpson," says Del Cielo.

Chicken or fish? More like cash or credit? Just seven years after she was nibbling on that tuna salad, Jessica had become Seventh Avenue royalty, with the most successful fashion brand of the new millennium. She was thirty-two when her fashion empire hit the golden mark—an estimated $1 billion in annual retail sales at the end of 2013. The array of Jessica Simpson products kept growing—handbags, sportswear, dresses, costume jewelry, bras, underwear, watches, baby clothes, fragrances, cosmetics.

Today, Jessica Simpson shoes are worn by women all around the world, especially in Greece, where high platform shoes worn with short dresses are a club uniform. She's a hit even in markets like South Korea, where women have never seen her on TV nor have any idea who she is.

In fact, it could be said that Jessica Simpson's biggest fashion achievement is having become invisible. Finally, she can let the shoes—and the rest of the merch—do the talking.

Chapter Seven

. . . .

THE INIMITABLE SOCIALITE

Tory Burch Gets Millions of Her BFFs to Walk a Mile in Her Shoes

In 2006, fresh from his launch of Jessica Simpson shoes, Vince Camuto got a call from Tory Burch, another pretty blonde with a talent for getting noticed. In Tory's case, her notoriety had been largely limited to the New York social circles. He took her call expectantly.

It was an era when Manhattan's prettiest well-dressed young social-ites had shifted into the spotlight of a celebrity-hungry world, becoming a kind of hybrid—half debutante, half celebrity: celebutantes. Celebu-tantes were widely recognized from their front-row perch at the runway shows of their favorite new-guard fashion designers, who included Mi-chael Kors, Tuleh (now closed), and Zac Posen. Starting in 2001, hotel heiress and former teen model Paris Hilton became the celebutante of the tabloids, where she was lampooned for her spoiled-rich-girl bad behavior and exhibitionism. In the process, she became world-famous, demon-strating the global reach of all those popular websites—such as Patrick-McMullan.com, Style.com, and NewYorkSocialDiary.com—which filled their webpages with all those alluring women, high-stepping through Manhattan to fashion shows, charity galas, and boutique openings.

Publicists worked hard to court the crème of Manhattan's coolest society girls of the moment—Tinsley Mortimer, Genevieve Jones, Fabiola Beracasa, and Zani Gugelmann were among the most visible starting in 2005—plying them with designer clothes and fine jewelry to get photographed in, as well as stylish products like champagnes for them to shill. Their social media–driven cool factor now made them worthy endorsers—better than some movie stars because they were so charming in public and they didn't demand big fees. It's no wonder that before long, these women began to see themselves as far more than mere spectators of fashion, or even arbiters—they deserved to create the fashions themselves.

So they marched straight into fashion land. Jones and Gugelmann hung out their shingles, promoting themselves as jewelry designers, while Mortimer signed on as the "it girl" image for Samantha Thavasa handbags in Japan.

A decade older than these women, Tory Burch was a society figure who had always set herself apart from the pack. Like the others, she wasn't a trained designer. But she had grown up steeped in the ways of high fashion and more confidently sophisticated than most about the nuances of the marketplace. What's more, she got there first, seizing the opportunity before everybody else.

A Privileged Upbringing

Ah, to be Tory Robinson, born in Philadelphia in 1966 to wealthy, good-looking parents who were enthusiastic jet-setters with fabulous wardrobes. Investor Buddy Robinson and his glamorous wife, Reva, lived with Tory and her two brothers on a thirty-acre estate outside of Philadelphia, with two full-time servants, German shepherds, and horses. Buddy Robinson inherited his seat on the stock exchange from his father, along with a paper cup company, which he sold. Buddy and Reva were pleasure-seekers who typically took six-week cruises to Europe each year. With her movie-star looks, Reva was a former aspiring actress who once lived in Greenwich Village and dated Steve McQueen and Yul Brynner. Tory gets to admire her mom every day: An enlarged black-and-white photo of Reva in a leopard-print bikini in Cuba in the 1950s hangs on the wall of her office. Tory was also close to her dapper dad, who once squired around Philadelphia's own Grace Kelly—and wore his custom tuxedos lined with Hermès printed silk scarves, as Tory told *Vanity Fair*'s Michael Shnayerson in 2007.

At the exclusive Agnes Irwin School, Tory was petite, popular—and rugged, the captain of the varsity tennis team, who also rode horses. When it came time for college, she chose Ivy League but close to home: the University of Pennsylvania, where she majored in art history, played on the tennis team, and actively dated lots of boyfriends. She stood out as an original dresser who could rock Grateful Dead T-shirts or exude an equestrian Hermès vibe, while chicly accessorizing herself the way European women did, with silk scarves, cuff bracelets, and interesting rings. Her look, which classmates described as half preppy and half jock, merited its own category: "Torywear," they called it, she admitted to Shnayerson.

Given her position in society and her strong sense of style, a career in fashion seemed like a foregone conclusion. So Reva Robinson rang up one of her favorite New York designers, Zoran, the Yugoslavian-born creator of a luxury take on Gap sportswear for the rich, to find a place for Tory to get started. Such were the connections of the society set.

Tory started by running errands and pouring champagne at Zoran's SoHo loft studio, where his famous clients like Lauren Hutton, Nancy Friday, and Gloria Vanderbilt dropped by.

With her charm and sporty, patrician looks, Tory moved on after a few months into her real calling: the fashion establishment—the publicity department at Ralph Lauren, then at Vera Wang and Narciso Rodriguez. She got married to Christopher Burch, thirteen years her senior, a wealthy Philadelphia venture capitalist and divorcé, the father of three daughters. Soon Tory took a break to have identical twin boys and then another son.

The Burches lived on Fifth Avenue at the posh Pierre Hotel—Chris Burch's bachelor digs, across from Central Park and Bergdorf Goodman—where they combined three suites to make a nine-thousand-square-foot mansion of an apartment, transformed into an exquisitely appointed home by interior decorator Daniel Romualdez, who also decorated their home in Southampton.

The Burches did the Manhattan social whirl, where Tory was now a presence at all the key fashion soirees. She was always captured by party photographers in a familiar, relaxed pose, gazing straight ahead, with a warm half smile, exquisitely dressed, so wholesomely pretty, like a Ralph Lauren model.

As her sons went off to school, Tory Burch was ready to go back into fashion, but no longer as an employee. This time she would be running her own fashion business.

A Sporting Chance in Sportswear

Tory saw the white space in women's fashion that could be her niche: What was missing were those hip, slide-around clothes that had a quiet, confident style, yet were far more feminine and embellished than, say, Banana Republic sportswear. Her own wardrobe was much more eclectic, patterned after the way rich continentals like her mother dressed: chic sporty, a mélange of vintage and designer styles—some picked up in Europe, a few pieces of J.Crew, some fabulous costume jewelry, unusual rings, dangling earrings, and cuff bracelets. She set out to commercialize her fashion vision, which read aspirational, to both rich women and wannabes.

From their New York living room, Tory and Chris Burch brought in fashion and retail experts and began holding meetings as she mapped out her ideas of starting a fashion business. Because of Tory's own notoriety and social connections, they weren't just any consultants. From just down the street, Bergdorf Goodman's president, Ron Frasch, and women's fashion director, Robert Burke, came over to advise the Burches.

Tory had closely gauged the market, noting that there was a demand for fancier sportswear—printed silk blouses and pants, embroidered sweaters, and casual knit dresses. She knew to revive the dickey—a 1960s classic and favorite of her mom—creating a detachable turtleneck to snap into a V-neck for a layered look. But more than anything, Tory was fixated on the tunic—an embellished print top that would be her iconic item, just like Diane von Furstenberg's 1970s print wrap dress.

Chris Burch, who had learned about manufacturing by running a family-owned sweater business, interviewed many of the initial employees, and through a referral found designer Stephanie von Watzdorf, who became their vice president of design. They aimed for the midtier women's sector known as "contemporary," with tunics and dresses from $250 to $400, shoes from $150 to $350, and handbags from $400 to $600. Tory hired a firm to create the double *T* logo, which was discreetly embossed on tote bags and put on as many products as possible. Chris Burch used his business connections to find five Hong Kong factories to make the initial products—about fifty units each. "Our first orders were so small and we had to beg—and sometimes pay premiums to get factory space," he told me in 2008 for *The Wall Street Journal*.

The Burches told me they invested about $2 million in the business, as well as investments gathered from friends, which bought them a lease on a 1,900-square-foot boutique on the Lower East Side of Manhattan and covered the production of the first shipment of products, all made in Hong Kong, to fill the store. They came out of the gate with products for fifteen merchandise categories—including those colorful tunics, bottoms, dresses, blouses, shoes, skirts, umbrellas, swimsuits, and handbags.

When the time came to throw a party to inaugurate the new boutique, it was by invitation only, beckoning fashion insiders. Tory's own celebrity pull ensured that a tony crowd of society swells from the Upper East Side converged on the opening, along with Manhattan's top retail executives and the fashion press. They all drank in the store's orange and green signature colors, the shiny brass fixtures, the double *T* logo—the clear vision of the Tory Burch lifestyle concept. Almost all of the store's $80,000 worth of inventory sold in a single day, and then the reorders lived on at toryburch.com.

Tunic Tour de Force

The signature item for her brand was the Tory Tunic, a split-neck blouse in printed silk with elbow-length sleeves and a loose silhouette festooned with embroidery and crystals, that was genius in its commerciality. The colorful tunics caught on because they flattered women of all ages (covering a woman's arms!), were suitable for many body types, and offered versatility as a swimsuit cover-up (the way her mother, Reva, wore them) or as a blouse over pants. Tory told me she used a print polyester tunic she had bought in a Paris flea market as the template for the line she made in China. Oprah Winfrey received some tunics as a gift from one of her producers for Christmas in 2004. She loved them.

And it didn't stop there. As Tory was among the influential Manhattan trendsetters with all the best connections, she got a call to appear on *Oprah* when the talk-show queen featured the $250 tunics on the "Oprah's Favorite Things" segment in 2005.

Tory and Oprah sat together during a little fashion show of the tunics while Tory gave a self-deprecating backstory about the craziness of starting a company with her six kids underfoot, weaving a tableau relatable to any working mom. The *Oprah* appearance triggered eight million hits on toryburch.com and thousands of orders for the tunic, which became an instant hit and a sturdy staple that could be updated every season.

Tory Burch LLC tallied first-year sales at a respectable $2 million—and by its second year in business, the company was earning a profit.

This quick turnaround was almost unheard-of in fashion start-ups, and provoked some who had labored long and hard to earn their credits as designers.

But Tory wasn't looking over her shoulder; she was focused on the steep upside ahead of her. She recruited Brigitte Kleine, the president of women's wear at Michael Kors, to be president of her company, while she and Chris remained co–chief executives. The company was now taking wholesale orders from department stores like Saks Fifth Avenue, Bloomingdale's, Neiman Marcus, and Nordstrom, allowing the Burches to achieve economies of scale and hold down production costs.

Going Camuto

By 2006, the Burches had brought in more experts to help exploit the company's fashion accessories to the hilt. That's when Tory contacted Camuto, who had nothing to do with the shoes and handbags she had sold at her opening. He was impressed with all her initial buzz—but he was also well aware how fickle fashion could be.

In the end, he could tell brush from timber. If Camuto felt confident enough about the potential for a simpleton-Texas-blonde-turned-failed-pop-singer-turned-reality-show-star to spend $15 million tying up licensing for Jessica Simpson's brand, imagine how certain he felt about Tory Burch, a prettier-than-a-picture upstart, who wasn't a designer but who had a high profile, a classy image, terrific taste, and loads of ambition and pluck. It was easy for him to see in Tory Burch the twenty-first-century version of Lilly Pulitzer, the first American socialite who made it big in fashion.

A half century earlier, in the late 1950s, Lilly Pulitzer, the wife of publishing heir Peter Pulitzer, wasn't thinking about fashion when she opened her very own orange juice stand in Palm Beach, supplied by vast local orange groves her husband owned.

Lilly set up her canopy on the corner of the tony Worth Avenue shopping street, where she was quite the vision: a tanned, barefooted bohemian, squeezing her heart out of those oranges. But it was the way she was dressed that made women pay attention. Lilly worked in these little-nothing shifts that her dressmaker stitched together, using dime-store cotton fabric in the boldest floral prints she could find to camouflage the fruit stains. Women who stopped by the stand started begging her to sell them the spare shifts she always brought along with her. On the spot, Lilly came up with a price: $25 apiece. Before long, America's Junior Leaguers from Palm Beach to Nantucket were sporting these chic print shifts that they dubbed their "Lillys"—including the new First Lady, Jacqueline Kennedy, whom Lilly knew from her boarding school years at Miss Porter's.

Lilly Pulitzer, a thriving $100-million-a-year fashion empire, was born and continues today—still trading on the socialite allure of Lilly Pulitzer, who died in 2013.

Buoyed by Lilly's example—and the fast-track fashion triumphs of socialites-turned-designers Diane von Furstenberg and Carolina Herrera—both Camuto and the Burches were thinking big and long-term. Tory first came to Camuto with an idea of marketing the elegantly minimal and casually sporty ballerina flats—she brought along some vintage samples—that were a vital component to her post-preppy Euro style. Designer Marc Jacobs was already making a trend out of his $300 ballet shoes that looked sleek with Capri pants, à la Audrey Hepburn in *Sabrina*. But like many ballerina flats on the market, those flimsy, too-soft, leather-soled Marc Jacobs flats lacked support and hurt after you walked around in them for a while—as the former supermodel Veronica Webb warned me when I zeroed in on the cute, red Marc Jacobs ballet skimmers I spotted in her closet.

But in the hands of Camuto Group's experts, out came a high-quality, affordable, comfortable leather shoe, which was made at Camuto's Brazilian factories. The ballet flat was sleek and low-cut but had a sturdy shank for support and a flexible rubber sole, which had previously been the sign of a cheap shoe but was imperative for comfort. Elastic gripping the heel area made the shoes fit snugly without gaping—a feature that made the shoes curl upward when they were out of the box—not a very upscale look, but highly functional. The punch line: the oversize buckle, a double-*T* logo in brass that jumped out like an Oreo cookie.

Ballet bonanza: the iconic Tory Burch "Reva" flats—more than five million have sold as of 2013.

Tory wasn't thrilled initially with that prototype—not as classy as she'd envisioned. "At first she was wondering if that logo was too big," Kleine recalled to me in 2013. "But it made a statement, so we went with it—some buyers gravitated to it and others didn't." Tory even named it Reva, after her mother.

It turned out that the response wasn't as ambivalent as Tory first feared. Without a smidgen of advertising, the Reva ballet flat, at $195, flew off the shelves and quickly turned into an icon, with more than 250,000 Revas sold after two years. The company kept going, rolling out dozens of variations in suede, patent leather, leopard, and metallic leathers—and it took care to keep them special by not flooding the market. That meant playing up scarcity and the "waiting list" game of short-shipping retailers—sending a store perhaps only ninety instead of the one hundred pairs it actually ordered.

"We instituted a policy that told retailers: Before you mark them down, we'll take them back," Kleine explained to me. The Reva fever spread to other Tory Burch shoe styles, namely her distinctive block-heeled pumps festooned with beads and brass trimmings, and to the company's best-selling "Tory Tote," a long-handled open satchel stamped with a big Tory logo, which was embossed to be more discreet.

The Tory Story

By 2013, Revas tallied more than five million pairs sold. It seems as though every fashionable teenager in New York wore Revas, which also became the flats that women carried along to switch out of their stilettos. Reva knockoffs were more rampant than dandelions in a backyard—and so were illegal counterfeit versions. The company spent millions fighting counterfeiters, and won a $164 million lawsuit against 232 websites selling fake Tory Burch flats, handbags, and accessories, believed to be the largest sum of damages ever issued to a fashion firm against online counterfeiters.

While Tony Burch LLC was building a fine business based on fundamentals, it maintained its essential spark through the cult of personality symbolized by Tory Burch, starring as Manhattan's classiest celebutante. It was the best of both worlds: a savvy businesswoman with exquisite taste who also fit perfectly into the celebrity mold that success was beginning to require. Her persona was the best advertising the company could ask for and ensured a continued high profile by appearing on the cover of *Town & Country*, doing a fashion show on TV with Martha Stewart, and even playing herself in a cameo on the MTV teen reality show *The Hills*.

And on her popular retail website, ToryBurch.com, shoppers click on the Tory Blog tab to steep themselves in Tory's world. She shares with her fans snippets of her own reality, intertwined with her fashion business. On February 12, 2014, the day of her nine A.M. fashion show, her diary began at six A.M. "Wake up, breakfast with my boys, then hurry into hair and makeup." She sounded like every mom by four P.M., with her entry: "Zipping uptown for my son Sawyer's basketball game. Sawyer did a great job!" On March 25, Tory is pictured in profile, in white jeans and a blue-and-white-print blazer when she introduces the "Robinson" powder-blue satchel next to her: "The whole silhouette is cleaner for a really understated yet chic look, and we added a removable luggage tag. I bring this bag everywhere with me—here I am at Palm Beach with it." Her jet-set mom, Reva Robinson, posts on the blog, reminiscing about that leopard bikini she once wore in Cuba—that has now become the inspiration for her daughter's swimwear collection.

"Tory has been very smart about branding herself," Anna Wintour told *Vanity Fair* in 2007. "I think she completely understands the power of image and marketing and branding. . . . Women find her clothes accessible and now they're buying into Tory herself."

Brigitte Kleine told me how impressed she has been watching Tory evolve and hone her fashion and business skills over the years. Having worked with trained designers like Michael Kors and Donna Karan, Kleine says that Tory's role is much the same: managing design teams who help turn out so many products. "Tory is right there with them, poring over fabric samples and mood boards, in fittings, and is involved every step of the way," she says. "She is leading a team to execute and create her vision."

Surviving a Split

Tory's celebrity tilted toward notoriety after she and Chris Burch separated in 2008. Chris Burch remained on the board of Tory Burch, where he and Tory owned equal 28 percent stakes in the brand. As they headed for divorce, Tory Burch started dating the very famous Lance Armstrong for a short while.

In 2010, Chris Burch launched his own new retail concept, C. Wonder, which knocked off many of the main elements of Tory Burch stores, including the signature tufted ottomans, wallpapers, lacquered and brass furnishings, and light fixtures. The merchandise was far cheaper, with C. Wonder's Reva-like pink and blue ballet flats selling for only $98. As tensions rose between the two, Chris Burch found a new girlfriend, Monika Chiang, and launched her as a fashion business, as if making a statement: *I created Tory Burch, and I can do it again.*

The squabbling came to a head in 2012 with dueling lawsuits: Chris

Burch accusing Tory of impeding him from running C. Wonder and interfering with his attempts to sell his shares in Tory Burch LLC, and Tory suing him for stealing trade secrets to produce C. Wonder.

But the sniping ended in 2013, when the Burches finally resolved their differences out of court in a confidential settlement. Chris Burch was left with a minority stake in the flourishing Tory Burch empire. Sales were $800 million in 2012, giving Tory Burch a market valuation of about $3 billion (making Tory herself now worth more than $1 billion).

Ending the litigation also meant that Tory Burch could proceed, as anticipated, with the likelihood of an initial public offering in the near future. Through early 2014, the fashion house stayed mum on its plans. But given the triumphs of Michael Kors Holdings Ltd. as a public company since 2011, whose market capitalization had more than quadrupled to $20 billion by early 2014, Wall Street investors had high hopes for Tory Burch, the fashion label solidly grounded in shoes and accessories. As for Tory, who was once typecast as the Manhattan socialite who had no business calling herself a fashion designer—she was the bold-faced name who personified the modern patrician glamour that millions of women coveted. Tory would continue her gallop far ahead of Marc Jacobs, Proenza Schouler, Alexander Wang, Zac Posen, and Narciso Rodriguez, all considered among America's most heralded creative fashion houses—to become fashion's most hotly awaited public company.

Chapter Eight

. . . .

HIP-HOP HOORAY

Sean Combs, Tommy Hilfiger, and the Rise of Urban Chic

Puffy was making an impact on the designer arena. . . . Whether or not he or his team were talented or not wasn't the point. The definition of a designer is when you can gauge the shift of a particular moment. Sean John was right there and moved that dial.

—Stephanie Solomon, senior fashion director of Bloomingdale's, 2012

In the end, we always knew that the revolution would be televised—just not in the form of a two-hour fashion special on E! Entertainment television.

On February 10, 2001, "Revolution" was the theme of the runway show for Sean John, the fast-growing casual menswear brand founded by rap mogul Sean Puffy Combs in 1998. Simulcast on both E! and Style cable channels, the breathless coverage of not only the runway, but all the backstage preparations, reached millions of TV viewers.

At just thirty-one, Combs presented tantalizing fodder for must-see TV. "It is that perfect combination for us where entertainment and celebrity meet fashion and celebrity," Mindy Herman, president and chief executive of E! Networks, told the *Los Angeles Times*'s Valli Herman-Cohen at the time.

Among orthodox fashion insiders, Sean John's TV special was considered a breach of protocol in 2001. By essentially inviting the public into the front row at his fashion show, he was dissing the retail buyers and the fashion press, who expected to have an exclusive first look before the masses could pass judgment on it. It would take almost a full decade before designers would start live-streaming their shows on the Internet.

Combs wasn't just ahead of the curve but operating on a different plane, proving at every turn that fashion was no longer a gated community where the public stood on the outside, waiting to get in. As always, when the elite no longer ran the game, the rules changed. And regular folks wanted to see celebrities, the people they knew and cared about, not designers.

To Be Seen

Appearances counted for Sean Combs, who chose his nicknames—first Puffy then Puff Daddy or P. Diddy or just Diddy—and carried his monumental success for everyone to behold. He was a spit-shined, brown-skinned brother, a sharp dresser in the old-school tradition of the black gentleman, who wore his Sunday suits any day of the week he felt like it. Since the 1990s, his Midas touch as producer, writer, packager, and performer had propelled his Bad Boy Records label—promoting hip-hop's blockbusters like the Notorious B.I.G. (Biggie Smalls) and Mary J. Blige—to sales of more than twelve million records and CDs, and he wasn't humble about it. He liked to style and profile, with the bravado of a rapper. "I've got that swagger," he liked to say. So when Combs put his first name and middle name—"Sean John"—on a fashion label, he hired a design team to interpret his ideas and visions, while he focused squarely on the packaging—the arresting presentation. He was well aware that his menswear label required more than the new colors, fabrics, and silhouettes; the Sean John brand needed to revolve around a persona and a *lifestyle*—a term that fashion people loved to throw around ("It's all about lifestyle merchandising!") without bothering to attach that "lifestyle" to one particular genre or individual whose life or style consumers knew and cared enough about to want to emulate.

Combs wanted to be that guy. He was a bona fide celebrity, and he had an evocative story to heat his runway. He poured about $1 million into that seventeen-minute televised fashion show—about twice what a major show would normally cost—for a presentation that would be drop-dead telegenic. Combs made it a point to participate in the casting of the models for his show: twenty-five buff guys who telegraphed as straight and rugged—fourteen of whom appeared to be black or Latino. They were styled in diamond-studded platinum dog tags, and crocodile-skin jackets and exotic furs (fox, lynx, mink, lamb, tanuki), their bare, muscular chests set off by tight leather pants. It made me wonder just what Puffy might have told them backstage, because each model hit the bright lights and *owned* that runway, walking tall and proud, exuding a palpable authority. It was his fist-in-the-air fashion statement of a black man in charge.

Sean "Puffy" Combs backstage before his fashion show in 2002.

"I have this searing recollection of seeing real men on his runway, not those superskinny Peter Pan boys that edgy designers use," remembered Robin Givhan, who was the fashion critic for *The Washington Post*. "I was fascinated how Sean John represented masculinity on the runway, the same way that hip-hop offered an expanded definition of how young black men were defining themselves and embracing their own success. It wasn't gimmicky. They were black men who looked sexy, expensive, and powerful."

TV viewers taking all this in knew they weren't shopping for clothes on Sean John's runway—which didn't matter because most of the styles paraded that night would never be manufactured or available for retailers to order. The runway clothes were props, delicious eye candy designed strictly for impact. The Sean John runway spectacle was all about Puffy—you knew him by his original nickname, and he had become a black folk legend.

Puffed-Up Street Cred

Born in a Harlem public housing project on November 4, 1969, Puffy grew up in Mount Vernon, New York, raised by his widowed mother, Janice, a teaching assistant. After graduating from a Catholic high school, he headed to Washington, DC, to historically black Howard University to major in business, where an internship at black label Uptown Records led him to drop out of school and join the burgeoning hip-hop music scene in the late 1980s, ushered in by a new generation of ambitious black entrepreneurs like Andre Harrell and Russell Simmons, who built the industry from the ground up. Hard work, hustle, and success had honed Puffy into a bon vivant and international jet-setter, who fell hard for his fine-as-wine trophy girlfriend, Jennifer Lopez.

Puffy's legendary hosting of parties and after-parties ruled the clubs. He also diced with danger, which built street cred, as he still faced criminal charges for gun possession and bribery in connection with a 1999 shooting accident at a club in New York that left three people injured. He even had a famous defense attorney, Johnnie Cochran, who had represented O. J. Simpson.

The Saturday night overflowing audience of 1,200 for the most anticipated fashion show of the week, of course, featured a celebrity-studded front row: Busta Rhymes, Bobby Brown, Luther Vandross, Mary J. Blige, Stephen Baldwin, Paris Hilton, Anna Wintour, and NBA star Kevin Garnett, as well as Cochran. J.Lo was notably absent, fueling rumors that her relationship with Combs was on the skids, but Combs's publicist explained that she was hosting *Saturday Night Live* that same night. Nevertheless, Combs made certain her presence was felt—just as if she were in the front row. In the printed show program, he dedicated the show to her: "Jennifer, thanks for showing me life."

J.Lo also made an unexpected cameo in the video reel that ran throughout the fashion show, projected on a huge screen as the backdrop for the runway. Amid the mash-up of newsreel footage from the civil rights movement in the 1960s, there she was in living color: J.Lo bouncing around in the surf, a scene from the video for her then-current hit, "Love Don't Cost a Thing."

Puffy recorded two rap verses to be played at the beginning and the end of his show. He was talking to *you*. As the lights went down, the audience hushed to listen to his recorded voice-over in emphatic staccato cadence:

"See, everybody always asked me why I started designing clothes. I basically just wanted to look good, man. You know, to be perfectly honest, I was just, like, looking in the motherfucking mirror, looking at myself and saying, 'Boy, Goddamn, you look good!' You know, I just wanted my pants to drape perfectly over my combat boots. I just wanted to walk down the street like I was Shaft or John Travolta. I just wanted to feel what it would feel like to be one of those superbad, superfly motherfuckers!"

The spotlights came up on the wide, mirrored runway with four models silhouetted against a large screen, where snippets of the video ran all during the show. The first model, a caramel-colored brother with a shaved head in a cream hooded jacket and pants, was densely swaddled in a lush eight-foot-long scarf of coyote skins and foxtails. The parade of macho men proceeded; some were bare-chested in jeans and those diamond-studded dog tags with unlaced combat boots, long fur coats dragging the floor. There were three-piece suits in plaids and sequined sleeveless muscle shirts with tie-dye jeans.

As the final models strode out, Puffy's voice-over returned, energetically polishing his cred, rapping about how he had to use his big money to hire Cochran to get him out of his legal jam and back on the streets. But that was all just setup for the real message: "I'm gonna dress each and every one of you cocksuckers. Fuck the white press. . . . Hip-hop forever."

Calling his public, his future customers, "cocksuckers"! Flipping off the white press! Who watching could resist that rebellious, defiant, badass spirit. Talk about lifestyle!

Combs ambled out onstage, dressed in a tame black pullover and white shirt collar with black pants—and his usual diamond studs in both ears. He smiled and waved to the wild applause—a standing ovation.

"The way he did it was so smart," recalls Emil Wilbekin, the former editor in chief of *Vibe*. "He broke through the barriers. 'We are here and inspiring and we have money and we are going to sell clothes.' To see it done with such swagger and bravado, it was exciting. I remember Paris Hilton, Anna [Wintour] was there. . . . He showed it like it was a big European brand."

As kudos and rave reviews poured in after the show, all Combs's wishes were about to come true. Weeks later, on March 16, 2001, Combs was found acquitted of all charges in connection with his criminal trial. Next, the Council of Fashion Designers of America nominated him for the "Perry Ellis," the best newcomer menswear designer for 2001. He would be the first celebrity designer ever nominated, and only one black designer—Gordon Henderson in 1991—had ever won the same award. Combs didn't win that year—but he could look forward to more accolades from the fashion establishment he desperately wanted to impress.

Thanks, Tommy!

After 2001, for Sean John the path to profits was immediate and steady—which would have been remarkable for any new fashion house in its first five years of business and was even more amazing considering Combs was inexperienced as a designer, and fashion was a sideline business for him. Already very rich and famous, he could afford and attract a team of seasoned designers, like a former Calvin Klein design assistant, Heather Thomson, hired as Sean John design director. Puffy benefited as the demand for urban fashions had already been stoked by other black-owned fashion labels—the first wave—namely Cross Colours, FUBU, and Phat Farm, founded in 1992 by his friend and sometimes rival, fellow hip-hop entertainment mogul Russell Simmons, founder of Def Jam Recordings.

Both Simmons and Combs would always be quick to publicly thank one man for showing them the ropes of fashion. It was in fact a white designer who put the whole big-logoed, oversize look on the map—the designer who the rap artists first wore on videos, the man who became a friend and a generous advisor to both Combs and Simmons when they started their businesses—even when it hurt his own. His name was Tommy Hilfiger.

Tommy Hilfiger's image is now so wedded to preppy and red-white-and-blue Americana that people forget that Hilfiger, who founded his business in 1985, was a pioneer of urban fashion.

As a classic men's sportswear brand, Hilfiger was initially derided by his designer peers as simply a marketer who reinterpreted the polo shirts and rugby shirts that were already out there, namely by Polo Ralph Lauren. Still, Hilfiger caught on big. After the Hilfiger label exploded from 1990 until about 1997, Hilfiger effectively hijacked the runway from every menswear designer in fashion, including Armani, when it came to designer jeanswear. Naturally, the fashion establishment deplored the way he pushed his way in. "He may have well-styled, well-made products, but I don't like the connotation that he is a creative designer," Jack Hyde, a veteran men's fashion writer and professor at the Fashion Institute of Technology, told me in 1992 for *The Wall Street Journal.*

Yet it was Tommy Hilfiger—a white guy from upstate Elmira, New York—who was the first designer on Seventh Avenue to tie his label to popular music, starting with rock and roll in the 1970s. He keenly understood that men weren't motivated to buy clothes because they were expensive or constructed of Egyptian cotton or the finest worsted wools. He knew that American menswear needed a strong identity that went beyond its label—an identity that could come from Hilfiger's long association with pop music. More than anything, Hilfiger saw fashion first and foremost as entertainment, and that vision kept paying off by keeping his label au courant and happening, spanning generations of consumers.

Born in 1951, Hilfiger was the second in a family of nine children, the son of a local jeweler-watchmaker. The Hilfigers were a rock-and-roll clan: Tommy and his younger brother Andy played bass guitar in a family rock group.

Tommy was a high school senior in 1969 when he and two friends pooled $450 and opened People's Place, the only store in town that carried trendy bell-bottom jeans. As People's Place thrived, Tommy began making crude sketches of exclusive jeans styles he dreamed up—and hired local tailors to make—to give their shop a cooler, more original edge. Rock and roll and Motown were always playing at People's Place, where local bands earned $100 to play live at the store's fashion shows. Such experiences taught Hilfiger early on that fashion needed the glamour and sizzle of entertainment to move the merchandise.

After People's Place closed—a small town like Elmira couldn't support it forever—Tommy moved to Manhattan, where he began as a freelance designer for Jordache jeans in 1983. There he caught the eye, and imagination, of Mohan Murjani, an apparel contractor from India, who had launched the hot-selling Gloria Vanderbilt jeans in 1970 and Coca-Cola sportswear. Murjani envisioned another fast fortune by turning Tommy Hilfiger into a menswear label in 1985. The positioning filled a void for classic preppy sportswear priced a notch below department stores—years before discount outlet malls existed.

Murjani hired famous New York ad man George Lois to come up with a shock-and-awe campaign to put Hilfiger on the map in a hurry. In the summer of 1985 a huge billboard high above Times Square flashed in bold letters: THE FOUR GREAT AMERICAN DESIGNERS FOR MEN ARE R— L—, P— E—, C— K—, AND T— H—.

Everyone knew the first three, of course—Ralph Lauren, Perry Ellis, and Calvin Klein. But who was "T.H."?

Fashion insiders were aghast; the nerve of this imposter! But the flood of attendant publicity led curiosity seekers by the droves into Macy's and Bloomingdale's to discover Tommy "Hil-FINGER"—as they kept mispronouncing his name. There was nothing bogus about the clothes—the polos, Shetlands, and khakis were indeed preppy at popular prices—and sales took off. Yet Hilfiger knew his success would fade quickly if he didn't keep his cool factor hot by wooing rock-and-rollers. His first big score came in 1993 when the Hilfiger brand sponsored British rocker Pete Townshend—who wore Hilfiger polo shirts and blazers during his Psychoderelict concert tour across North America.

That was just a year after Tommy Hilfiger Inc. had reached the magic $100 million threshold—$107 million in sales, to be exact—and gone public on the New York Stock Exchange, one of the first fashion houses to jump into the bull run of the 1990s on Wall Street. Great timing: The initial public offering raised $100 million—used to expand rapidly across department stores.

Hilfiger gave preppy a strategic spin: Hilfiger's logos grew LARGE: his name spelled out in big block letters, bigger than the *E* on the eye chart—designed to see from far away across a crowded room. The big logos had everything to do with optics: designed expressly to drive eyeballs over to Hilfiger's section in stores like Macy's—which at first was only a few racks buried in a sea of apparel on circular racks and T-stands—across the vast men's sportswear floor. Those logos were as good as arrows, leading shoppers right to the spot. What's more, the huge graphics were novel—the only clothes people wore typically with big lettering back then were university sweatshirts.

Hilfiger probably didn't sense it at the time, but his combination of bold red, white, and blue color-blocking and the catchy logos were catnip to all those swaggering young black rappers, who were already showing off with status logos like Puma, Adidas, and Gucci. "Everybody loved Tommy. It was totally about the swag," said June Ambrose, fashion stylist to Jay Z, Mary J. Blige, and other hip-hop stars. Hilfiger made uniforms for the Lotus Formula One auto racing team—all those colorful decals slapped on the jumpsuits. The hip-hop kids went nuts when they saw rapper LL Cool J decked out in one onstage. Rapper Grand Puba wore a dark green Tommy jacket and Tommy T-shirt on his *2000* CD cover. Then came the *ka-ching!* moment in 1994, when Snoop Dogg wore a rugby shirt with TOMMY across the front and HILFIGER across the back on *Saturday Night Live*. Retailers from coast to coast called the following Monday morning begging for those rugbys. Tommy was officially on fire.

Hip-Hop Santa Claus

Such fortuitous plugs were part organic, part staged, and worth millions of dollars in publicity—and cost the company hardly anything. It was the power of the giveaway, peddled by Tommy's brother Andy Hilfiger, who was living in East Harlem, working as a lighting man for rock bands and music videos. He made fast buddies with all the video and music people as he showed up on sets like Santa Claus with free stuff, handing out an array of Tommy shirts and caps and duffel bags. Like grass seed, he knew it would take root somewhere. As Andy told me in

1998, "I never pushed for them to wear Tommy onstage. But you know, when you give away clothes, somebody's going to wear them somewhere where they will be noticed." Rap performers could call Hilfiger's showroom and be welcomed to come over and help themselves. Grand Puba and his posse walked out with three hundred free items. Hilfiger also began making clothes looser and oversize, the way the rappers liked them.

The hip-hop crowd also loved Polo Ralph Lauren and Timberland boots, as well as Burberry, Gucci, Versace, and Louis Vuitton—but none of those brands in the early 1990s would ever think to reach out and connect with them. Of course, those companies' execs saw who was wearing their merchandise, but they blithely ignored it—some fearing any association with rap and hip-hop, which many still perceived to be a thug culture. Fashion marketers back then took a while to believe in the crossover appeal of hip-hop.

Hilfiger was different. He and Andy had close black friends since high school, and their comfort level had always been apparent. When his clothes became a hit with hip-hop artists, Tommy was tickled. He loved to hear his name popping up in rap lyrics. Meanwhile, Hilfiger's company spent millions sponsoring rock concerts and creating original on-stage gear for the Rolling Stones, David Bowie, Sheryl Crow, Rod Stewart, Lenny Kravitz, and Britney Spears. The stars—including Crow, Bush, Sugar Ray, and Usher—put on live performances on his runways during Fashion Week. "I believe in entertainment

Hip-hop rocked Tommy Hilfiger's runway in 1996, featuring rapper Treach of Naughty by Nature.

on the runway, instead of a boring show. [Menswear] clothes are plain, you have to jazz them up," Hilfiger told me in 2012.

At one menswear show, Hilfiger sent rappers dancing down the runway, including Coolio and an up-and-comer who most of the audience didn't know was Sean Combs.

Using the power of celebrity, Tommy was raking in all the money and kudos, positioned as the hottest American designer in the early 1990s. This fact wasn't lost on some of the more enterprising celebrities. They wanted in. Around 1991, Russell Simmons called on Tommy to teach him how to become a fashion brand too.

"Russell came and said, 'I want to do my own line'—his own version of casual wear targeted to the young, urban hip-hop kids—and I said, 'Come over and I will show you how this works,'" Tommy recalled. Thus began a series of meetings and introductions, with Tommy delving into the nitty-gritty details, such as telling Simmons about the difference between ten-ounce and fourteen-ounce denim fabric.

But why would Tommy deign to share all his valuable institutional knowledge with a new competitor in his very own lane—one, in particular, who was well financed and could get up to speed in a hurry? "I liked him and he had been helping me all along, connecting me to artists who we were dressing. By that time our company was rolling along, we didn't feel threatened," he told me.

The House of Sean John

In 1997, looking for help launching his fashion business, Sean Combs asked Andy Hilfiger to connect him with Tommy. "We hit it off immediately," said Tommy. "I showed Puffy everything we were doing behind the scenes; I hooked him up with Brett Meyer, an attorney who understood fashion and music," who introduced him to Ashok Sani, the Indian apparel contractor who became Combs's business partner in fashion.

Sean John was a fashion start-up with the right infrastructure, in-house designers, and financing—with Puffy's celebrity always as the calling card that made the difference. At MAGIC, the huge Las Vegas menswear trade show that drew all the major retailers looking to place orders, Sean John debuted as an unknown, yet bigfooted in with an oversize booth, displaying a huge poster—a faded photograph of a young boy about nine years old, dressed in a suit and his mother's fur coat. The caption read, WHO IS SEAN JOHN? Retailers combing the aisles couldn't resist the intriguing come-on and wandered in in droves to meet the man behind the boy.

The initial Sean John collection for men was mainly dark denim jeans—plus T-shirts and caps and a few shirts in the $30 to $120 range. The clothes had a relaxed fit but weren't oversize. The signature item was a $120 velour tracksuit with zip front, a flat baseball-style knit collar, and elastic at the ankles. It came in rich, heathered shades like wine, charcoal gray, and navy. The all-important insignia—the logo appeared on the right chest—was relatively discreet: Combs's neat, cursive "Sean John" signature, either embroidered in thread or embossed in a rubbery relief on the fabric. Combs—who liked to wear suits a lot—was attuned to being his own billboard. Soon he was always wearing—and being photographed in—a Sean John velour tracksuit in burgundy, black, or navy, worn with black sneakers and, sometimes, with a big gold medallion. (Combs posed in the tracksuit, on a gigantic vertical billboard in the heart of Times Square, with his fist in the air—in the seminal Black Power salute that American track star medalists Tommie Smith and John Carlos made on the podium at the 1968 Summer Olympics.)

What distinguished Sean John from Phat Farm and its other urban-wear predecessors was Puffy's singular ability to engage the fashion establishment, from Kal Ruttenstein, the influential senior fashion director at Bloomingdale's, to *Vogue*'s Wintour, who recalled to me in 2013 that she always encouraged him "to go for it."

She said: "Puffy is a superstar. I admire that drive and that ambition and that belief in yourself and maybe [he is] over-the-top and says things [he] probably shouldn't, but . . . these larger-than-life personalities are good for fashion. We can't all be well behaved and perfect all the time. Life would be so boring."

As for Bloomingdale's Ruttenstein—the former president of Bonwit Teller and one of the most prescient retail trend-spotters in fashion—he was already in sync with the infectious appeal of hip-hop and signed on early to carry the likes of FUBU, Cross Colours, and Phat Farm. Always ahead of the curve, Ruttenstein got busy in 1995 creating exclusive hip-hop bling for Bloomie's—pendants with oversize dollar signs en-crusted with crystals—that flew off the shelves. In 1998, when Combs was ready to introduce Sean John, Ruttenstein was at the front of the line. The retail sharpshooter fell into a swoon, as he could now envision celebrity dollar signs about to flash in Bloomies' young men's sportswear departments, for he knew that Puffy Combs was hip-hop royalty, a rap mogul marketer with real Hollywood cachet.

So Bloomie's took the lead, introducing Sean John exclusively for a few weeks, before the line was available to other stores. Ruttenstein hosted a cocktail presentation for the fashion press at Bloomie's in New York, where Combs showed off his collection of jeanswear items, which were straightforward and attractive—and mainly distinctive because of their logo. The party favor was a black Sean John baseball cap. André Leon Talley, *Vogue*'s influential African American editor-at-large, was in the house, dressed in a Sean John T-shirt, cheering Combs on—another indication that the brand was on its way. Everybody left the store and headed over to a dinner at Mr. Chow's on East Fifty-Fourth Street—one of the favorite see-and-be-seen restaurants of New York's hip-hop kingpins.

Ruttenstein was confident that Combs's crossover celebrity would make him palatable to the white mainstream—and even the upscale crowd, unlike the other urban brands, which skewed more Middle Amer-ica and heavily black and Latino. Track clothes with bright colors and logos "really resonated strongly at the moment," remembered Stephanie Solomon, who took over the women's fashion directorship after Rutten-stein died in 2005. "It was novel and cool and kind of rebellious. All of us felt [Combs] was making an impact on the designer arena. . . . Whether or not he or his team were talented or not wasn't the point."

Solomon said that Sean John was coming out of a fashion culture and making a statement to the world. "That's the definition of a designer, when you can gauge the shift of a particular moment. Sean John was right there and moved that dial."

The Sean John velour tracksuits—worn with a variety of the trendi-est sneakers—became bestsellers. They also became the uniform for Rut-tenstein, a heavyset man who liked to dress comfortably. Given his stature in the industry, he became a walking billboard for the brand.

Play It Again, Sean

After the 2001 Fashion Week, when Sean John's fashion show had been televised and shown again and again, sales of Sean John kept soaring at retail, as many fans of the ubiquitous Tommy Hilfiger had switched their loyalties to Sean John, whom they saw as fresh and happening. What's more, black folks in particular took great pride in watching Sean John soar to the top of the fashion heap.

This was a difficult time for Hilfiger, whose brand was starting to suffer from overdistribution and fatigue. Any hot fashion brand was inevitably going to flatten over time. As the saying went on Seventh Avenue, "Live by the buzz, die by the buzz saw." Hilfiger was also the victim of a hideous smear campaign, an urban myth that came out of nowhere. The smear was that Hilfiger had made an appearance on *The Oprah Winfrey Show* in which he allegedly said that he didn't want blacks wearing his clothes. The rumor was false, of course. He'd never even appeared on *Oprah* in his life. But as the lie kept circulating on the Internet, it kept gaining more traction, and many black customers began to boycott the brand. Finally Oprah invited Tommy to come on the show to quash the hateful rumor once and for all. But the ugly publicity hit the Hilfiger brand when it was down, during a corporate restructuring that closed boutiques and reined in Hilfiger's distribution across America as it focused on building its trademark across Europe.

Combs, who of course had nothing to do with any of this, nevertheless benefited from Hilfiger's slump, signing new licensees, as America's youth now had a new status marker.

After Sean John's big TV runway moment in 2001, his next million-dollar runway show in February 2002 easily became the most anticipated moment of New York Fashion Week. Celebrities begged for invitations to see what everybody had been buzzing about: the gorgeous male models, all that fur and diamond bling, and a thumping hip-hop sound track—this time on display at Combs's glossy new venue, the opulent Cipriani 42nd Street, a luxurious event space at the landmark 1923 Bowery Savings Bank building, with its magnificent sixty-five-foot-high frescoed ceiling and chandeliers. Combs delighted in sending out the most lavish invitations that guests had ever seen (and which I saved): a black velveteen box containing a linen square, embroidered with all the fashion-show details, and a pair of black silk knot cuff links—at a cost of $60,000 for one thousand invitations.

That fashion show lasted a tingling—but fleeting—ten minutes. And as Sean John needed to resonate on a permanent stage, in 2004 Combs inaugurated Sean John's first retail store—a Manhattan flagship on Fortieth Street and Fifth Avenue—featuring all of Sean John's logoed sportswear, including luxurious $600 "snorkel" down jackets, whose hoods were trimmed in raccoon. A few suits and tailored clothing pieces rounded out his collection. Given that Combs didn't have a women's line yet, the store felt incomplete—more like a boutique than a real flagship. Still, it was a stand-alone store—and another marker that Sean John was a bona fide fashion brand.

It was also in 2004, after three consecutive years of nominations, that Combs finally won the CFDA award for best menswear designer of the year, beating out finalists Michael Kors and Ralph Lauren, both veteran CFDA winners. When Marc Jacobs opened the envelope and announced, "Sean Combs," Puffy, tuxedoed in a white dinner jacket, jumped up and went ecstatic. Inside a theater at the stately New York Public Library, he bopped across the stage, doing a little jig as the live orchestra played along to his steps. He gushed: "I'm from Harlem, New York. This is crazy right here. . . . A couple of years ago I was in a Polo store saving my money to get a polo shirt, Ralph Lauren, and now I'm nominated. This is like the American dream."

Many others reveled in his victory. "Puffy had captured the imagination of the traditional fashion space," remembered Jameel Spencer, the former chief marketing officer of Combs's Bad Boy Records. "He was doing multipage spreads in *Vogue*. . . . It was street wear that had met the runway. There was a certain level of prestige and pride that Puffy was there. He was damn near Gucci to urban America at the time."

Unforgivable

The dream just kept getting crazier. Rounding out his fashion designer portfolio, Combs signed on with the venerable Estée Lauder Companies to introduce his first fragrance, Unforgivable by Sean John, in

2005. Like a hit record, Unforgivable soared straight to the top of the charts and ruled the men's fragrance counter, as sales exceeded $100 million in the first year.

Combs was the right star at the right time for Lauder, which needed a new vehicle to connect with a wide swath of that core millennial demographic. At Lauder, "we needed to modernize and diversify our image, and Sean gave us the ability to do that," said Karen Khoury, creative director and senior vice president at Lauder in charge of developing the Sean John brands.

In preparing his fashion collections, Combs—a multitasker who just won't quit—was known to float in and out of the design studio, unavailable for the steady, tedious decision making that goes into the creative fashion process. He ended up infuriating the folks on his design team, who were forced to keep crazy hours to accommodate Combs, a night owl, who would schedule a drive-by meeting with them to start at, say, nine thirty P.M.—only he would keep everyone waiting, blowing in an hour or two late, as he juggled his packed schedule with four of his own reality TV shows, including *Making the Band* and *P. Diddy's Starmaker*.

But when it came to developing Unforgivable, Combs rolled up his sleeves and didn't allow distractions. He was the consummate consumer expert who had worn fragrances his entire life, and thus became obsessive about creating his own, according to Khoury. He even got into the tedium of sampling and trials to build the right scent. He was well aware that the bar would be high among his most exigent fans—black and Latino men—who were heavy users of fragrances and expected only the best from him, a scent that smelled luxurious and sexy.

Khoury and her team at Lauder were forced to work on Saturdays—the only day that the overcommitted Combs could manage regularly—as well as fly to his home in Miami for meetings. From the very first, Combs came teeming with specific ideas of what he wanted. "He chose the fragrance direction—the idea was all his," Khoury confirmed. "He had worn scents that were citrusy and he liked the idea of freshness . . . of sexy woods. In his mind that smelled 'elegant and money,' and that's what he wanted. I sat in a meeting when he was working with us and he was sampling fifteen types of bergamot. He was incredibly involved in creating what he liked, and he knew what would sell and what his customers would like."

The TV commercial for Unforgivable, starring Combs—shirtless as a sex symbol, cavorting with different women—was hokey, almost like a spoof. It ended with Combs's voice-over purring: "Do you love me?"

In addition to the retail party launch to big crowds at Saks Fifth Avenue, Lauder spent millions kicking off Unforgivable in Europe, sponsoring Combs's legendary annual "White Party," a tradition he began at his East Hampton home overlooking the ocean, where the dress code was all white for party guests, who included his neighbors Martha Stewart and Donna Karan. In 2005 the venue was a private home in St. Tropez. For Sean John's Unforgivable, the party was "a big part of building that brand in Europe . . . the whole image—jet-setter king-of-the-world image that was aspirational—that is what he was selling," Khoury said.

The Fat Cat Pack: Buddying with Ron Burkle

Combs's cadres of major league players grew ever wider, including Ron Burkle, the Ralphs supermarket mogul and private equity investor, known for once being BFF with President Bill Clinton. Born in 1952, Burkle, who liked to party in the fast lane, was a wonky and pudgy divorcé who resided in the landmark Greenacres, the lush Beverly Hills estate built in the 1920s by silent-film star Harold Lloyd. Combs got to know Burkle during an off-chance meeting, when Combs hitched a ride to Las Vegas on Burkle's 757 jet. Burkle invited his new friend to host one of his famous after-parties following the MTV Movie Awards in 2003. Combs recalled to The New Yorker's Connie Bruck in 2012 that Burkle's guests that night were a high-watt assemblage, including David and Victoria Beckham, Beyoncé, Ashton Kutcher, Cameron Diaz, Chris Rock, Will Smith, and Jamie Foxx.

Not long after the MTV after-party, Burkle's investment arm, Yucaipa Companies, invested $100 million for a minority stake in Sean John, from a fund reserved for financing "underserved areas and minority businesses."

For a billionaire like Burkle, such expenditures were more hobby than investment, a few million that he could afford to throw at pet projects—in the words of writer Bruck—"to enjoy the dividend of glamour."

I was one of the rare journalists who got to interview the reclusive

Burkle during a thirty-minute breakfast meeting at the New York Palace Hotel when he was passing through Manhattan in 2005. He was visibly impatient having to sit through this quick meeting—which I insisted upon to prepare for the *Journal*'s first major feature on Combs. Burkle's investment in Sean John was intriguing to me, but he sloughed it off as just another investment, while underscoring that he and Combs were personal friends.

"I don't like to spend a lot of time with people who do what I do because it is boring to me," Burkle told the writer Bruck. "By surrounding yourself with diverse people, I think you find yourself."

Burkle's largess allowed Combs to surprise the fashion community by announcing in 2004 that he was investing in Zac Posen, a struggling menswear designer. Posen, who is white, happened to be another wunderkind discovery of Bloomingdale's Ruttenstein.

It struck me as curious that Combs didn't choose a black designer to mentor instead of Posen. But as fashion writer Givhan and I mused about this, she observed: "Puffy did not want to be pigeonholed. His decision to back someone like Posen meant: 'I am playing in high fashion—nobody is gonna put Puffy in the corner, [the hip-hop ghetto].' Puffy did not come to change fashion, he wanted to be in the club. He brought an esthetic with him, but he didn't come in to upend the industry. He wanted to be in the thick of it."

But Puffy's ambitions had their limitations—something that he would be forced to face as his brand aged. He had been the beneficiary of a pop-culture, rap-music-infused tidal wave—a prolonged fashion moment of big logos and oversize silhouettes, which happened to match up neatly with Combs's own oversize celebrity.

But all fashion has a half-life, and Combs was forced to move out of his comfort zone as the original urban street-wear crowd entered their thirties and grew tired of baggy, logo-emblazoned garb.

Sean John had hit a wall, as many celebrity fashion brands inevitably did—most sooner than his. Menswear silhouettes had gone skinny, which had forced Sean John and many other urban fashion labels, such as Sean John's archrival—Jay Z's popular Rocawear—to slim down, minimize or hide their logos, and look for an updated marketing hook.

Combs, who had always personally preferred the elegant tailored look for himself anyway, used the lull to play to his tastes, putting up lavish suits and tuxedos, textured leather pants, and fur jackets on the runway, to big applause at his shows. But he believed the fashion bible of menswear, *GQ*, dissed him, refusing to feature any of Combs's sharp runway looks in its editorial pages.

Jim Moore, the astute, longtime creative director at *GQ*, reminded him just how fashion magazines worked. *GQ* only depicted clothes that were actually produced and existed in the marketplace—such as Sean John cardigans and sweat suits and other basics—and not the fantasies from the runway stage. Moore told him the Sean John collection would benefit from producing scaled-down versions of what Combs put on the runway and wore himself.

"I told him, 'You always look so great, just make the clothes you wear, maybe have it for a reasonable price, a Sean John deluxe line, for example,'" Moore recalled to me.

It's not that Combs didn't like the idea—he'd always wanted to be a bigger deal than a velour tracksuit and a cursive logo on jeans sold on metal T-stands at Macy's. But the retailers, who'd always thought of Sean John as being in the urban-young-male box, just couldn't see his brand in a dressier mode.

What's more, the hard truth was there wasn't any real volume in high-end designer menswear—nothing like the multimillions in sales he'd been used to. Puffy never had to scour to find a market for Sean John—his fan base followed him straight into fashion. So naturally he was unprepared when he was forced to keep innovating season after season. He lacked the tenacity and patience of a professional fashion designer, such as CFDA menswear award winner Thom Browne—whose idiosyncratic skinny, high-water suits and tailored clothing vision drove him to beat his head against the wall for years before the world was ready to buy his creative concepts. And even then, Browne, wedded to his convictions, was willing to settle to be a smaller niche brand.

Instead, Puffy pursued new gimmicks. He even ginned up a collection of racy leather getups for women on his runway. The controversial look was supposed to be a high-impact tease for his foray onto the main stage—women's fashion—which he hoped to get off the ground in 2007. But once again, Combs's lack of authentic vision, persistence, and patience ran smack into the wall of business realities, and he ended up settling for a lackluster juniors' collection of women's sportswear from $40 to $299 for Middle America chains like Dillard's. After a couple of lackluster seasons, he shut down his women's division altogether.

As Sean John faded past its prime in casual sportswear, Combs shuttered Sean John's New York boutique due to slow sales and entered an agreement to sell Sean John fashions for young men and boys exclusively to Macy's, where it found a niche alongside brands like Marc Eckō and Jay Z's Rocawear—all still viable sportswear businesses, just no longer the big deal they once were. Combs, having bagged his CFDA award, was no longer as invested in the business as a real designer might have been. Yet he could still enjoy all the trappings—he clearly got a kick out of appearing in the holiday commercial spots he did for Macy's, joining celebrities like Jessica Simpson, Martha Stewart, and Carlos Santana, all of whom had merchandise at Macy's.

It was clear that Combs had new priorities to excite him as he pivoted into the world of premium vodkas, taking an equity stake in Diageo's struggling Cîroc brand (vodka made of grapes instead of potatoes) and turning it into a premium seller. It was another testament to his deft ability to market his own hip-hop, continental brand of cool, as he continues to throw his famous Cîroc New Year's Eve parties and other Cîroc-branded events.

Who needed fashion? Combs could again fulfill his James Bond fantasies posing as the head of his own multicultural twenty-first-century Rat Pack of handsome guys and sultry women in numerous videos for Cîroc "ultra-premium vodka" to the vintage recordings of Frank Sinatra crooning: "Luck be a lady tonight."

Chapter Nine

. . . .

MAKING DOLLARS OUT OF SCENTS

The Sky's the Limit for Jennifer Lopez

Sean "Puffy" Combs dedicated the televised February 2001 fashion show to his lady love, Jennifer Lopez. But as the Sean John men's collection of jeans and fur-trimmed parkas the show promoted hit the retail sales floors that fall, J.Lo, thirty-two, surprised everybody with her sudden marriage to Cris Judd, also thirty-two, a former dancer who had directed her latest video—just months after she and Combs ended their two-year relationship.

But even in the heat of a whirlwind romance, the busy megastar couldn't stop thinking about getting a long, sleek leg up on the fashion business. She was fully committed, as she had already begun sniffing out her first fragrance.

The Lopez-Judd nuptials took place at a low-key ceremony in Los Angeles, after which the newlyweds fled to Milan for their honeymoon at Donatella Versace's grand nineteenth-century villa on Lake Como.

What a romantic getaway for the happy couple! But solitude wasn't what they had in mind. Their Italian holiday would be a working honeymoon, a time for fashion photo ops and a critical planning meeting for the new J.Lo perfume.

Their trip coincided with Milan Fashion Week, when the hub of this stylish, compact city became a hive of celebrity buzz, with sightings of supermodels, led by Naomi Campbell and Linda Evangelista—not to mention all the famous faces Armani, Gucci, and Versace flew in to embellish their front rows. Only this time, just three weeks after the terrorist attacks of September 11, the mood around town was positively downbeat. Missing were scores of journalists, American retailers, and celebrities—most of whom pulled out. But the planners of Fashion Weeks in Milan and Paris resolved to carry on in a muted version of the usual bacchanal, calling off the festivities and after-parties. There was little to celebrate in any case. Every fashion house in the United States and Europe took a hit, as women across America—high fashion's most influential marketplace—had lost interest in shopping, forcing retailers to cancel orders and take early and steep markdowns—in some cases as high as 75 percent—on all the new fall fashions.

The house of Versace—still struggling to find its way five years after the murder of Gianni Versace—refused to succumb to America's doom-and-gloom scenario and spoil one of the two critical seasons on the fashion calendar. Versace's vital publicity machine subsisted on celebrity hype, and so Donatella Versace, forty-six—Gianni's younger sister and the creative director of Versace—soldiered on to host the lavish wedding party, to which she had devoted months of expensive preparations, for her favorite Hollywood muse.

Versace's runway show would thus sparkle, with the tabloid "Get of the Week" starring on the front row: newlywed Lopez, looking splendid in a deep V-neck, pearl satin gown with gray suede stiletto boots, together with her groom, Judd, in a pale beige suit and tie. As if on cue, they were constantly touching each other, all lovey-dovey. The fashion-show audience couldn't stop staring at them. Earlier, Lopez told inquiring reporters backstage that her wedding to Judd was "magical, really romantic," and why they decided to honeymoon in Como: "Donatella has been very generous to say we could come and stay with her and we just couldn't turn it down." Naturally, they wouldn't miss the show. She told *WWD*: "Everyone knows I love fashion. I don't think that's a secret. As for Versace, I think it's really sexy, very feminine."

Honeymooning in Milan:
Jennifer Lopez and Cris Judd at
the Versace fashion show, October 2001.

After the show, a fleet of cars ferried about 150 fashion editors, models, and Milanese socialites—virtually none of whom knew Lopez personally—to Villa Fontanelle on Lake Como, wrote *The Wall Street Journal*'s Milan-based Deborah Ball in *House of Versace*. Donatella spared no expense, hiring a hundred guards to secure the party and installing special floodlights projecting on the lake to thwart any enterprising paparazzi who might try to crash the wedding celebration in boats.

Guests strolled about the gorgeous gardens, amid three thousand yellow roses, and hundreds of white candles lined the driveway, where live violinists entertained. There was Cristal champagne, heaps of caviar, and supper. Around eleven P.M., Donatella, in a leopard-print gown, led the honeymooners outside to join the party, where everyone ogled La Lopez, stunning in a jade jumpsuit with plunging neckline. (Partygoers immediately flashed back to that iconic green Versace number she'd worn a year earlier—the racy plunge-to-the-navel jungle-print gown that put J.Lo on the map when she accompanied Combs to the 2000 Grammy Awards.) Under a full moon, she and Judd cut a giant wedding cake, feeding each other in front of invited photographers, who also captured them smooching on a red velvet sofa at the party, according to Ball.

Jenny from the Block

Back in Milan on Via Gesù, next door to Versace's headquarters at the Four Seasons Hotel, the couple holed up in the honeymoon suite. That's where Coty's senior vice president of marketing, Catherine Walsh, headed, right after she landed in Milan, for her first meeting with Lopez.

With her fame skyrocketing following her hit 2001 romantic comedy *The Wedding Planner*, and *J.Lo*, her number one pop album, Lopez would never let her private life get in the way of taking care of business. Just like Madonna and Beyoncé—both famous for a tireless work ethic—Lopez was a champion multitasker: a dancer, singer, and actress who was ready to start marketing all types of merchandise. To get to the top, you couldn't just be talented, you had to be relentless.

She'd watched Puffy move shrewdly to position his Sean John fashion label carefully. As Lopez mapped out her fashion future, she would follow Puffy's lead to seek advice from Tommy Hilfiger, who, together with his brother Andy, was prepared to become her benefactor in her fashion and cosmetics ventures.

Her gorgeous looks and talent notwithstanding, Lopez was also a woman who benefited from the serendipity of impeccable timing. She reached her peak just as Latinos had become America's fastest-growing demographic, not to mention increasingly well-off. Being the most visible Latina in the mainstream entertainment industry, she was perfectly positioned to transmute her popularity into riches.

Jennifer Lopez, born July 24, 1969, in a working-class Bronx neighborhood to Puerto Rican parents, had set her sights on the American dream. You can imagine her as an ambitious third grader—probably always on the front row of her dance classes—dreamily posing at home before her bathroom mirror, reciting: *I'm gonna be a movie star.* In high school, Lopez excelled on the track team, but never cottoned to academics. She dropped out of college after one semester so she could make her show business dream a reality.

She spent her early twenties doing gigs as a backup dancer in stage musicals, in music videos, and—after winning a tryout—as one of the break-dancing "Fly Girls" on the hit 1990s TV series *In Living Color*.

She became a star in Hollywood in 1995 after her Golden Globe–nominated title role in *Selena*, the biopic of the Latina singer. By 1998, she was a $1-million-a-picture actress and the pride of Latinos everywhere, with another hit movie, starring opposite George Clooney in Steven Soderbergh's *Out of Sight*.

A string of bankable romantic comedies and pop music moments would follow, but J.Lo didn't need to win an Oscar for her greatest contribution to womanhood: her capacious booty. Beyoncé's trio Destiny's Child might have made "Bootylicious," a catchy club tune in 2001, but it was J.Lo's own dangerous back curves that were the catalyst for this major cultural swing in the everybody-can-agree-upon beauty standard, as rounded butts started to displace big boobs—to the hoorays of genetically endowed black women everywhere.

She was a sight to behold on a single page of *Vanity Fair* in the July 1998 issue that showcased the back view of her glorious rump in vintage laced-up briefs. Novelist Erica Kennedy reminisced on *Huffington Post* on May 10, 2010: "I remember being awestruck by this image and thinking, *Who is this girl?* . . . This image, and others like it, changed women's lives. Seriously.

"Because J.Lo was not one of these women who was modestly embracing her curves like, say, Kate Winslet. . . . Well, J.Lo has always been the bad bitch whose message was clear: *I'm the shit. I know it and you better fucking know it too. Love me or leave me alone.*

"She was the Sex Symbol, the chick who became a prize to the hottest dudes in the game, the chick who showed up on red carpets in body-hugging [Hervé] Légers and generously served up backshots, the chick who . . . hustled to #1 through sheer force of ass. She was the dark-haired, pale-skinned okay-looking back-up dancer on *In Living Color* and *Yo! MTV Raps* who transformed herself into a bronzed, honey-haired A-list glamour girl and sex symbol right before our eyes."

Now she was ready to transform herself into a fashion mogul just as impressively. Lopez, who knew Andy Hilfiger first from music videos, asked him to introduce her to his brother. Tommy Hilfiger initially envisioned Lopez becoming a new label within publicly traded Tommy Hilfiger Inc., where he was the principal designer and honorary chairman. But when Tommy checked in with the board of directors, they decided to pass, because management was fully engaged with closing scores of Hilfiger boutiques and restructuring the brand, he reminisced to me in 2012.

But Andy's enthusiasm for Lopez was catching, and Tommy didn't want to let it go. His employment at Hilfiger Inc. allowed him to have personal ventures, after he got board approval. He asked, and the board gave him a green light. Tommy said: "Andy resigned as head of Tommy Jeans and I funded the whole thing. We did the fragrance deal with Coty and the clothes. And today we are still 50 percent partners with Jennifer."

Even with the backing of the entrepreneurial Hilfigers, Lopez got off to a rocky start in fashion in 2001, with her J.Lo by Jennifer Lopez line of sportswear togs—velour tracksuits and skimpy tops—which never really clicked at retail during its six-year reign in a classic case of a celebrity name that lacked a strong identity to her brand.

Jennifer Lopez was fully committed and engaged when she started shopping her name to perfume makers. Yet launching a celebrity fragrance in 2002 was a roll of the dice: no hits since Liz Taylor's White Diamonds, and a slew of celebrity fragrance flops in her wake. Estée Lauder (Hilfiger's fragrance marketer) and then Elizabeth Arden (Liz Taylor's marketer) were both rumored to have turned down Jennifer Lopez.

But the beleaguered Coty Inc. smelled an opportunity when J.Lo came knocking. In dire need of a home run, Coty was a stagnant $1 billion business of drugstore makeup and cosmetics and Sally Hansen nail polish, with a few lackluster designer fragrances. Seeking a corporate makeover in 2001, Coty hired a new chairman and CEO, Bernd Beetz, the former president and CEO of LVMH's Parfums Christian Dior. Beetz—a Procter & Gamble packaged-goods veteran—had skillfully turned around Dior cosmetics. Coty also hired Catherine Walsh, a veteran marketing executive from Estée Lauder Companies, as senior vice president. Beetz and Walsh were in hot pursuit of a game changer—a unique fragrance that would surprise everyone and become a blockbuster.

When Lopez's people approached Coty, Walsh and Beetz got it immediately. They saw her as a hot Latina icon, with crossover, global appeal. And even though celebrity fragrances were dicey, Beetz was committed. He gave Walsh carte blanche to spend whatever she needed—and she got busy. It was fortuitous that Walsh was in her midthirties with spiky black hair and a downtown vibe—she wore a lot of black and combat boots. She was the perfect hipster executive to click with Lopez.

Giving Good Neck

Walsh recounted the scene to me when she arrived at the Four Seasons Hotel, taking a private elevator to the penthouse suite, which she was surprised to find noisy with bodyguards, assistants, and friends when the newlyweds were supposed to be honeymooning.

Walsh was surprised when J.Lo greeted her in a Four Seasons terrycloth robe, hair dripping wet from the shower. She leaned her neck in to Walsh and told her, "This is what I want to smell like."

Soapy clean and fresh. It didn't take a focus group to conclude that Lopez was on to something. The green movement encompassing everything from bottled water to farm-to-table eating had been leading a backlash against heavy fragrances—and scents that suggested chemicals. Estée Lauder saw this coming and introduced a natural skin-care product in 1990 called Origins, which became a hit.

Dress-Down Nation had also caused people to gravitate to subtly scented products instead of perfume, like $8 shower gels and $15 lotions, led by Bath & Body Works, Victoria's Secret—and $10 Axe body spray for men. These scented products were less than half the price of the usual colognes and felt easier to wear when people were always in tank tops and flip-flops.

So Walsh's initial reaction to Lopez was: Terrific! A modern scent wrapped around a glamorous woman whose star was still rising. And breathtaking she was. Walsh remembers staring in that first meeting as she took in the stunning beauty without makeup that was Jennifer Lopez.

Movie stars are generally good-looking—the most memorable the ones with some quirky feature that gives them a signature. Jennifer Lopez is that elite class of bombshell that radiates sex appeal, like Elizabeth Taylor in her prime: star power overlaid on an arresting beauty. Her caramel complexion is luminous, fine-pored, and exquisite. Her speaking voice has a streetish, Latina lilt—pleasant to hear because it sounds sultry and so New York. I remember seeing her in person for the first time at a fashion event in New York more than a decade ago—and yes, I sure did lean around to inspect her slammin' body from the rear view. Va-voom.

No wonder Puffy Combs was once so deeply smitten. He was known to have wooed J.Lo with grand gestures: enlisting the velvet-voiced Luther Vandross to serenade her in a New York recording studio, and another time sending over to her one hundred white doves. Combs fantasized to *Vanity Fair*'s Ned Zeman in 2001 that his and J.Lo's was among Hollywood's most passionate romances:

"We'd always say to each other that I was Frank and she was Ava, you know what I'm saying? I can understand why there was a lot of media attention because there was a lot of energy in the relationship. . . . For me, it was the most energy I gave to a relationship. Sometimes when two people get together, you feel a certain type of spark that's like, *Yo!*"

Lopez was a girly girl who liked to strut her stuff, who traveled with $90 Diptyque scented candles imported from Paris, who loved mixing fragrant oils from boutique vendors to concoct her private signature. Walsh's objective at that initial meeting was to tease a lot from Lopez, to get a real sense of what she loved. Walsh came prepared with Lucite bottle shapes and color mood boards. J.Lo loved the fuchsia and bright shades that felt very Latina and feminine. But she also had a minimalist streak; she wore beige lipstick. As they walked around the beige hotel suite, Lopez singled out the long, narrow-necked lamps.

They ended up in the oversize bathroom, where Walsh said she felt like an intruder—staring at the square bathtub full of water with rose petals floating on top for the honeymooners. But Lopez was all business. Walsh took out a piece of paper and drew a perfume bottle with a round curved shape with one side thicker than the other—explaining about the side that protruded: "This is your butt."

Lopez loved the concept. She suggested that the bottle should be tall, with frosted glass, and how about "a little bling, like a rhinestone collar?" Walsh demurred, puzzled. She didn't understand the slang: "I had to ask her, 'What is *bling*?'"

Weeks later Walsh flew to Frankfurt to catch up with Lopez and Judd, who were performing in a concert. It was now time to come up with the name of her fragrance. They began brainstorming, tossing out words almost randomly. Finally, Cris Judd jumped up: "Honey, you just glow. Look at you! You glow!" Lopez clapped her hands and said, "That's it!" Glow by J.Lo was born.

There was more to do—and Lopez was on it, reviewing hundreds of bottle shapes and sampling more than three hundred scent blends. Walsh describes Lopez as the consummate professional, who arrived on time for meetings, didn't take phone calls, and always came prepared—the opposite of Puffy. "She's an excellent decision maker," Walsh says. Lopez finally decided on sample number 24B for her fragrance. It resembled the fresh, soapy smell, with notes of orange blossom, pink grapefruit, rose, sandalwood, with a light musk. The soft carton box was translucent and texturized to feel like skin—that concept was all Lopez's idea.

Coty positioned Glow by J.Lo at $39—premium, but still accessible to her young fans as well as women thirty and up—pulling in all those shoppers at Macy's, where J.Lo Glow would be launched.

One hitch with Glow by J.Lo: Lopez refused to film a commercial at the last minute. She and her advisors worried that her movie was out there and that a commercial would be overexposure. The result was a commercial without her, with just fans all talking about "Get the glow." In the end, Walsh wished they had nixed that idea, which she says didn't really resonate with people.

Exceeding Expectations

With the fragrance all ready to go to market, Coty ran the scent by key retailers for an early reaction. Macy's and Boots in the UK were luke-warm at first, still not confident that Lopez could do the trick to make people fall in love with a celebrity fragrance all over again. Coty ratcheted down its expectations for Glow by J.Lo to sales estimates between $20 million and $26 million in the first twelve months, reported *WWD*.

Walsh recalled to me: "There is no way we knew what was coming"— which was an avalanche. Sales started modestly but before long, word of mouth took over. Glow by J.Lo exploded: $120 million in sales in the first nine months. "Oh my God, I see it. . . . It is really moving. . . . We hit number one!" Walsh exulted when the figures came in.

Glow by J.Lo benefited from the element of surprise. Nobody was expecting a new generation of celebrity fragrances—least of all with

Lopez leading the way. But as it turned out, Glow exuded hip and young; it had bling on the bottle, and an atomizer that lit up—everything that shouted novelty and specialness.

The juice also happened to smell good on a lot of women. But the bigger thing that Coty was selling was Jennifer Lopez, the Bronx-born Jenny from the block—who was gorgeous, who could sing and dance, and whose life was busy and complicated with a revolving door of boyfriends and husbands to keep people wondering and talking about her constantly. Most important, she exuded sex, which is the clincher when it comes to fragrance.

Lopez filled everybody's sexual fantasies. "Good girls go to heaven, bad girls go everywhere," explained John Demsey, the group president of Lauder. Just like Liz Taylor, J.Lo had that fast image. Men fantasized about going to bed with her. Women fantasized about being that vixen. Jennifer Lopez was that woman.

Like Liz Taylor, the public would root for J.Lo during her string of love-'em-and-leave-'em romances. People tuned in to her (missing her first quickie marriage when she was a nobody) during her torrid and very public romance with Puffy. When he got in trouble with guns, they wanted her to leave him. Fans secretly hoped her rebound marriage with Judd would last, but when it didn't (they divorced eight months later, around the time Glow by J.Lo landed in stores), the fans swooned at her romance with Ben Affleck. When "Bennifer" got engaged, they cheered.

After Bennifer crashed and burned, that cleared the way for her to marry singer Marc Anthony (born Muñiz). Latinos loved seeing her return to her roots. The four-year union resulted in twin daughters. Her latest romance, with Casper Smart, a dancer seventeen years her junior—was a May–December fantasy that many women over forty loved. But after two and a half years, the couple broke up in 2014. So, yes, J.Lo's soap opera life made her fans care about her.

A Fragrant Tsunami

After the J.Lo juggernaut in 2002, every cosmetics house once again raced to put out its own celebrity fragrances. After an era of so many celebrity fragrance bombs, now it seemed the formula couldn't fail. So many of the new brands rung up respectable first-year sales of more than

$50 million. Elizabeth Arden rushed in with Britney Spears, Usher, and Halle Berry. Parlux had Paris Hilton. Estée Lauder went slower, adding a Daisy Fuentes fragrance, sold exclusively at Kohl's, and later, in 2007, Sean John's Unforgivable. Coty, which had started the ball rolling, zeroed in on the always-lovable woman who represented the Carrie Bradshaw in every fashionista with Lovely by Sarah Jessica Parker.

By 2005, as many as seventy new celebrity fragrances had hit the marketplace, according to industry experts. Most came and went so fast they never made it inside department stores—and went straight to the discount bins.

But the Glow by J.Lo franchise stayed strong, and Jennifer Lopez was number one on the *Forbes* celebrity list of the most powerful people in entertainment in 2012, with an estimated income of $52 million due to her "smart positioning and a whole lot of hustle." She rebounded from all those middling *Maid in Manhattan* and *Monster-in-Law* romantic comedies to stay in the limelight on prime-time TV as a popular judge on *American Idol*.

Meanwhile, no one has the perfume drill down better. J.Lo introduced an average of two new scents every year since 2002. Miami Glow, Blue Glow, L.A. Glow, Rio Glow, Still, Glow After Dark, Deseo. None of the follow-ups have performed as splendidly as the original Glow— and a few were downright duds—but the die of J.Lo as a hit at the perfume counter had been set. With every new fragrance curious fans would check it out—just as if it were a new song. Shoppers weren't buying a fragrance as much as they were buying the persona, whose megawatt career kept her as current as the latest iPhone apps.

For Coty Inc., Jennifer Lopez fragrances were more than a blockbuster franchise. Jennifer Lopez created huge momentum at Coty, which became the world's biggest fragrance marketer, more than doubling its 2002 sales from $2 billion to $4.6 billion in 2012.

In the after-Glow, the Coty people now looked like the smartest folks in the room. It wasn't that celebrities were going to displace designer fragrances—they would never be more than 10 percent of the entire marketplace. But they did what celebrity association always does: attract attention. Designers who for years had never paid any mind to Coty put the company at the top of their list. Designer brands now represent about two-thirds of Coty's business. Coty snared the big ka-huna, Marc Jacobs—the hottest American designer on the planet, who now markets his fragrances through Coty. Coty also now owns the kingpin of American designer fragrance brands, Calvin Klein. But Coty also maintains the largest roster of celebrity brands, including Lady Gaga, Sarah Jessica Parker, Kimora Lee Simmons's Baby Phat, Shania Twain, and David Beckham.

None of it would have happened without the original spark of Jenni-fer Lopez. Coty became the house that J.Lo built. And quite the house at that: In 2013, Coty became a public company listed on the New York Stock Exchange, with a market valuation of $17.8 billion.

The magic of Glow by J.Lo extended beyond a single company or even a single fashion category. Celebrity scents were novelties that pulled shoppers into department stores, where they might buy lipstick and foun-dation, a new top, shoes, or a party dress. They reached a hard-to-engage demographic, young people between eighteen and thirty, who increas-ingly had been bypassing the cosmetics counters at chains like Macy's, Bloomie's, or Nordstrom altogether in favor of fast-fashion purveyors like H&M, Forever 21, and Zara.

The momentum from J.Lo fragrances helped give Lopez second and third chances in the apparel business. In 2011, she finally hit pay dirt when she rebounded with a new Jennifer Lopez fashion collection aimed at women over thirty, including the underserved large-size market, launched exclusively at the 1,100-store Kohl's chain. As Jennifer Lopez drove to the front of the fashion business, breaking new ground and making huge profits, grateful retailers joyfully lined up behind her, en-joying the view.

Chapter Ten

. . . .

THE RED STAR THAT STARS BUILT

Macy's Celebrity Moment

You've got a better chance getting in the door with a product under a celebrity name as opposed to an unknown designer name. The truth of the matter is that many of the designers that we carry today are less known by the average consumer than you would expect.

—Terry Lundgren, chairman and CEO of Macy's, June 2005

Celebrity fragrances—there were new ones always coming out from J. Lo, Taylor Swift, Rihanna, Lauren Conrad, Justin Bieber, Lady Gaga, Britney Spears, Kim Kardashian, and the rest—forced young women back into department stores to at least smell the tester and perhaps buy a bottle too. Shoppers didn't need to be pried away from one celebrity fragrance once they got hooked on it. They were often ready to move on anyway, to the new, shiny bottle—to the new, shiny celebrity. These young women bought two or three new fragrances each year—it was *so last year* to stay with the same scent—which kept them coming through the doors.

Of all the big chains, Macy's Inc. seemed to grasp this new dynamic best. The company has parlayed the fragrance counter into a strategic advantage in its quest to become a nationwide powerhouse.

After mergers and acquisitions across the department-store sector in the early 2000s, Macy's emerged as Goliath in 2007, a $26 billion chain with 850 stores and a burgeoning online division, Macys.com. Macy's would continue to gallop ahead of the pack as the strongest better department-store chain in America, getting celebrity buzz starting with its fragrances that extends to fashion collections from Jessica Simpson and Madonna, to menswear from Donald Trump, to bed linens and towels from Martha Stewart, and to pots and kitchenware from Food Network celebrity chef Rachael Ray. Macy's formidable lineups of celebrity brands have served it well, especially as the bridge to shoppers under thirty, who had eluded Macy's for years.

The gateway drug at Macy's, right on the ground floor, has been around twenty celebrity fragrances introduced with great fanfare at the Herald Square flagship store in Manhattan from 2002 to 2013. The gal who headed to Macy's to sniff Justin Bieber's Someday is just as likely going to stay there for a while, to browse "Shoes and the City"—an entire floor devoted to women's shoes, as well as other contemporary fashions.

"We started to recognize that we had to get the millennials (those born in the 1980s and 1990s) back, that they were going to be the biggest marketing opportunity for us," says Martine Reardon, executive vice president of marketing at Macy's.

In 2012, Macy's estimated that about forty million of America's millennials spent more than $65 billion on the kind of merchandise sold by Macy's—considerably more than what boomers spend, making them a fertile consumer group worthy of Macy's undivided attention. At the end of 2013, Macy's said it planned to add thirteen new millennial brands in apparel to expand upon the existing eleven millennial fashion brands it already carried.

Reardon told me: "Once we get her at eighteen, she stays with us through all her life stages—through her interview suits and bridal and beyond. The way to get to her is to have really exciting products and exciting launches that appeal to her. We started to get into celebrity fragrances because we saw how fast they could appeal to everybody, mainly the millennial woman."

For Macy's there's no denying that celebrities—as brands and as endorsers—made good scents together.

Do You "Belieb" in Magic?

It was at Macy's Herald Square and at Macy's San Francisco in Union Square in 1991 where the one and only Liz Taylor would make cosmetics history as she appeared in person to launch White Diamonds—surrounded by photographers and video crews—to the delight of hundreds of her awestruck fans.

But for a decade, the White Diamonds phenomenon had to be considered pretty much a one-off, based entirely on Liz's unique persona: an extraordinary movie star the likes of whom might never come again. That's why the success of Glow by J.Lo in 2002 and beyond came as such a revelation. Macy's jumped all over it, corralling all the big celebrity fragrance launches from then on. Today, the fragrance kickoffs have become colossal marketing efforts, hyped for months with news stories planted everywhere; YouTube videos, TV commercials, and other gala events leading up to the big unveiling, with the media and thousands of young shoppers converging at the Herald Square Macy's for the big photo op—the in-store celebrity personal appearance, featuring stars like Lopez, Mariah Carey, Christina Aguilera, Britney Spears, 50 Cent, Usher, Queen Latifah, Paris Hilton, Taylor Swift, Beyoncé, Rihanna, Madonna, Lady Gaga, Nicki Minaj, Selena Gomez, and Adam Levine.

Once the celebrated star was on the premises, the amped-up shoppers didn't just stop at the cosmetics counter. The celebrity fragrance of the moment made the whole store smell good, conferring that subliminal cool halo that captivates and engages consumers and makes them plunk down their charge cards. Of all fashion and beauty merchandise, fragrance probably generates the most impulse buys—and from Macy's point of view, that's pure gold. The right celebrity perfume can drive sales for the whole chain.

Macy's proved expert at finding the "right" celebrities, landing the two biggest celebrity fragrance debuts of the new age—Justin Bieber in 2011 and Lady Gaga in 2012. Both produced catchy pop-music videos that garner hundreds of millions of views on YouTube. Both enjoyed cult followings of tens of millions of followers on Facebook and Twitter—giving them a unique ability to instantly connect with their fans, including millions of millennials, steering them straight into Macy's.

Introducing: Justin Bieber

Justin Bieber, the young Canadian pop singing sensation, was all of sixteen in 2011 when *Forbes* named him the second top celebrity under thirty, earning $53 million in just twelve months. (Lady Gaga came in first, earning $90 million.)

He was twelve when he began posting homemade webcam videos of himself on YouTube, singing and guitar playing in his bedroom. He was wholesome, poster-boy cute with his signature forward swirl of thick bangs, and blessed with a big soulful voice and hip-hop moves. He became the protégé of pop singer Usher, who led him to a recording contract, after which Bieber began to sell out concerts and record a nonstop string of platinum hits. Bieber's secret sauce was his interaction with millions of fans—his "Beliebers"—through his YouTube videos and his Twitter feed, which established a new benchmark in consumer marketing and turned the teen heartthrob into the twenty-first-century Elvis.

Justin Bieber launches
Someday at Macy's in June 2011.

Bieber was the real deal, the grand prize marketers salivate over: an instant, can't-miss connection to young people, many of whom had never shopped at Macy's. For the debut weeks of Bieber's kickoff scent, Someday, Macy's would have a sales exclusive—compelling all those teen fans and their parents to be hooked into Macy's.

It was only fair that Macy's got first shot—it was Macy's that steered Bieber into perfume in the first place. Three years earlier, the powers at Macy's began talking to Bieber's people about launching back-to-back fragrances a year apart. The agreement would include Bieber appearing in Macy's TV commercials, which would run nationally. Bieber's handlers made an easy calculation. The more exposure Bieber got through Macy's, the more money his fragrances would generate for his charities; he planned to donate all the proceeds through his partnership with Give Back Brands.

"To their credit, they realized what a marketing machine this was and how we could take this to a new level," says Reardon of Macy's. Needless to say, Macy's braced for a mob scene on June 24, 2011, when Justin Bieber showed up at Herald Square to promote Someday, whose round bottle with a rose-petal top was destined to become a bedroom trinket for millions of girls. "I picked out the bottle and everything," a vivacious Bieber volunteered on camera during an MTV interview inside Macy's.

A number of Bieliebers had camped outside on the sidewalks surrounding Macy's for a couple of nights before the event. Such were the giddy groupies who improvised a pep rally during their long wait, reciting the lyrics to Bieber's hit songs in unison. They even erupted into a spirited call-and-response: "SOME!" shouted the teens standing in the front of the line. Then, right on cue: "DAY!" from fans way behind them.

Scores of true "Beliebers" lined up outside of Macy's to catch a glimpse of Justin Bieber when he came to meet fans.

Full-On Frenzy

If Macy's publicists imagined tons of images of Bieber waving to his fans as he strolled into Macy's, they were disappointed. The scene outside in front of the store was pure mayhem. Shaky amateur videos on You-Tube posted by fans barely caught glimpses of Bieber, who was engulfed by security guards shielding him from the mobs of screaming teens. But the important part of the launch, the sales figures, went as planned: Someday soared into the untold millions of dollars within a couple of weeks, "by far the biggest fragrance launch we've ever had," Reardon says, declining to elaborate. A year later, in June 2012, when Bieber's encore fragrance, Girlfriend, debuted at Macy's, demand for both fragrances spiked, as expected.

I stopped into Macy's to sample a spritz of both fragrances, whose scents smelled as teenybopper and toylike as the bottles they came in looked. Girlfriend, in particular, was a cloying cotton-candy scent that managed to smell sticky—hard to imagine even a teenager wanting to spray that on her skin. Not that this mattered to the Beliebers: "They just come in wanting to buy it; they don't always ask to smell the tester first," a young saleswoman at a Macy's fragrance counter explained to me. She then cheerfully returned to her spiel, reminding me that for a limited time only, with the purchase of Girlfriend, I could take home a cool gift-with-purchase: a candy pink–and-lavender padded case suitable for an iPad or laptop computer.

In 2011, between the two fragrance launches, Bieber starred in a hilarious TV commercial to promote Macy's after-Thanksgiving storewide sales—starting at midnight instead of the usual four A.M.—on Black Friday, the biggest shopping day of the year. Macy's had previously tested the midnight opening a year before at only six locations. The results couldn't have been more encouraging: The bewitching-hour crowd was predominantly big-spending teens and young adults, actually outnumbering Macy's more conservative core boomer shoppers.

To capitalize on what they thought was a winning formula, Macy's designed the spoof, a thirty-second TV spot in which an unassuming Justin Bieber enters a limousine in the dark of night. The chauffeur in a black suit and tie turns around, recognizes his famous passenger, and belts out a shrill scream—reminiscent of the fans at the Someday launch. After the limo pulls into Macy's back entrance, two burly workers on the loading dock spot Bieber walking by—and suddenly they scream and jump around like teenyboppers. Finally, a Macy's security guard squeals as he holds open the door for a bemused Bieber, who chuckles as he walks into . . . Macy's.

(Macy's got the full ripple effect from this gem of a commercial as TV news shows kept airing it. Then the commercial went viral, as fans began producing their video parodies of "the Bieber screamers at Macy's," posting them on YouTube. "That's when you know you've hit it big-time," says Reardon.)

The crescendo of Bieber cross-pollination came on Thanksgiving night, when Macy's Herald Square became a magnet for teen shoppers. The cheese in the trap was the nine hundred Justin Bieber perfume gift packs, displayed at the main floor perfume counter. Anticipating that many young women would scout for fashion markdowns, Macy's had painstakingly planned accordingly, with a number of irresistible deals aimed at them, including thousands of pairs of Rampage boots, marked down to the door-buster price of $19.99 instead of the usual $49 and $59.

"I'm betting on the $19.99 boot we have. It's an absolutely ridiculous price," Macy's chairman and CEO Terry Lundgren told *The Wall Street Journal*'s Dana Mattioli, standing next to him while waiting for Herald Square to open. At last the clock struck twelve and hundreds of wide-eyed shoppers, including lots of young people, came barging through the doors right on cue. "Just look at this," he said. "We knew the younger crowds would stay up all night, while the baby boomers went for a nap."

Minutes later, crowds of young women began to congregate around a life-size Justin Bieber cutout beside the fragrance counter where those gift sets were displayed. The frenzy was full-on. A half hour into the sale, the young women's juniors' floor was disheveled, with toppling shoe boxes, stray boots, and paper stuffing scattered around. Teens were lined up at the dressing room. There was a run on those Rampage boots as young women called out their sizes and colors to employees working in a roped-off section around huge stacks of shoe boxes. "I just knew," a satisfied Lundgren told Mattioli.

In June 2013, Justin Bieber returned with Justin Bieber The Key, his third fragrance, launched again at Macy's, with the Twitter hashtag #Unlockthedream. Timing was everything, as the squeaky-clean Bieber would prove to be a moving target. Seven months later, on January 24, 2014, Bieber was posing for a mug shot at the Miami police station when he was arrested for DUI and bad behavior. Press reports in the coming weeks would reveal he was carousing and drinking, visiting brothels, and smoking so much marijuana on a private jet that the pilot complained and Bieber was kept for questioning when the plane landed. Would his Beliebers stick by him through all of this entitled bad-boy behavior? The powers-that-be know that celebrities are moving targets and that timing is everything. They also have morality clauses in their contracts so that if a star falls, their large investments won't be a total loss.

Going Gaga

Skewing a bit older—but every bit as passionate as the Beliebers—was another cult fan group, the "little monsters" of Lady Gaga, the exhibitionist pop diva and eccentric fashionista who once trussed herself in a dress made of raw steak.

Gaga was another original for the books—a pop singer whose genius was marketing her personal brand as the Mama Monster, the leader of her flock of little monsters, her rabid fans, giving them a sense of family in a world where the nerds, the ugly, the lonely, the unpopular—all races and persuasions—are welcomed and belong. They repaid Gaga's devotion to them by screaming and crying hysterically at her concerts, throwing themselves onstage, and sending her supertanker loads of mail. Starting in 2008, the "Born This Way" wunderkind blazed into the spotlight, branding herself as a high-concept curiosity, with sold-out concert tours and music videos that rivaled Bieber's in popularity. A five-time Grammy Award winner, Gaga was named 2011's style icon by the Council of Fashion Designers of America—the same award Sarah Jessica Parker won in 2004.

In the fall of 2012, Lady Gaga was ready to roll out her first fragrance, marketed by Coty, at Macy's—a sure-thing bestseller, if ever there was one. Gaga called her fragrance Fame, harking back to *The Fame*, her hit 2008 debut album, where she first introduced the concept of her little monsters. And Gaga had entrusted her Fame with Coty—and Walsh again—to blow it out in a high-octane Gagapalooza.

Months before Fame hit Macy's, Coty played Gaga's eccentricities to the hilt, promoting Fame as "the first-ever black eau de parfum." The stylish association—head-to-toe black is de rigueur among the fashion cognoscenti—came through loud and clear.

But Gaga was playing for more than just chic. Her perfume had to be outrageous, in keeping with her ability to shock and awe. "You must want to lick and touch and feel it, but the look of it must terrify you," she told Vogue. Fame's listed ingredients read like a witch's brew: "Tears of belladonna, crushed heart of tiger orchid with a black veil of incense, pulverized apricot and the combinative essences of saffron and honey drops." Fame was a black-tinted liquid that miraculously sprayed on as clear; Coty even had a patent pending on Fame's opaque-to-clear technology.

Months before the official unveiling of Fame, Gaga teased and titillated, claiming that Fame contained extracts from her very own blood, as well as sperm from an anonymous donor. She trash-talked to WWD: "You just get sort of the after feeling of sex from the semen and then the blood is sort of primal. . . . It's like a sense of having me on your skin. . . . Actually, the perfume smells like an expensive hooker." And to CNN: "I want it to smell slutty." Fame played on YouTube in a five-minute commercial—a macabre fun-house fantasy, punctuated with screams and black liquid oozing everywhere. "WTF?!!" wrote several viewers in the comments section.

At the end of New York Fashion Week, Coty hosted an all-black masquerade gala, the official launch party for Fame—to be followed the next day when Gaga would make her appearance at Macy's. The gala took place at the Guggenheim Museum, where invited guests—mostly the fashion press from all over the world who were already in town—swanned through the spiraling exhibition space, drinking from black goblets and gawking at celebrity guests Marc Jacobs, Lindsay Lohan, Yoko Ono, and Paris Hilton.

The evening's carpet was black, of course—and Gaga channeled Morticia Addams in a tight black gown, with a gold crown atop her cascading Rapunzel hair. Her usual sky-high heels looked even more foolish when cameras caught Gaga in a clumsy stumble as she headed inside the Guggenheim.

The evening's "art performance" was billed as "Sleeping with Gaga," during which Gaga reclined inside a gigantic replica of Fame's black-and-gold bottle while guests filed by, sticking their hands through a hole to pet her while she "slept." David Bowie's rock classic "Fame" filled the air—and so did Fame, which Gaga spritzed from a flacon. This staged pomposity managed to impress even jaded fashion partygoers, who became as giddy as Gaga's little monsters.

"It was a strange party that was pretty silly, but after you were there for a while, everybody kind of got into it," said Elizabeth Holmes, a *Wall Street Journal* fashion reporter, who wore a black mask in joining the revelers.

Coty and Macy's counted on all those chattering fashionistas spreading the word and tweeting up a storm about Gaga's party antics (a tattoo artist engraved an actual tattoo on the back of her neck in real time), supplying the viral buzz that teed up shoppers for the following evening at Macy's—which had already primed its Facebook page and sent off targeted e-mail blasts and other well-aimed advertising to reach the very shoppers it knew would be interested in Gaga's hot new fragrance.

Gaga made a dramatic entrance at Macy's that afternoon, alighting from a black-and-gold perfume bottle–shaped carriage, pulled by two black horses. She was all Wonder Woman–meets-Goth in a black patent gown, a bronze headdress, and scary, skyscraper platform boots. Moving gingerly, Gaga once again stumbled on her way inside the revolving doors. Cordoned off near the entrance were hundreds of fans, who whooped and hollered: "Ga-ga! Gaga, we love you!"

Now Smell This!

Eager and fidgety, the two hundred or so lucky shoppers who had bought $125 gift sets of Fame—about a third of whom were men—came all dressed in black a full two hours early, as they awaited the meet-and-greet with Gaga that started around four P.M. New Yorker Lisa Murphy, twenty-five, a pretty blonde in a black leather jacket with sequin lapels, came across like a celebrity fragrance connoisseur: She had already worn perfumes by Britney Spears and Beyoncé. But to her, Mama Monster was in a class all her own, as she asserted: "Other celebrities' perfumes, you can just tell that they put them out there, but [Gaga] worked hard for a while on hers."

Vogue's whopper 916-page September issue featured Lady Gaga as the cover girl, all statuesque in a fuzzy platinum wig and a pink fishtail gown by Marc Jacobs. *Vogue* contained a profile on Gaga and an advertisement for Fame with a scratch-and-sniff scent strip. I rubbed it on my wrist—and had my own *aha!* moment. Gaga's eau de hooker was instead a rather humdrum floral bouquet, about as tame as a virgin. Gaga had psyched us all.

Lady Gaga was surprisingly honest—not to mention astute—when she blithely admitted to *WWD* that her blood-and-semen yarn was nothing but a lie—and went further to coldly dissect the whole celebrity fragrance biz:

"I don't think it really matters how it smells. I'm not trying to be funny, but I guess I'm trying to say that in the celebrity fragrance world you're buying a fragrance because you like the celebrity. . . . I don't really give a shit about perfume. That's sort of the point of it."

Gaga was indeed the most ingenious and calculating of marketers. Who really gave a hoot what Fame smelled like? All her little monsters were buying a piece of Gaga—the product that would bring them into the bosom of their beloved Mama Monster. Whether Gaga was peddling patchouli, bergamot, or rosewater, her trusty audience was buying Gaga, her Fame, her perfume. And Macy's could chalk up another celebrity moment—a marketing gift that would keep on giving. Until something better came along.

The month after Gaga's Fame orgy, it was platinum-blonde rapper Nicki Minaj's turn to introduce Pink Friday, which was the name of her debut studio album and, presto change-o, her debut perfume. Macy's publicity team gamely donned pink wigs and Nicki Minaj T-shirts on the afternoon Minaj blew in for her meet and greet.

Only One Star at Macy's

By cosmic coincidence, Macy's had always featured a red star in its logo. It was there when the retailer was founded in 1858, based not on celebrity worship but on a red-tinted tattoo that Rowland Hussey Macy got as a teenager when he worked on a Nantucket whaling ship—a memento of the bright star in the sky that guided his boat to safety during a fog. He made the star the apostrophe in Macy's, one of the best-known trademarks in retailing.

A century and a half later, that star would come in handy. Starting in 2007, Macy's began using the tagline "Only one star can put it all together" and #onlyonestar as a Twitter hashtag. This was a clever way to underscore that Macy's had broken away from the pack of look-alike department stores—with its mix of private-label brands and its exclusive or limited distribution brands, but most notably with its association with celebrity brands. It was designed to one-up those clever fast-fashion chains like H&M and Forever 21.

Jessica Simpson—who dated back to 2005 with Macy's—was the anchor among celebrity fashion brands in the women's department, with her shoes and fashions and fragrances hitting all counters.

Other celebrities would join the women's lineup over the years, including Gwen Stefani's L.A.M.B., Carlos Santana, Madonna's Material Girl and Truth or Dare, Beyoncé's House of Deréon, Marilyn Monroe, Lauren Conrad, and Thalia Sodi (in spring 2015). The top celebrity endorsing menswear at Macy's with his name on fragrance, suits and ties, and watches was none other than Donald Trump—who'd beaten Simpson to Macy's a year earlier and had been "an unbelievable runaway success," Macy's CEO Terry Lundgren told me for *The Wall Street Journal* in June 2005. "You've got a better chance getting in the door with a product under a celebrity name as opposed to an unknown designer name," he said. "The truth of the matter is that many of the designers that we carry today are less known by the average consumer than you would expect."

Suit Yourself

Whom did mainstream shoppers know instantly?

The Donald, of course.

Trump was already a household name in 2004—certainly throughout New York, where the Trump name was slapped on so many buildings, starting with the marble-and-brass Trump Tower on Fifth Avenue. Trump had his *Apprentice* reality TV franchise; bestselling books, such as *The Art of the Deal* and *Think Like a Billionaire*; a Trump board game; and even Donald Trump talking dolls, complete with his fold-over coiffure, which spoke seventeen phrases such as: "Have an ego. There's nothing wrong with ego."

But America's most famous real estate mogul, known for his braggadocio, had gone all soft goods on us in 2004 when he introduced his $60 Trump the Fragrance—marketed by Estée Lauder—and $400 Donald J. Trump collection suits.

It didn't matter that the Donald was never known for his sartorial flair. His Trump suit brand would be an instant hit, a bestseller in Macy's men's department in its first year. By the very next year, Trump had managed to become regarded as one of America's most favored fashion designers. In a 2005 survey conducted by New York marketing company Brand Keys, of five hundred adults across America asked to rate 1,200 brands—ranging from banks to fast-food chains to apparel and consumer electronics—Donald Trump beat out Giorgio Armani and Donna Karan among the most trusted fashion names in America. The Brand Keys survey also put Trump brands ahead of his competitors in having the qualities that consumers most desired in clothes, namely comfort, style, and fit.

It all happened because Sheldon Brody, whose Marcraft Apparel Group made private-label suits and licensed brands like Jones New York for chains like Macy's, was in desperate need of a new brand. Dress-Down Nation had forced Brody to scour for a new way to push men's suits. He knew better than to scout for another designer name like Armani— ordinary guys weren't going to respond to a fashion warhorse. Brody needed a high-profile, red-blooded man who could energize the very image of a suit, reconnecting it with entrepreneurship and corporate success. Someone who had the panache of Wall Street but was not too highfalutin, in order to capture the mainstream guys for the $400 suits Marcraft needed to move. I marveled as Brody in 2006 told me this story in his New York office.

The answer was none other than Donald Trump, who immediately came to mind for a simple reason: The man was always in a suit. "When did you ever see him in a sport shirt?" he asked me. "Every photo of him with a shirt and tie and jacket on—usually buttoned." When Brody made his initial overture to Trump—to front a suit line—the Donald was mildly amused and turned him down flat. But the seed had been planted.

Trump would have a change of heart after he completed his first season of *The Apprentice* in 2003–2004. The popular reality show drew twenty-eight million viewers on its season finale—many of whom had watched him for a running fifteen weeks sit tall behind his broad desk and deliver that trademark blow, "You're fired," with such executive brio. Trump was America's most famous corporate suit, and he just *had* to do a suit line, Brody implored when he circled back to Trump, who finally said yes.

Trump, the Art of the Fashion Deal was about to happen—but only after Brody talked the blustery, could-be billionaire back down to earth.

Initially, Trump had lofty and unrealistic expectations for his suits. Given that Trump himself wore the finest Italian $5,000 Brioni suits, Trump dreamed that his suit line should be on par with, say, $1,500 suits by Giorgio Armani.

No way, Brody recalled telling him. The wholesale customer was Macy's, after all! The suits carried a list price averaging around $450 but were often promoted at 50 percent off. The Donald J. Trump suit collection would have the trappings of luxury, such as an elegant satin label inside the jacket and handmade details like pick stitching—a subtle running stitch around the lapels, which is the hallmark of finer garments, now easily doable on high-tech machines. Brody had to explain to Trump the economics of fashion retailing. The main point was that the objective was volume, as in BIG—something that Trump could relate to.

The Trump suits wouldn't even be top of the line in Macy's men's department—but they were treated like the celebrity exclusives that they were. At Herald Square, Trump suits had their own alcove, featuring a long boardroom table with high-backed chairs, imparting the ambiance of an executive suite. Each suit jacket contained a little card that said that the Trump garments were the "ultimate achievement in clothing manufacturing and carry Donald's own seal of approval," and a pithy declaration from Trump himself: "I searched the world to procure the

finest imported fabrics. Expert tailors have crafted suits to my rigid spec-
ifications. The result is a garment worthy of the Trump name."

Hokey, and a colossal load of BS, but effective.

Trump-Struck

Rodney Bullock, a thirty-nine-year-old fashion design student, was
among the crowd at Macy's who showed up to see Trump in person at
the launch of his new suit line at Macy's. He told Tim O'Brien, author of
TrumpNation: The Art of Being The Donald, that he was considering
buying a suit. Bullock told O'Brien why he admired Trump: "He's about
money. He has a name. He means money. I want to go after that look.
People are all here [at Macy's] because they want to see the man who's on
TV firing people. . . . Living in a city with millions of people and we're
all starstruck. That's what it boils down to."

I got to see this for myself in 2006 when the Donald came back to
Macy's for the lunchtime launch of Donald Trump Watches. The first
floor was packed with shoppers who had been lining up for an hour or
so, all waiting for Trump with their cell phones and cameras aimed at the
door where he would enter. Folks piled up around the entrance on Thirty-
Fourth Street and perked up once they heard, "Money, money, money,
money!"—the opening lyrics from the O'Jays' '70s hit, "For the Love of
Money." Trump ambled in like a prizefighter. The scowl, the bravado—
he made a slow, full turn, cocking his arm in front of his chest, in an
exaggerated gesture to show his wristwatch to a barrage of flashing cameras. Then he went over to cut the ribbon at the watch counter and pose
for more pictures with Macy's executives.

I followed the Trump entourage to the third-floor suit department
right next to Trump's boardroom of suits, where the Donald got busy
signing autographs and posing for pictures with the first hundred shoppers who had bought his watches. This was the hoi polloi—probably not
an investment banker or attorney in the bunch—and Trump turned into
a politician on the campaign trail, being downright friendly to these
starry-eyed TV fans, including a middle-aged tourist from England
who bought three watches so he could meet Mr. *Apprentice*. Brody
walked me around to check out one of the suit displays, a pinstripe on a

mannequin. "A lot of value for the price," he assured me, pointing out the pick stitching on the lapel.

As the Trump dress shirts and silk ties came on board, Trump won a fan I would have never expected: Hollywood stylist Phillip Bloch, who'd dressed the likes of Halle Berry and Sandra Bullock. "I use the ties in shoots, I've worn them and they are quite good," he said, adding that they weren't freebies. "I buy them just like everybody else, at Macy's."

Trump had nothing to do with the designing of his suits, and he wasn't the reason for the end of the suit slump. It just so happened that in 2004 young men were starting to dress up for work again. Sales of suits increased 34 percent that year, halting an eight-year decline, according to NPD Group Inc. market researchers.

So Trump—without the creative adeptness to lead and influence clothing trends—was merely the beneficiary of lucky timing.

New York Times fashion critic Cathy Horyn wrote of the Man Who Would Be King of Fashion: "It couldn't be true. Mr. Armani has worked his fingers to the bone to be a world-renowned designer; spent a fortune advancing the idea too. And what about Valentino, Karl Lagerfeld, Stella McCartney and . . . Domenico Dolce and Stefano Gabbana? They don't even make the list. Shut out of America. Ignored. Trumped. It's true. . . . He may have been surprised himself to learn that he had done in a year of light lifting what has taken Ralph Lauren nearly forty years to accomplish."

Exploring the Galaxy

Macy's started to showcase its lineup of famous celebrity brands in splashy TV commercials in 2007 and 2008, executed by JWT New York, Oscar-winning director Barry Levinson (*Rain Man*), and Oscar-winning cinematographer Bob Richardson (*The Aviator, JFK*). One Christmas holiday commercial was filmed on location in a Brooklyn studio where a custom-built, two-story set was created to resemble the actual Macy's. The video was edited to feature fast cutaways of Tommy Hilfiger, Jessica Simpson, Donald Trump, Emeril Lagasse, Martha Stewart, Kenneth Cole, Usher, Russell Simmons, and Sean Combs—all of whose branded products were sold exclusively at Macy's.

Each celebrity was busy decorating the store to the tinkling notes of

The Nutcracker Suite when suddenly the lights and music went off. The camera zoomed in on the heel of Jessica's tall black boot as she stepped on the electrical cord, pulling it from the wall socket. "Oops," she squealed.

"Jesssssss-i-ca? Darling?" said Martha Stewart, who tapped her fingers together, scolding in the semidarkness. Wide-eyed and sheepish, Jessica grimaced as she pushed the plug back into the wall, and as the store lit up, so did the music. An announcer said: "Only one star can bring all these stars home for the holidays; that's the magic of Macy's."

The humorous ads telegraphed a powerful message that set Macy's apart from all other retail chains: All the celebrities featured in Macy's commercials weren't just hired pitchmen but genuine stars who marketed their namesake products, sold at Macy's.

Macy's red star became bigger, even more prominent. In her corner office at the Herald Square store, executive vice president Reardon has a big red star affixed to the wall, as do many other Macy's employees.

Macy's was known for its events; the dynamic retailer crackled with year-round in-store buzz from the cooking demonstrations, fashion shows, and numerous celebrity appearances—all associated with the merchandise they sold. Even if you didn't live in New York, you could get a taste for all these events because Macy's videoed them and put them on Facebook and YouTube.

In Shoes and the City, the behemoth second-floor shoe department, which stocked up to three hundred thousand pairs of shoes in its inventory, there was an outpost for E! Live from the Red Carpet shoes—yes, there was such a brand for satin and sparkly shoes for weddings and parties. Macy's christened the brand with a little red-carpet fashion show in January 2011, amid the season of the Oscars and Golden Globes. But the first celebrity shoe brand to the party—a full three years ahead of Jessica Simpson—was Carlos by Carlos Santana shoes.

Abraxas, God of Sling-Back Pumps

It seemed strange that a rock-jazz artist from the 1970s—a laid-back guy, no less—would lend his name to a line of high-heeled pumps, sandals, and tall boots that sold for between $110 and $250. Macy's introduced

Carlos Santana shoes in 2002, when few women associated the name of the rock star with shoes.

It didn't matter. The footwear built a following first, heavily among Latinas and blacks, as it became a $200 million a year brand in 2012.

At a time when the 1970s legend was having a twenty-first-century renaissance with his bestselling Grammy Award–winning *Supernatural* album in 1999, Santana got the idea to use his name to market women's shoes in order to generate funds for his Milagro Foundation for children. His quest led him to one of America's biggest traditional footwear marketers, Brown Shoe Company, based in St. Louis. Brown, the supplier of Naturalizer and LifeStride shoes mainly to department stores, didn't have a label for fast, sexy high heels—which had come in demand during the reign of *Sex and the City*. So instead of a designer hook, Brown chose a celebrity one—an unexpected one at that.

Carlos Santana plays his guitar in front of a display of Carlos Santana shoes at Macy's in 2012.

"Carlos was our first fashion brand at Brown—and everybody thought we were crazy," because middle-aged Santana had no connection to fashion or women, recalled Rick Gelber, the head of Brown's Carlos Santana division. But Gary Rich, Brown's president of wholesale at the time—and an avid guitarist—was intrigued with the idea of fusing footwear with a hip, musical image. It was Latino, sexy, colorful, urban, Miami—and it didn't hurt that he had a bit of hero worship for Santana, with whom he would become close. "Gary had the vision and pushed it through," Gelber told me.

Brown's designers developed hot styles, and the brand became famous for its high-heel, crochet-embellished dressy western boots and high-heel pumps. Macy's became Santana's first retail account, and the brand became instantly popular in Miami and Texas border towns, buoyed by Santana's personal appearances at stores.

The presence of the Latino music legend at the big footwear trade shows in Las Vegas was a big plus. The Carlos Santana show booth featured runway fashion shows with lots of Latina and black models—and Santana threw a concert at the Vegas Hard Rock Café, where he signed shoes and gave away CDs.

Macy's pushed the success even further, paying for a commercial that shows Carlos Santana in his signature black fedora seated on a stool strumming his guitar next to his wife, Cindy, conversing about his shoes while models show his fashions. Carlos says: "Music inspires my collection. The beauty of color, of symmetry and real passion."

Not to mention the power of celebrity.

Chapter Eleven

. . . .

CELEBRITY BY DESIGN

Project Runway Fits Michael Kors Like a Glove

Fashion schools should spend less time on working with [students] on doing sketches and more time on media training and how to package themselves.

—Michael Kors, September 2007

Michael Kors needed *Project Runway* like a sewing machine needed a needle. He just didn't realize it at first.

It was 2003 when his Manhattan neighbor—TV producer Desiree Gruber—phoned him about an exciting new concept for a reality show with fashion designers as contestants that she had cooked up with Hollywood producer Harvey Weinstein and supermodel Heidi Klum. Their brainstorming would become *Project Runway*, a reality show featuring start-up fashion designers competing for cash and the chance to show their designs during New York Fashion Week.

Gruber sketched out to Kors the recurring roles they envisioned: Heidi Klum would be the host judge, joined by Kors and *Elle* fashion director Nina Garcia—along with different guest judges each week. As the only veteran designer among the critics, Kors would give the show credibility and gravitas.

Since 1981, when he launched his namesake fashion label, Kors had seen it all. His high-end sportswear collections had won critical acclaim— which translated into modest success as he had tenaciously climbed the rungs for years, only to suffer a setback in 1990: a Chapter 11 bankruptcy reorganization—alongside all of his "best designer" accolades.

But Kors bounced back and was holding his own in 1997 when he experienced the dream of every American designer: He was appointed to be creative director for a prestigious fashion label in Paris. No less than the founder of the world's largest luxury goods conglomerate, LVMH chairman Bernard Arnault, picked Kors to take over the reins at Céline, a dusty-but-respected accessories label where Kors tirelessly toiled for five years, successfully creating a fashion signature for Céline in apparel— as well as continuing to design for his own label, in which LVMH eventually bought a 33 percent stake.

In 2002 when his contract ended, Kors gave up Paris to focus exclusively on his modest eponymous label in New York. His experience at Céline left Kors more sure-footed than ever as he plowed himself back into developing his luxurious American sportswear niche brand, which had an elite following of affluent women and Manhattan socialites like Blaine Trump, Tory Burch, and Aerin Lauder. He also had an avid following of Hollywood celebrities, women like Gwyneth Paltrow, Sigourney Weaver, Debra Messing, and Rene Russo, who loved his clothes enough that they didn't demand a big check to wear them in public.

Kors had become something of a culture hero to influential members of the fashion press—notably Anna Wintour. I always looked forward to interviewing him because he was so affable—such a "quotron," a raconteur who regaled everybody with his pithy comments, colorful observations, and nonstop humor.

Just think how splendidly you would play on TV, was how Gruber propositioned him. A flattered but skeptical Kors turned her down. "A flat-out no," recalled Anne Waterman, Kors's top marketing executive at the time and his longtime confidante. Kors had reason to be cynical when it came to the reality-show genre, and he doubted that *Project Runway* would somehow manage to escape descending into the foolishness and outrageous pranks of shows like *Survivor* or *Big Brother.* "I had this fear it was designers eating bugs, or something weird like that," he reminisced on video to the *Hollywood Reporter* in 2010. "Fashion is tricky to get on film—to get it right," he said. "Fashion in and of itself is glamorous—and you don't want to turn it into a joke, so how do you have that balance?"

He figured that all that designer shoptalk about "fabrications" and bias cuts would be boring to ordinary TV viewers. He said: "We can't believe anyone cares about what we love."

And that was precisely the point. Outside the fashion pond, Kors was nearly invisible. Michael Kors was just another label hanging on the designer floor at Saks Fifth Avenue or Neiman Marcus. That's why John Idol, the chief executive of Kors Inc., pleaded with him to reconsider. Kors needed to do *Project Runway* to be seen and heard, to put himself on the map before the millions of regular folks whom the company was now courting as customers. The house of Kors was on the verge of adding lower-priced merchandise and, most important, developing a lucrative accessories business. The company was poised to become a powerhouse player, in the league of Gucci and Prada; it all boiled down to selling those shoes and handbags to the masses. By going on TV as a regular, Kors could quickly be visible to a young audience of fashion influencers.

Nobody at Kors could predict whether *Project Runway* would be a hit or a miss. In any event, it was a low-risk gamble—if the show flopped after a season or two, it would be forgotten in a hurry. The only shot that a boutique brand like Kors had at becoming a billion-dollar industry player was for Kors to become a household name—something that he hadn't accomplished in more than twenty years so far. It wasn't enough just to bask in the reflected glory of dressing the Hollywood "it girls" of the moment. Michael Kors needed to become a celebrity in his own right.

The Next Big Thing

Kors was now moving forward, with a laser-like purpose that he'd never had in the twenty years before. In 2003, Silas Chou and Lawrence

Stroll—the investors behind the Tommy Hilfiger juggernaut in the 1980s—took controlling interest of the Kors fashion house for $100 million. The new benefactors were squarely focused on growing Michael Kors Holdings Ltd. into a billion-dollar public company.

I always marveled at the fashion business instincts of Chou and Stroll—both billionaires who came from wealthy families sired by fashion industry industrialists: Chou from Hong Kong and Stroll from Canada. At heart, these guys were garmentos—the old-school nickname for apparel manufacturers in New York's "rag trade" Garment District—who had mastered the intricacies of production and merchandising. They approached fashion strictly as big business, a strategy they'd proven successful with Tommy Hilfiger Inc. Tight like brothers, Chou and Stroll were also great fun and loved to entertain on a grand scale.

I happened to be in London on business in 2002, when they invited me to lunch at their New Bond Street headquarters, where we enjoyed champagne, Dover sole, and freshly shaved truffles on pasta served by an English butler. At the time, they owned two stellar luxury British labels, Asprey and Garrard, which they were struggling to turn into major players, starting by spending millions to build a palatial New York flagship store on Fifth Avenue next door to Trump Tower. But this would prove to be a business adventure doomed to fail because, despite their storied heritage, both Asprey and Garrard were practically unknown to New Yorkers, let alone American shoppers. Chou and Stroll weren't infallible—and they were losing millions on this miscalculation.

Backstage close-up: Michael Kors, Lawrence Stroll, Michael Douglas, and Silas Chou, in 2013.

During my London visit, when Chou and Stroll began musing about the next big thing in American fashion, the conversation really got interesting. The business partners were adamant when they told me that they would never invest in a fashion start-up—no matter how promising—because it always takes years to establish brand recognition with a new name (as they learned to their dismay with the Asprey and Garrard misfortune). The only American brands worth pursuing, Chou said, were two designers who had been in business since the 1980s: Marc Jacobs and Michael Kors.

Jacobs had by then become a big star as the creative director of Louis Vuitton, so owner LVMH was also tethered to his Marc Jacobs fashion business.

That left Kors.

This turned out to be far from idle lunch chat. Months later, in 2003, they swept in to buy Michael Kors—and three years later they cut their losses and unloaded Asprey and Garrard.

A Charmed Life

Born on August 9, 1959, in New York, Michael Kors was an adorable, platinum-blond, blue-eyed toddler who appeared in Lucky Charms cereal and Charmin bathroom tissue commercials between the ages of four and six. His mom was a showroom model on Seventh Avenue, and he grew up steeped in the world of fashion.

By the time he was in college at the Fashion Institute of Technology he worked as the in-house designer at Lothar's, a chic French Manhattan boutique with clients like Jackie Onassis, where he designed everything from tie-dye jeans to swimsuits. Ambitious and fast-tracking, Kors dropped out of FIT and started his fashion business in 1981, without ever having worked for another designer.

His first retail customer was the tony Bergdorf Goodman, where he mastered the art of trunk shows: retail events where he waited on wealthy women who placed special orders from a collection of sample garments. He learned how to deftly critique a woman's fashion choices with honesty and diplomacy. That experience put him on the path of the legendary Bill Blass, the standard-bearer for America's socialites. Kors's signature wasn't avant-garde or show-offy but quiet luxury with flair—the French have a mellifluous word for it: *soigné*. Think of the look of his clients, like model-turned-actress Rene Russo, whom he dressed when she played opposite Pierce Brosnan in the 1999 remake of the stylish caper *The Thomas Crown Affair*. The film portrayed the epitome of the jet-set lifestyle, just like in the original 1968 version starring Steve McQueen and Faye Dunaway, who was stunning in her picture hats and miniskirted ensembles.

"Rene knew that the wardrobe was essential to this movie, and when they started filming, she felt that the film wardrobe wasn't chic enough," recalled Waterman. Russo rang her designing BFF Kors directly. Soon Russo was at the Michael Kors showroom, trying on samples from Kors and Céline collections—past and present—in front of *Thomas Crown* director John McTiernan and the movie's wardrobe people. There was no time to make costumes in triplicate—as movies typically require—so they just picked from the samples: chic cashmere turtlenecks, tweeds, pantsuits, and coats, the expensive career components befitting Russo's character, a high-end specialist insurance claims investigator. (Kors didn't create Russo's sexy black translucent gown; it was designed by Randolph Duke and shot before Kors's looks were added in the film.)

Kors's reputation was already soaring with Céline and his own namesake collections. But Russo's chic clothes showcased in a hit movie surely helped Kors in 1999, when Kors won the CFDA award for best women's-wear designer.

It was also in 1999 that he launched his first namesake perfume—which became a bestseller—and E! Entertainment ran a documentary on him, which raised his profile even more. "The exposure from that program was bigger than any of us had realized," he told me in 2007.

Michael Kors was high-chic sportswear—a brand that I admired but always seemed overpriced to me ($1,800 for a double-faced wool sheath dress!)—another reason his company had yet to crack the $500 million sales threshold before 2004. The Kors label had a lot of growing to do, especially in the lucrative handbag-and-shoe category, the very same business model that Prada, Gucci, and Louis Vuitton used to make a killing.

Like most designers, Kors channeled his energies into runway presentations with his original signature: He put fresh-faced all-American women, wearing casually messy hair, and men together, striding tall in clothes that reeked of wealth and sophistication—sumptuous cashmere and silk turtlenecks, updated peacoats, fox vests, sable chubbies, suede jeans. He had a penchant for bold, bright primary colors, stripes, and nautical themes. The Kors impact was so very town-and–country club, ski-lodge resort, and Palm Beach—or "Palm Bitch," as he playfully dubbed his spring 2004 collection. Under its new benefactors, Michael Kors Holdings Ltd. now did expensive ad campaigns—spending $25 million a year to impart the jet-set vibe in print ads showing glamorous couples to-ing and fro-ing aboard private jets, yachts, and limousines.

But his *Thomas Crown Affair* aspirational stance was hardly enough to move the needle among a new generation of millennials. Women in places like Oklahoma City, Charlotte, or San Diego needed to be aware and excited about Michael Kors—to choose him over Tory Burch or Diane von Furstenberg or Theory—among the designer brands chasing the same shoppers.

BFA

Front-row regulars Michael Douglas (right) and Catherine Zeta-Jones join Michael Kors (left) backstage after his fashion show on September 12, 2012.

Kors CEO Idol was already leading Kors to the masses by beefing up Michael by Michael Kors, his midtier label, and introducing shoes, handbags, sunglasses, and watches, effectively lowering his prices with the addition of all those $200 handbags and watches and $100 shoes. Kors rolled out hundreds of in-store shops across Macy's starting in 2003, as well as three hundred freestanding Kors boutiques, which the company would open around the world by 2013.

To sell on that large a scale, it was more important than ever for Kors to become a celebrity. And the path to get there had already been blazed by the king of America's celebrity designers—his contemporary, Isaac Mizrahi.

Les Mizrahi

Mizrahi, whose women's sportswear collections were modern and very original, was deemed American fashion's next big thing throughout the 1990s—ahead of Kors, Jacobs, and everybody else. In addition to the acclaim he received for *Unzipped*, the 1995 documentary that tracked his path through the business of launching a collection, he was a contestant on *Jeopardy!*'s celebrity invitational, and always popping up in cameos on TV and in movies playing a fashion designer, of course. His critics couldn't stop clucking about the fame-obsessed Mizrahi—if only he had put the same energy into making his fashion collections profitable and commercial. If only . . .

Their critiques proved prescient when Mizrahi was forced into liquidating his company in 1998 when his financial backers, the French House of Chanel, pulled the plug on the famous but perennially unprofitable label. It showed the limitations of celebrity. Mizrahi waxed on about how his collections were full of "fabulous clothes, the only kind that will sell," but in truth his clothes weren't selling at all—a business that at its peak was estimated never to be more than $10 million a year. Ultimately, he was like the pop singer whose fans didn't buy his music.

But Mizrahi's going-out-of-business drama turned out to be only a hiatus of sorts. Fashion designers are famous for second and third reincarnations, and Mizrahi would have his too. But first, he was on to his next curtain call. I caught him at a gig in the East Village at Joe's Pub when he was playing the piano, swaying while he crooned the Fred Astaire vintage number "I Left My Hat in Haiti."

By 2000, he was appearing off-Broadway, starring in his one-man confessional, *Les Mizrahi*, a charming performance where he sketched on a big easel—and constructed a dress in muslin onstage, while prattling wistfully about his fashion career.

His Hollywood the-show-must-go-on attitude was nothing but savvy. He made his love of the limelight work for him. Fashion people were surprised—though it only reflected on their cluelessness—when he resurfaced in the mass market, in Target of all places. In 2002, Target hired him to translate high fashion for budget shoppers with his own label, Isaac Mizrahi for Target.

It was the first cheap-chic designer collaboration—where Target counted on Mizrahi's élan and showmanship to seal the deal with shoppers. Michael Francis, Target's senior vice president of marketing, who helped broker the deal, told me back then that Mizrahi's celebrity was just as important as his design credentials.

Isaac learned to love his Target gig quickly. He was a bit testy at first when he was forced to eliminate design details in order to keep the prices down. His new creative challenges had nothing to do with being cutting-edge and everything to do with being commercial: The $14.99 stretch poplin wrap blouse he designed had to be made to fit women from size XS to size XL.

And speaking of commercial—Mizrahi was born to star in Target's TV advertisements. There he was, Mr. New York, dashing through his fashion showroom, across a Manhattan street, then into a Yellow Cab, while talking in a vivacious flutter:

"Wait till you see these clothes I've designed for Target! It's like chic! Affordable! *Divine!* Fifth Avenue meets Main Street USA. Classic, fresh, clothes to make women all across America fab-ulous!"

Mizrahi's novelty Target collection played as a smash hit at retail from the get-go, and over the next five years mushroomed into a $300-million-a-year business. How clever he was to use Target as his bridge back to high fashion. Mizrahi did a fashion show with Bergdorf Goodman, mixing his $1,000-and-up couture designs (he had revived his high-end label somewhat, with a few garments—a "capsule" collection) with Target's budget under-$50 clothes to graphically illustrate the high-low manner in which modern women were now dressing.

Cheapskate chic: Isaac Mizrahi, here in 2003, brought high fashion to the mass market when he began designing women's collections for Target.

Target's slogan: "It's fashionable to pay less." Indeed, the fashion editors invited to the runway show that day were often fooled (me included), frequently checking the program's cheat sheet to distinguish the $29 Target togs from the luxurious Bergdorf components. Mizrahi had unwittingly changed the high-fashion drill from now on—as designers like Karl Lagerfeld, Stella McCartney, Versace, Phillip Lim, and Proenza Schouler would all start turning out one-time-only capsule cheap-chic collections for Target and H&M.

Mizrahi was the first to be admired and respected in a new way, as the pied piper for a populist movement—where mainstream women felt validated by the fashion cognoscenti at last. Women stopped him everywhere asking for his autograph or to take a picture with him.

The relentless trooper who loved to entertain as much as he loved designing clothes had landed in the right place at the right time. He taught every designer in fashionland a valuable lesson: It takes a celebrity to sell fashion on a big scale.

Of Kors He Can!

Kors was every bit as endearing as Mizrahi—minus his breathless shtick—and always serious when it came to selling clothes. Upon further reflection, Kors finally said yes to *Project Runway*, for the greater good of his brand. Waterman explained to me: "We didn't do it for the fun of it. We needed to get into a *gazillion* homes at once. TV was the way to do it."

Project Runway emerged fortuitously at the intersection of fashion and pop culture. By around 2005, viewers were tuned in to *Project Runway* the same way fans were entertained watching chefs prepare a dish on the Food Network. So when Heidi Klum challenged designer contestants to make a party outfit from live foliage and flowers from the flower district, or to make an outfit for Carrie Bradshaw on an episode when Sarah Jessica Parker was a guest judge on the show, with only $15 worth of materials, TV viewers were locked into the process.

Kors initially feared that the show would be watched by only "fashionista freaks, gays and men wanting to see Heidi Klum in a short dress." But he knew the show had hit critical mass when he kept hearing from all the non–fashion people who had become loyal fans of the show, from septuagenarian jazz musician Quincy Jones to construction workers.

Project Runway was one of those shows that people liked to discuss the next day at the office, and Kors's opinion seemed to count more than the other judges', because he was the only professional designer among them. (I was even invited to be a guest judge in 2007.)

By season three, the show had tripled its audience from the first year to an average of 3.4 million viewers every week, according to Nielsen— and stayed at around three million viewers until the ninth season, giving Kors a long stretch of TV face time to become a household name. Indeed, he had fast become a pop-culture celebrity—a fashion designer who dazzled with his command of techniques with fit and fabric, while glibly critiquing in hilarious metaphors such as:

"This [dress] looks like toilet paper caught in a windstorm."

"It's like a hairdressing smock. Like she was cutting her hair, there was a fire in the beauty salon, she belted it, and she ran out in her zebra dress."

"I mean, she looks like a transvestite flamenco dancer at a funeral."

"All the curtains from Tara ripped off the wall and put into one dress."

By 2007, the fourth season of *Project Runway*, Kors was in demand everywhere. He was on Martha Stewart's show talking about fashion and whipping up spaghetti and meatballs or pineapple upside-down cake in her kitchen. Just like the tabloid stars who were polled about every aspect of their lives, Kors was now telling *Harper's Bazaar* and *Elle Décor* about his favorite vacation haunt and his floral preferences or what he was going to serve at a summer barbeque.

His schedule now pulled him in every direction during Fashion Week: In September 2007, for example, he conducted at least forty-five interviews, attended two book parties, and appeared onstage at the Fashion Rocks pop concert in front of thousands at Radio City Music Hall. Sandwiched between all the publicity that week: his Michael Kors spring collection fashion show.

All the celebrity splash pushed his company into the forefront of cool and ensured the success of CEO Idol's plan to introduce twelve lifestyle stores containing mostly handbags, shoes, and watches from Kors's lower-priced Michael label. In every store opening where he appeared, bands of screaming teens brandishing cell phone cameras queued up for him to autograph the $70 belt or $300 handbag they were buying.

"TV has definitely spread the gospel," he told me in 2007, commenting about his new fan base of young TV watchers. He once visited a Nordstrom store in suburban Los Angeles, spending two hours signing autographs on fragrance boxes and "on every piece of paper that wasn't nailed down," he told me.

As Kors's success spiked with the popularity of the show, people started calling it "the *Project Runway* effect." It proved that you could have all the fashion-forward concepts in the world, but business success required that good design be accompanied by designers who were telegenic and media savvy—celebrities in their own right.

Kors, finally, was a believer. "Fashion schools should spend less time working with [students] on doing sketches and more time on media training and how to package themselves," he told me.

He also discovered that celebrity attracted celebrity: He told me in 2007 that he created five times as many red-carpet gowns as he had in the 1990s, dressing stars like Jessica Simpson, Fantasia Barrino, Jennifer Lopez, and Jennifer Hudson. First Lady Michelle Obama wore Kors for her official White House portrait in 2008. It all helped draw attention to his brand.

"In order to make noise on the newsstand, you have to bang some pots," he told me.

And that was the domino effect—the more interest people have in celebrities, the more they pay attention to fashion and the more they become aware of designers like Kors.

In December 2011, Michael Kors became the most successful fashion initial public offering in history, valuing the brand at nearly $3 billion. By 2014, the company's valuation had bumped to $20 billion, with 2013 annual revenue of $1.5 billion and net income of $176 million, with 303 stores around the world and sales across 2,800 department stores and specialty stores.

In 2013, after ten years as a judge on *Project Runway*, Michael Kors, citing scheduling conflicts, left the show.

But not before he sold more Kors shares valued at more than $700 million. At fifty-four, Kors rarely appeared in public anymore without his black wire aviator glasses, looking every inch the multimillionaire movie-star mogul.

Chapter Twelve

. . . .

WE'LL ALWAYS HAVE PARIS

Reality-Show Stars Join the Stampede

By 2011, the "I think I'm a celebrity; therefore, I have a shoe line" zeitgeist had filtered all the way down from Jessica Simpson to Adrienne Maloof, one of the original Housewives on *The Real Housewives of Beverly Hills.*

Maloof had no apparent talent or experience in fashion design and marketing—the main aptitude she showed on TV was her ability to get into hissing spats with her girlfriends and neighbors—yet she must have brimmed with optimism when she launched her namesake shoe line at Lord & Taylor that year. A wealthy heiress (the diverse Maloof family holdings include the Sacramento Kings basketball team), the fetching-at-fifty, honey-blonde Maloof was a shoe fiend in the Carrie Bradshaw/Imelda Marcos league, as evidenced by her showroom-of-a-closet, where she said she stashed most of her five hundred–odd pairs of designer shoes and boots.

Lacking her own bona fides, Maloof strapped her shoes to a designer legend, as in "Adrienne Maloof for Charles Jourdan." It wasn't that

Charles Jourdan, the fabled-but-faded 1970s maker of stilettos from Paris, came looking for her. It was Maloof who approached Charles Jourdan.

Maloof tracked down the executives of Titan Industries, a footwear marketer based in Huntington, California, whose licensed brands include Charles Jourdan shoes designed exclusively for the US market. Based on Maloof's TV visibility, they agreed to give it a try, pairing Maloof's name with selected Charles Jourdan styles that Titan created for the brand.

"What we did was a side deal with Adrienne—which was unusual, given that we specialize in high-fashion shoes"—names like Badgley Mischka as well as celebrity Gwen Stefani's L.A.M.B. footwear and, for a short time, Jennifer Lopez shoes—Titan's president, Brad Bailey, told

me. He said: "Adrienne didn't design the shoes," but under the agreement she stood to collect royalties on the Jourdan styles marketed with her name. Lord & Taylor promoted Maloof like a TV star at its New York Fifth Avenue flagship store, where she signed photos of herself and the soles of the new shoes purchased by her TV fans.

And of course, the footwear was fodder for the reality show. In a 2012 *Housewives* episode, Maloof hosted a black-tie charity fashion show that doubled as a launch for her new shoe collection, held outdoors at her Beverly Hills mansion, in the lush

The Real Housewives of Beverly Hills's Adrienne Maloof and her signature shoes in 2012, at the MAGIC fashion trade show in Las Vegas.

backyard garden: a splendid, candlelit setting amid the roses and topiaries. But why did so many of the runway models wear flowing chiffon gowns hiding their feet, when their shoes were supposed to be the stars of the show?

Lisa Vanderpump, her Beverly Hills sister Housewife and frenemy on camera, huffed in her imperious British accent: "I thought the whole point of the fashion show was to see the shoes, and everybody is in long dresses. . . . Only Adrienne would have a fashion show for her shoes and not show them. I came to see the Maloof hoof."

It was a catty dig that made the Bravo TV producers ecstatic. Vanderpump carried on: "Watch out, Maloof hoof, the Vander pump is on its way to kick your ass."

It was the wisecrack that lit up the Twittersphere and propped up an entire season of otherwise tedious tit-for-tats by sparking another semi-scripted feud among the high-heeled Housewives.

While the Maloof for Jourdan collection was pricey—shoes from $195 to $395—and mimicked the trendy, towering platform pumps on other designer shoe lines, the label never gained traction with upscale shoppers. Even the vintage Charles Jourdan cobranding couldn't turn a TV Housewife into a Sarah Jessica Parker. It came as no surprise that the Maloof styles landed on the markdown rack, selling at steep discounts for as low as $69.99 online at sites like Zappos.com.

Maloof's three seasons on TV were forgotten in a flash. She was dropped from the *Housewives* cast in 2012—the same year she divorced from Dr. Paul Nassif, her plastic-surgeon husband of thirty years—and Titan Industries phased out the Maloof line. Side out, rotate. Another reality-show fashion cautionary tale.

Gossip, catfights, divorces, and the rest of the high jinks emerging from the luxe lifestyle of the rich bitches of reality-show land had become standard fare, but the result was nonetheless hilarious, eminently watchable and addictive, escapist TV. The women personified the pampered trophy wife, with their spray-on tans, impossibly long and lush hairdos, cleavage-flashing frocks, and diamonds on demand. Accenting their skyscraper stilettos was that familiar queen of message handbags: the Hermès Birkin satchel, a handmade status symbol (starting at $7,400).

TV viewers salivated with closet envy looking at these women's plus-size wardrobes, customized spaces with all kinds of drawers, shelves, and three-way mirrors that were at least as big as New York studio apartments. Mary Schmidt Amons, one of the Washington, DC, Real Housewives, showed off the lengths she took to keep her same-size grown daughter from filching her fashion treasures. Her locked closet was secured by a biometric fingerprint scanner.

So much of the content of the shows revolved around fashion that the TV characters became fixtures at charity fashion shows and sometimes scored coveted front-row seats at New York Fashion Week—even when the TV cameras weren't around. As they all became more convinced of their own fabulousness, inevitably some dared to evolve from crocodile-toting weapons of mass consumption to—you knew it—fashion designers in their own right. Or wrong.

The booby prize for the Housewife impersonating a designer goes to "She by Sheree," the half-assed attempt by Sheree Whitfield, a member of the cast of *The Real Housewives of Atlanta*, who decided to initiate her own fashion collection—but failed to get her sample garments ready on time. Her solution? Displaying fashion sketches on easels, which pissed off her invited guests, who'd expected to view a runway show. Unbowed, Whitfield pushed her way into New York Fashion Week in 2009, where "She by Sheree" bombed, this time with real clothes on live models at an event before an audience comprised of her TV groupies. Freelance fashion writer Karyn Collins wrote that the Sheree-designed collection was "the unfortunate combination of poor design, shoddy execution and sloppy presentation."

Making her excuses on *The Wendy Williams Show*, Sheree whined: "I've taken a hiatus, Wendy, because *it's a lot of work!*"

At least a few of the other reality-show celebrities actually got their fashions into the marketplace. And not just shoes, like Maloof and NeNe Leakes, the cheeky Atlanta Housewife who decided her humanitarian mission was to stand up for women who had big feet—sizes nine to thirteen (she's a ten)—and could never find trendy styles that would fit. Others couldn't resist the pull—or rather the push—of shapewear: New York Housewife Bethenny Frankel came out with Skinnygirl Shapers, while her fellow cast member Jill Zarin too cutely called hers "Skweez Couture."

And then there were the complete lines of clothes and accessories for women from the Kardashian sister-act trio at Sears.

But don't think for a moment that popular retail brands such as Steve

Jessica Simpson's bankable casual look: Daisy Duke shorts with Western boots, 2005.

Movie star shades: Rachel Zoe (top) and Jessica Simpson (bottom).

Jessica Simpson models her namesake shoes and handbags, 2006.

The Michael Jordan effect. Before: The 1970s look of Julius "Dr. J" Erving (far left, 1977). After: Jordan introduced long, baggy shorts and Air Jordan sneakers and made shaved heads trendy (left, 1995).

Fendi's famous "Baguette" handbag, launched in 1997, came in hundreds of patterns, enabling fashionistas not to see themselves coming and going.

For the Golden Globes and Oscars, Giorgio Armani has been known to send personalized sketches of the gowns he proposes to create for select leading ladies.

Brand new: Tory Burch inside her original NoLIta boutique in 2004. On day one, the shop was filled with tunic tops, handbags, shoes, and accessories—a splashy spread that sold out immediately.

Tory Burch (left), with her business partner in shoes and accessories, Vince Camuto, and his wife, Louise Camuto (right), in August 2010.

Tory Burch (center) with Jessica Alba (left) and Ginnifer Goodwin (right)—all in Tory Burch gowns—at the Metropolitan Museum of Art's Costume Institute Gala in 2013.

Sean John's billboard, starring Sean Combs, in Times Square in 2004.

A $70,000 flourish: Embroidered linen invitations and silk knot cuff links in black velvet boxes sent to one thousand guests for the Sean John fashion show on February 9, 2002.

Sean Combs (center) with Tommy Hilfiger (left) and Calvin Klein (right) at the opening party of the Sean John boutique on Fifth Avenue in September 2004.

Lady Gaga launches her Fame perfume at Macy's in September 2012.

Jennifer Lopez promotes Glowing, celebrating her ten-year partnership with Coty Inc. in 2012.

Jennifer Lopez and Michael Kors at the Met Museum's Costume Institute Gala in 2013.

Lovely in leopard (from left to right): Kourtney, Khloe, and Kim Kardashian launch their collection at Sears in September 2011.

Kanye West at the Mark Fast men's runway show at London Fashion Week in 2012.

Fashion victim: Victoria with David Beckham in London in 2005. Victoria wore Roberto Cavalli's "Dragon Ming Vase" couture gown to Elton John's Annual White Tie and Tiara Summer Ball. She asked Cavalli to alter the gown to be so narrow at the bottom, forcing her to remain standing throughout the entire event.

Victoria Beckham in front of a mood board in her design studio in 2010.

Sleek and fitted: Victoria Beckham wears one of her signature designs in 2012.

Twin winners: Supermodel actress Lauren Hutton (center) joins Mary-Kate (right) and Ashley (left) Olsen, whose The Row collection won the award for best women's wear designer at the Council of Fashion Designers of America gala in June 2012.

Fashionable wattage (from left to right): Anna Wintour, Tom Ford, and Julianne Moore, together at the CFDA gala in 2013.

Madden (shoes), Spanx (shapewear), or Theory (women's sportswear) lost a wink of sleep over any competition they might get from these ersatz designers. Sure, celebrity was a force to be reckoned with in fashion retailing, but the reality-show-celebrity brands hadn't a joule of the megawatt celebrity sparkle of Carlos Santana or Daisy Fuentes, whose fashion collections effectively hijacked the established order of things, nor the serious fashion business chops of Jessica Simpson.

What the Housewives had was just enough celebrity fairy dust—and connections—to put them in business. Young fans, in particular, seduced by the hype of their new offering, might buy a glittery $40 Kardashian Kollection T-shirt as a souvenir. But the pan flashed, then went dark. The combination of C-list celebrity and average to below-average merchandise—neither distinctive nor consistently innovative—just can't survive in the pressurized atmosphere of today's marketplace.

Yet these overreaching reality stars are still worth talking about because . . . well, because people love to blab about them. Macy's wasn't going to pass up a chance to tally yet another TV name on its roster. The store promoted New York Housewife Jill Zarin's Skweez Couture shapewear for about a year, while Lord & Taylor enjoyed the burst of publicity from Maloof's launch in its store—and the bump in sales that followed. Such brands were among the trendy flourishes that retailers typically feature to tart up their assortment—as they ride the wave of the celebrity moments of the season.

I'll Have What She's Having

Retailers have nothing to lose from grabbing a little novelty value from time to time. Like it or not, reality-show stars have become arbiters of style who have the ability to excite shoppers and move lots of merchandise. The more popular the name, the more merchandise she can sell—just not necessarily merchandise bearing her name. Even Snooki and her tanorexic posse, with their frat-house antics in MTV's former reality hit *Jersey Shore*, revived many people's interest in tanning like never before: Stars Snooki, JWOWW, and Pauly D each signed deals with different companies to market tanning and self-tanning cosmetics under their own names. And the critics had claimed that *Jersey Shore* had no redeeming social value!

There's also tangible evidence that reality-show stars help push the sale of clothes. RealityTVFashion.com is a popular website founded by Yakini Etheridge, a New York clinical psychologist who found a way to pocket some extra dough from her love of fashions worn on reality shows.

In 2010, Etheridge kicked off her site as a fashion blog, which she refined further by zeroing in on the shows that black and Latino audiences watched the most—which turned out to be around twenty different reality shows, including *The Real Housewives of Atlanta*, *I Dream of NeNe*, *Basketball Wives*, *Love & Hip Hop* (Atlanta, Los Angeles, and New York), *Tia & Tamera*, and fourteen shows on VH1. While every other mainstream website was chronicling the moves of the most popular white stars like Bethenny Frankel, none were paying close attention to following the black or Latina women, led by Leakes and Evelyn Lozada (*Basketball Wives*), who had strong, loyal consumer followings—including white women. Etheridge spotted a void she could fill—but admitted she thought it was only a small niche market at first.

Her blog, RealityTVFashion.com, which got as many as five hundred thousand page views a month in 2013, is where women go to locate the designer clothes—or look-alikes—that the shows' stars wear on TV. Every night at her Harlem, New York, home, starting around seven thirty P.M.—after seeing off the last of her psychology patients—Etheridge watches the shows and shoots images of the fashions directly off her TV screen, then downloads them onto her site. The images are far from high resolution, but they're clear enough for her readers to see and recognize from their own viewing.

Etheridge uses Google images and places like ShopStyle.com to quickly locate the same fashion items—or, more likely, similar items—which she can link directly to an online retailer. An independent service company keeps track of all the sales generated by the links on her website and processes her commission checks. Her cut of sales varies widely—she may collect as little as $1 for every item that clicks through to a sale or more typically between $5 and $10, and sometimes higher.

Her biggest coup in 2013 was with Atlanta Housewife Porsha Stewart, who wore a $70 multicolored beaded necklace in one episode. Etheridge tracked the necklace down to the website of Dillard's department stores. "I sold so many—maybe two hundred of those—and I received like four or five dollars for each necklace," she told me.

She also makes money from advertisers who run ads on her site. That all adds up to tens of thousands of dollars. It's still shy of six figures, she says, but double what she earns as a clinical psychologist.

For her ingenious new career, leveraged on American women's fascination with the wardrobes of the rich, tucked, and Botoxed divas of reality television, Etheridge can ultimately thank none other than Paris Hilton—the quintessential spoiled rich party girl.

Screen grab from the
RealityTVFashion.com website in 2014.

Paris Is Burning

When Jessica Simpson's Southern-belle persona lucked into a fashion groove from her exposure on the millennial reality show *Newlyweds*, it was by accident. But in 2003, Fox Entertainment went straight for the reality-TV fashion jugular—the high-end conspicuous consumption so brilliantly evoked in the fictional world of Carrie Bradshaw's *Sex and the City*. For the role of the sport-shopping glamour girl with an apparently bottomless Birkin pocketbook, they chose Hilton, whose Los Angeles estate featured mirrored, vault-size closets, teeming—no, bursting—with designer clothes.

Paris represented more than just another superficial-but-photogenic exhibitionist. She was a marker of the zeitgeist and a needle mover, introducing the world to a shallower, coarser kind of American socialite.

The very word *socialite* once indicated a woman who was a model of social decorum—whose style of dressing, entertaining, and comportment were all expected to be an impeccable example of gentility and good breeding. Paris Hilton was the polar opposite—someone who was labeled a socialite because she spent her life socializing, aka "partying." She was a madcap heiress, a teenage train wreck—bouncing from private schools to boarding schools, and ultimately, at sixteen, doing a year at Provo Canyon School for troubled teens. When she eventually managed to crawl across the finish line with a GED, it couldn't have been clearer that she didn't give a damn about getting a college degree or shielding her reputation from negative publicity. She wasn't looking for a husband; she was looking for a party and to score some coke in a nightclub bathroom.

Buttressed with her trust-fund millions, Miss Thing didn't need a man to take care of her either. Paris could blithely break the rules and still come out on top; she would always be the stylish, pampered, naughty princess who some women secretly envied for her daring, reckless ways. Even more women admired her designer clothes. And that would be her saving grace: No matter what nastiness she got up to, there would always be those who coveted the Paris lifestyle and wanted to buy whatever the hell Paris was selling.

One Night in Paris

Paris Hilton was born in Los Angeles on February 17, 1981, the first child of third-generation Hilton heir Richard Hilton and his wife, Kathy, who chose to name her firstborn after her favorite city. And just like the City of Light, Paris would be a glittery presence who had ambitions of rocking in the limelight—being a movie star—from the time she was a child.

And who could blame her? Generations of Hiltons had been drawn to the flame of celebrity. Conrad Hilton, Paris's great-grandfather, who began building his hotel empire in 1919, never used his burgeoning wealth to ascend into Junior League circles. He preferred the fast company of showgirls and Hollywood starlets. His second wife for five years was the foxy Zsa Zsa Gabor, a Hungarian beauty queen who made a sport of catching eight rich husbands. ("Eat, drink, and remarry" was one of the sayings on her needlepoint pillows.) Conrad Hilton was hardly hoodwinked by the gold-digging Gabor—simply content that he could afford her. "Glamour, I found, is expensive, and Zsa Zsa was glamour raised to the last degree," Hilton wrote in his 1957 autobiography *Be My Guest*. Conrad's son Nicky did his dad one better. He went celebrity chasing for the grand prize—MGM's dream girl, eighteen-year-old Elizabeth Taylor, whom he wed and divorced in the span of eight months.

Along came Nicky's son Richard, who met Kathy—a former child TV actress née Kathleen Avanzino, who appeared in shows like *Bewitched* and *Happy Days*—when he was nineteen and she was fifteen. They married five years later, and the couple spawned Paris and three more children. Living in the forty-room Hilton Los Angeles mansion, Paris had early childhood BFFs the likes of Nicole Richie, child actress Lindsay Lohan, and Kim Kardashian, who would remain chums for many years.

The Hiltons began living in New York when Paris was fifteen, at the family's room-service-equipped Manhattan flagship: the Waldorf-Astoria Hotel on Park Avenue. Living in the New York tabloid fishbowl in the 1990s meant those pretty Hilton teenagers—Paris and her kid sister Nicky—quickly became paparazzi favorites. Although Paris was underage, the fast-tailed teen managed to get into all the nightclubs, where she cruised the high life.

As adulthood beckoned, Paris made a play at a career. She cobbled together a smorgasbord of stylish gigs—starting with fashion modeling, of course. She signed with Donald Trump's agency at nineteen, followed by inconsequential acting roles. Her dramatic talent was neither great nor necessary. This was a new millennium, and her most intriguing role would be the one she was born to play: herself. Paris, it turned out, could make a career by dolling up in designer finery and acting out in public.

Her performances were memorable on the runway of Heatherette, a celebrity-centric label that became famous for doing the sparkly CARRIE T-shirt that Sarah Jessica Parker wore on *Sex and the City* and outfitting clients like Pamela Anderson, Alicia Keys, and Gwen Stefani. During

New York Fashion Week, Heatherette's showpieces were mainly skimpy, sequined party frocks—perfect for Paris, Heatherette's unofficial poster girl, who sashayed, posed, and carried on, making a spectacle of herself and reliably generating viral photos and publicity for the show.

She jumped on top of nightclub tables to dance and ran through a string of tabloid-worthy boyfriends, including Leonardo DiCaprio, and still had the energy to get into public tiffs with Shannen Doherty and everybody else, it seemed. Paris popped out from her limo in oversize shades, toting her pocketbook Chihuahua, Tinkerbell. With an angelic face and a rail-thin body, she used her no-expense-spared wardrobe allowance to create a fashion signature that could only be called "high skank"—nipple-baring see-through tops, high-slit skirts, stilettos, and ultra-low-rise pants. She wore the slutty look as a badge of honor, and she became pied piper as thousands of Paris wannabes imitated her style—including carrying a tiny fashion dog as an accessory.

But in the end, Paris's true style was her lifestyle. In 2003, Fox TV was prescient enough to see that all that sparkled was gold. The cable network approached Paris Hilton with a novel role, right up her alley: *The Simple Life*, which would take the hedonist princess outside of her coddled element and set her loose in Middle America among the rubes. Paris loved the concept and invited her bestie Nicole Richie to come along for the ride.

They were rich gal pals in low-rise pants and midriff tops, enthusiastically slumming (and giggling and pouting) their way through eye-rolling menial tasks like pumping gas, grooming dogs, and living with a family of seven in a small town in Arkansas. The hit show played the goldfish-out-of-water plot for laughs and surprises, lasting four seasons. During that time, real life overtook art. In 2005, she did a little reality show of her own: *1 Night in Paris*, a sex tape she made with a former boyfriend whose "unauthorized release" sold more than a half million copies online. An indiscretion that would once have destroyed a woman's reputation and made her a social pariah only made Paris even more of a titillating curiosity, further inflating her bad-girl cred. Tabloid shows on every conceivable platform lapped it up—and so did her mushrooming public.

Far from scolding her, her mom, Kathy, joined her on reality television.

By 2005, Kathy Hilton had her own show, *I Want to Be a Hilton*, where the contestants were divided into two teams: "Park" and "Madison," after the swank avenues in Manhattan. These ordinary young people competed in challenges such as organizing a fashion show and a charity event, while Kathy Hilton served as their mentor, coaching them on the fine points comme il faut—the protocol of etiquette, art, and culture, because, clearly, she had done such a great job with Paris. The grand prize at the end of the season was generous: a $200,000 trust fund, a rental apartment, a new wardrobe, and—the ultimate in solipsism—the opportunity to hang out with the Hiltons. Each week, as contestants were eliminated, Kathy Hilton fired off her parting shot: "You're not on the list."

Paris's next reality show, *The World According to Paris*, followed her to exotic locales around the world, where the scene was all too familiar: At a crowded Madrid nightclub, the natives went ecstatic when minidressed Paris sat suspended on a swing onstage and shouted into the microphone: "Bitches, I'm Paris!"

Paris, now an ultra-famous millionairess fashionista, had developed such a potent "it girl" aura that clubs and evening events were willing to pay her "appearance fees" for any drive-by stopover—starting around $100,000 for a few minutes and a photo op. "Every B-list celebrity has Paris to thank for making the paid photo ops a big deal, because she raised the rates," a New York fashion publicist told me.

Paris was in hot demand in 2007, when she agreed to pose at the end of a runway show in Moscow for "designer" Kira Plastinina, the then fifteen-year-old daughter of a wealthy Russian dairy magnate who spent millions turning his daughter into a local fashion phenom. Paris was rumored to have collected as much as $2 million for that Moscow photo op.

Paris and Kathy Hilton's reality TV show, and all the other fashion-centric shows it competed with, had a tremendous cumulative effect on fashion. As a foot soldier in the fashion trenches covering the industry for *The Wall Street Journal* during those years, I can heartily attest that TV—with its endless stream of look-at-me celebrities, real and created—did far more to push fashion into the forefront of pop culture, making trends accessible and entertaining, than fashion designers could ever do.

But as the first decade of the new century waned, the question became whether Paris Hilton, the attention-getting personality, could become a bankable fashion brand. We knew she was raking it in for parading her image, but could she sell actual clothes? She tried.

In 2007, Paris started dabbling in fashion with what could at best be called souvenir party clothes for fans, such as sequin-covered tops and minidresses and metallic finishes on blouses and logo T-shirts, priced from $30 to $130 under her Honey Bunch label. Her biggest footprint was in fragrances—sixteen scents as of 2013, with names such as Dazzle, Tease, Heiress, Can Can, and Fairy Dust, marketed by Parlux Fragrances LLC, where Paris Hilton fragrances tallied more than $80 million in annual sales, from which she collected royalties.

But who can remember the size and shape or price—indeed the very *existence*—of Paris Hilton handbags? Outside of the United States, fashionistas in more than forty other countries can. In 2014 there were about sixty "Paris Hilton Handbag & Accessories" stores worldwide, mainly in the Middle East (Jordan, Dubai, Abu Dhabi, Saudi Arabia), Asia (Malaysia, the Philippines, India, Indonesia), and South America (Brazil, Colombia, Peru, Venezuela). The bags sold in the Middle East on Paris Hilton's website looked pretty cheesy, as they mimicked the all-over logo patterns of Louis Vuitton (the brown LVs) and Gucci's GG stamped look. The Paris Hilton versions of quilted mobile phone cases resembled the pattern on Dior bags.

It was hard to imagine Paris carrying her own bags in Beverly Hills or New York. Yet the ubiquity of her shops and breathless copy on the Paris Hilton Stores website from the Middle East distributor showed just how enthralled—and seduced—the locals must have been with the myth of Paris Hilton:

> Paris Hilton—the brand and the persona needs no introduction. It is a brand associated with style, elegance, and a distinctive embellishment for the stylistically conscious. The charisma of Paris Hilton reflects in her collection of fashion accessories that are a hybrid of elegance, refinement, chic and timeless style. The legacy of Paris Hilton brand transcends age, purpose, geographies and invades your senses to sweep you off your feet.

Despite the multimillions Paris pocketed mostly internationally—including as a club DJ—she would never manage to move the fashion needle, nor even register a blip in American fashion circles. Her often vulgar shtick of erratic behavior was no longer shocking—it became stale and predictable after a few years. Overexposed in every conceivable way, there wasn't much new that Paris Hilton could do.

"Paris didn't evolve; she didn't have a baby or get married or give people another reason to keep interested in her," said Jo Piazza, author of *Celebrity, Inc.*, who noted in 2013 that Paris's latest antics no longer caused a ripple in the tabloids.

Yet Paris would always be singled out as the party-girl haute fashionista who made young women covet luxe labels. Inside her LA home, her very own mirrored closets were stuffed to the gills with millions of dollars' worth of such couture paraphernalia—all on full display in the 2013 movie *The Bling Ring*, a satirical black comedy of real-life events, the true story of a Hollywood Hills ring of celebrity-obsessed teens who coveted the luxury fashion labels worn by their idols.

In this truth-is-stranger-than-fiction tale, a gang of Valley high schoolers targeted the homes of Paris Hilton, Audrina Patridge, Megan Fox, Lindsay Lohan, and Orlando Bloom and Miranda Kerr, from which they filched more than $3.5 million of designer clothes, jewelry, and cash in 2008 and 2009. Dressed in their stolen designer loot, the kids nightclub-hopped and posted pictures of themselves on Facebook.

They chose Paris Hilton as their first victim—smartly typecasting her as the celebrity most careless about her home security. And they were right. They showed up at her home and guessed that she might have a spare key stashed under the doormat for those nights when she staggered home in confusion. *Bingo!* No burglar alarm went off after they walked through the door. They strode right in and helped themselves to jewelry, cash, and handbags, only to return five more times with friends to ransack her closets, cherry-picking their favorite outfits and accessories. Once they even stayed a while, drank her liquor, and partied in the "nightclub" room in her home.

The real Paris Hilton not only appeared in a cameo in a nightclub scene in the film, playing herself, but also generously lent her home—the actual place where the burglaries took place—to Sofia Coppola for two weeks so the director could accurately re-create the burglaries for the movie. Paris's opulent digs were a gold mine for any location scout—a shrine to Paris so gaudy that you couldn't make it up; throw pillows emblazoned with images of her face, and dozens of framed cover shots from magazines like *Glamour*, *Us*, and *Playboy*, where she appeared, as well as a trove of sumptuous designer loot and jewelry. Coppola said later, "She is larger than life, and her house is like Paris World."

Hilton told the blog *Vulture* she was shaken when she watched the teen actors claw over her personal belongings. She said: "It's so violating. It just made me really angry and upset, and when I see these kids, I want to, like, slap them."

Nancy Jo Sales, whose 2010 *Vanity Fair* article "The Suspects Wore Louboutins" was the basis for the movie, called the real-life heists the "perfect crime of pop culture" in a social media age. "They were trying to steal their stuff and become them and become their fame," she said on a video packaged with *The Bling Ring* DVD.

On the same video, Leo Braudy, the author of *The Frenzy of Renown: Fame and Its History*, said, "It's intriguing to me how similar the celebrities—that the bling-ring targets—are to the bling ring themselves. They have the same preoccupation with objects. They have the same preoccupation with surface, the same preoccupation with being cool—with being trendy."

And the same goes for millions of ordinary consumers, seduced by the hype of designers and luxury totems, who maxed out their credit cards to buy much of the same stuff at stores or online.

The K. K. K. Clan

It was now my turn to keep up with the Kardashians, live at the one-year anniversary of the Kardashian Kollection of women's fashions at Sears on September 14, 2012.

America's most wanted reality-show sisters—Kim, Khloé, and Kourtney Kardashian—were making a rare appearance at a Sears branch store in Yonkers, New York, to meet their fans and stoke the interest in the hottest fashion turn at Sears in years. It would be another intersection of celebrity worship and fashion—a rock-star atmosphere of screaming mobs of middle-class women.

A year earlier, the Kardashian Kollection enjoyed a splashy rollout at seven hundred of the more than eight hundred Sears stores. The struggling retail chain, whose shabby interiors and spotty customer service had contributed to its decline in recent years, had suddenly spawned this glossy new KK oasis. Each store's shop-in-shop was an island of plush charcoal carpeting and KK wallpaper with individual KK dressing rooms. Think Las Vegas kitsch: Hanging from the ceiling were black cutouts faking chandeliers, beaded curtains, and artificial red flower bouquets, and a red velvet rope in front of an oversize poster of the glamorous trio.

The Kardashian Kollection was an all-out effort by Sears to play catch-up. Sears Holdings Corporation—since 2005 comprised of Sears and Kmart together—had been generating net losses for years. In 2010, Sears's domestic stores reported $22 billion in revenue, with a net loss of $1.4 billion. Sears's private-label apparel brands included Canyon River Blues, Lands' End, and Joe Boxer—hadn't been on the fashion radar in decades. It had missed the boat on trying to woo all those young fashion customers whom Macy's, Target, Kohl's, and Kmart had long been chasing with their own celebrity lures.

In his February 2011 annual letter to shareholders, Sears CEO Eddie Lampert wrote that the apparel business at Sears "has been disappointing for a long time and continues to be underproductive compared to our competitors. . . . We believe that we have better talent in place now, and we expect them to make an impact immediately." He singled out the Kardashian Kollection as one of the two new labels that "must work to improve the productivity and profitability" of the chain's apparel offerings. Terms weren't disclosed for the deal, but it was easy to assume that the high-profile Kardashians commanded multimillions from Sears, which thrust this Hail Mary pass to woo the millennials back to Middle America's once-most-reliable retailer.

The Kardashian sisters were worth their weight in Twitter followers: Kim was ranked among the top ten on Twitter, with more than fifteen million followers. Khloé had seven million, and Kourtney six million. Their combined power in the Twittersphere alone could effectively lead throngs of shoppers to the trough. The troubled Sears might have shuttered 170 full-line stores in 2011, but with more than seven hundred remaining stores, the Kardashians knew Sears was nonetheless still a huge platform for selling fashion, bedding, home accessories, and sundry goods across America and beyond.

Though Sears hadn't kept up with their competitors in exploiting celebrity power, the storied American catalog retailer had been an early adapter. Way back in 1981, Sears boosted its sagging apparel sales by developing a fashion line around Cheryl Tiegs, a popular *Sports Illustrated* swimsuit model. According to Sears's online archives, Tiegs—who at the time was also the $1 million face of CoverGirl cosmetics—became "very involved in the design and styling and fit" of the women's sportswear that was advertised with the tagline "It's got to be Cheryl Tiegs." The Cheryl Tiegs collection developed into a $100 million juggernaut that expanded into clothes for women of all ages, until the line was discontinued in 1989. Sears's fashion authority would erode over the years as the mighty chain failed to keep up with savvier competitors. Back then, Sears was still so massive in electronics, home goods, and other areas that it wasn't so preoccupied with chasing the young fashion marketplace.

The Kardashians were meant to spearhead the long-overdue Sears Komeback.

Starting in the spring of 2011, Sears began promoting the coming of the Kardashian Kollection with a slick advertising campaign shot by *Vanity Fair* photographer Annie Leibovitz, who styled the Kardashians as though they were modeling for Versace or Dolce & Gabbana. The kaptivating trio stood abreast and a-butt: Kourtney in a leopard-print blazer, Khloé in a leopard jumpsuit, and kurvy Kim in a leopard bustier sheath with a retail price of $99—twice the price of similar dresses selling at H&M or Forever 21. Of course, there had to be a "Making of the Sears ad"—behind-the-scenes videos for YouTube, further fanning the Kardashian buzz. If the clothes looked half that good in person, everyone agreed, Sears was destined for a home run.

Growing Up Kardashian

Like the gorgeous Gabor sisters, Magda, Zsa Zsa, and Eva—Hungarian-born beauties who were famous for being famous and sometimes-actresses who were popular TV talk-show guests in the 1960s—the exotic

Kardashians were beautiful and fixated on catching and keeping the men in their lives. No singing or acting talent was required. Their rocket ride to rock-star status was one of the most remarkable of the reality-show era, based on terrific packaging of the life and times of the wealthy members of the blended family of beauties in Los Angeles.

The girls owed their inherited wealth and the exotic cast of their good looks to their late father, a second-generation Armenian named Robert Kardashian, a wealthy businessman and attorney, who famously joined the legal defense team of his longtime buddy O. J. Simpson. The Kardashian kids, including a son, Rob, grew up in affluence, but only Kourtney and Rob graduated from college. Kim ran in the fast lane of Hollywood with kids like Paris, Nicole Richie, and Lindsay Lohan. Kim's teenage boyfriend for several years was T. J. Jackson, son of Tito of the Jackson 5. So although not born celebrities, they were only one degree removed from birth.

Ryan Seacrest, the host of *American Idol*, told *The Wall Street Journal*'s Melissa Marr that he came across the K family, his first subject for a TV show, after meeting the Kardashians socially. After seeing video of the family's antics at a barbeque, he proposed a show following the lives of Kim Kardashian and her family to E!, where he was hosting *E! News* and other red-carpet events. *Keeping Up with the Kardashians* debuted in 2007. Critics initially panned the show as a display of the voluptuous Kim Kardashian and not much more, but the show caught on. The Kardashians were willing to let it all hang out, allowing TV cameras to invade their private lives. No other reality series had ever come close to this level of exhibitionism.

While interest in Paris Hilton had ebbed and flowed over the years, she served as inspiration to every pseudocelebrity hoping to make a footprint in pop culture, starting with the Kardashians. The entire Kardashian clan was "willing to push the boundaries of personal exposure for the sake of bolstering brand Kardashian," wrote Jo Piazza in *Celebrity, Inc.* It was TV keyhole voyeurism at its most explicit, as viewers watched the Kardashians fight, marry, divorce, and Khloé get arrested in handcuffs for drunk driving. The family members worked every angle to collectively earn an estimated $65 million from the show and other endorsements in 2010—and were, in the words of Piazza, a "guilty pleasure who inspired less guilt" than the often obnoxious Paris Hilton. True, Kim and Paris both had sex tapes that helped propel them to the forefront, but Paris came across as a curiosity: idle rich, spoiled, and not someone whom women looked up to. Kim managed to quickly move past the prurience and present herself and her sisters as aspirational role models—hardworking entrepreneurs, family-centered—all while remaining sexy as hell.

Paris Hilton (left) and Kim Kardashian (right), here in 2006, grew up as friends in Los Angeles.

For once, blondes didn't have all the fun—the exotic Kardashians, of Armenian descent, were the hottest raven-haired babes since Cher, forty years before. In fact, a big part of the sisters' appeal was that they were an ethnic Rorschach—they could read Latina, Arabic, Jewish, almost anything a fantasy could require. And they were curvy—not stick-skinny like the runway models most women can't relate to.

Their influence in beauty and pop culture was huge. Suddenly young women were imitating the Kardashian look—dark, smoky eye makeup with false eyelashes, high-heeled shoes, and the tightest bustier dresses in animal prints. At beauty salons the most requested looks became variations of the Kardashian sisters' thick, layered tresses—often achieved with hair extensions. Online retailers sprouted an abundant selection of Kardashian wigs named "Kim" and "Khloé."

In pursuit of Kardashian kurves, women wore padded shapewear—or went to the extreme for butt implants—and plumped lips with collagen. The branding of Kardashians went *K* krazy—Kardashian Khaos, a souvenir "lifestyle" boutique in Las Vegas; Kardashian Kolor nail polish; and Lash Dash luxury lash collection from Kourtney Kim Khloé Khroma Beauty.

Kim's interest in fashion actually preceded her TV fame. She'd had a knack since right after high school, when, with the help of family backing, she opened Dash, a high-end neighborhood boutique in a Cala-basas suburb not far from their home. "Sure, my parents were generous. I got a nice car at sixteen, but at eighteen I was cut off," she told *Complex* in January 2007, when she posed on the cover in a skimpy black bikini. "I've worked really hard. I opened up the store myself." But Dash was very much a family affair, with mom, Kris, helping to keep the books and Kourtney designing clothes for it. Kim extended her fashion reach as a stylist, starting with her Hollywood buddies Richie and Lohan as clients—and Khloé assisted her.

Pop singer Brandy liked Kim's sexy style and asked her to become her stylist. When Kim began dating Brandy's younger brother, Ray J, they made the sex tape that went public in 2007. Kim had no problem flaunt-ing her voluptuous hourglass figure and wide, curvy backside—and her calculated risk paid off: Instead of being written off as a sleaze, Kim managed to make her booty as famous as J.Lo's. (Kim would be a cover girl on *Harper's Bazaar, W, L'Uomo Vogue,* and *New York* magazines.)

And like J.Lo, Kim and her sisters wanted to parlay all that love from the public into cash from the public. It was impossible for Kim to sell her booty directly, so she monetized the next best thing—the clothes, acces-sories, and scents that adorned that booty.

Dashing into Fame

In pushing Dash on their weekly reality show, the sisters became more credible in fashion as they were shown designing and strategizing at the store. During a video interview in 2012 with *The Wall Street Journal*'s Lee Hawkins, Kim spoke earnestly about their working fashion career: "The show is our platform. The show is our best commercial, we show everything from the creative process to the finished product on our show."

And Dash became a mecca for Kardashian groupies, as dozens of young women lined up outside before the store opened, waiting to get in, especially on weekends. Dash spawned branches in Miami and New York, attracting hordes of women who seemed more interested in gawk-ing than shopping.

I was disappointed when I discovered that there wasn't much to buy at Dash—at least the afternoon that I stopped into the Los Angeles store in August 2012. What began as a trendy LA boutique in the suburbs had turned into a souvenir shop—a tourist trap for the Kardashian brand. In Los Angeles, Dash had moved to the tony Melrose Avenue in West Hollywood, in the same block as a Marc Jacobs boutique—and it felt as flimsy as a movie set. The afternoon I was canvassing Melrose, I walked past a burly security guard and wandered inside Dash. I headed to the back of the store, where the clothes—but no customers—were. There were racks of cheap-looking harem pants and minidresses with labels I didn't recognize. Totally underwhelming.

In the front of the store, there were three or four other shoppers milling around the displays that were a shrine to the Kardashians: $34 Kardashian Kollection logo T-shirts, shelves with stacks of *Kardashian Konfidential*, the bestselling coffee table book penned by the sisters; Kardashian candles and fragrances, including three scents by Kim and two by Khloé and Lamar—Unbreakable and Unbreakable Joy—with their photos on the package (undoubtedly collectors' items by late 2013, when the couple split).

Taking Bebe Shots

Kim was the fashion meal ticket—the middle sister, who *People* had anointed as one of the best-dressed celebrities. After a hot couple of years of the reality show, Kim cofounded ShoeDazzle in 2009, an innovative online retail club that quickly attracted more than three hundred thousand members, whose $39.95 monthly fee gave them access to a selection of affordable private-label shoes recommended by Kim, who initially served as the site's "chief stylist." The strength of her name helped ShoeDazzle raise more than $60 million in venture capital. Yet by 2013, Kim's role as chief stylist was taken over by Rachel Zoe—a fashion reality-show star in her own right with *The Rachel Zoe Project*, which aired from 2009 to 2013. Kim tweeted that she was sticking around as ShoeDazzle's cofounder and was "thrilled" to be working with Zoe.

The very same year, the Kardashians created a capsule fashion collection of a dozen or so pieces for Bebe—a midpriced mall chain of club wear—Lycra leggings, leather minidresses, and sequins. "Of course, with Kim, Khloé, and Kourtney behind this collection, you know there's only one unifying factor to be counted upon: this collection is going to be blazing HOT . . ." said Bebe's press release.

With Kim Kardashian in tow, the Bebe collection hit the runways of New York Fashion Week in 2010, showcasing a parade of the usual tight and spangled party wear, some of which was the Kardashians'. Kim sat conspicuously in the front row wearing a gray hooded minidress with a black leather bustier. During the applause at the end of the show, Kim stood up on the front-row seats, turning from side to side and waving her black leather–gloved hands like Queen Elizabeth.

How well did the Kardashian togs sell at Bebe? The retailer didn't disclose and didn't return calls seeking comment. Bebe's president, Emilia Fabricant, sounded skeptical after only one year of the Kardashian

Kim Kardashian in February 2010 taking a bow at the Bebe runway show, which included styles designed by the Kardashian sisters.

collaboration. She told *WWD*: "The sisters do still have relevance. But at Bebe, we need to move with fashion and we want to be first in the fashion world with everybody else and not fall behind. We are definitely assessing the situation." Translation: Weeks later, the Kardashian deal was kaput.

K Is for Knockoff

But a year or so later, in the early months of the Sears deal, which was said to be going swimmingly, a drama worthy of a reality-show moment popped up backstage as the Kardashians were accused of copyright infringement. In August 2011, under the headline "K is for Knockoff," handbag designer Monica Botkier posted this item on her blog at Botkier .com: "We just discovered how our Botkier 'Clyde' 2004 was simply copied by Kardashian Kollection for Sears. They say imitation is the highest form of flattery but we don't think so."

The bag in question was a black pleather bag trimmed in faux leopard with slanted pockets and drawstring sides—an original silhouette that Botkier claimed it had gone to the trouble to register as its trademark design earlier. Botkier told *WWD* that she sent Sears a cease and desist order and said she would seek help from the Council of Fashion Designers of America's "You Can't Fake Fashion" campaign against counterfeiters. According to *WWD*, the Kardashian look-alike bag disappeared from Sears.com.

In the Kardashians We Trust

The Kardashian fans who came to that celebration in Yonkers on September 17, 2012, weren't thinking about copyright infringement when they showed up to meet their favorite reality stars at Sears. The night before, many had slept in their cars in a nearby parking lot, to make sure they'd be among the first two hundred in line to be allowed inside Sears to meet the K sisters.

I walked in and headed straight over to the busy Kardashian section with around a dozen shoppers going through the racks, where everything in the collection was 40 percent off that day. I thought the variations of the bustier dresses—made of cotton-Lycra—looked pretty good, though they seemed pricey at $79 to $99, even with the discount. I had to laugh at the Kardashians' rendition of $58 premium denim jeans with three distinct "fits": The Kourtney (boot cut), the Kim (the tightest and skinniest, of course), and the Khloé (with bigger back pockets). The $69 pleather handbags, with too many rivets, looked cheap, and the costume jewelry—earrings and bangles priced under $30—looked thin and downright brassy, not as cool as the styles you could buy at a street fair. But if I had to grade on a kurve—the fact that Sears offered so little that was appetizing—well, then the Kardashians were C–.

As the fidgety fans (mostly female, between fifteen and thirty) camped out on the floor, waiting for the Kardashians to arrive, I wanted to know if they were buying the fashions or the Kardashians, so I informally surveyed the crowd, speaking to about a dozen women. They were hardly naïve. Everyone I spoke to believed that design teams probably created the Kardashian merchandise—while Kim and her sisters supervised what they did. There were enough leopard prints and bustier dresses that looked like the clothes the Kardashians would wear, so they seemed satisfied. One twentysomething shopper insisted: "The Kardashians wouldn't put their name on something if they didn't believe in it."

Then I ventured: "Why are you willing to pay $79 or $99 for a Kardashian body-con dress, when right in the same strip mall at H&M and Forever 21, there are similar dresses a third that price? Are you just paying for the Kardashian name?"

And that's when they showed they were loyal fans who were making an emotional purchase that had little to do with intrinsic value. One woman said: "I think they probably use better materials. It's worth it; it's not a rip-off."

Here Come the Kardashians

Roped off by security people and Yonkers policemen, the fans shrieked nonstop, starting around four fifteen, at the first sight of a Kardashian bounding down the escalator toward the stage. "Khloé, I love you!" "Kim!" "Kourtney!"

Kim, in a long-sleeved black top and tight straight skirt, with her hair in a high ponytail, strained to speak into the microphone over the deafening shouts. "We can't wait to meet all of you," she said. They then pulled up chairs at a table and proceeded to autograph stacks of their own publicity photos while starstruck fans were swiftly herded past the table where they sat.

Kardashian Kollection a Year Later

What a difference a year makes. I returned to Sears adjacent to Cross County Mall in Yonkers, and what I saw was jaw-dropping. I couldn't believe that it was even the same store.

It was only a couple of weeks into September, and the new fall merchandise in the Kardashian Kollection looked virtually untouched. On practically every rack there were signs that said 50% OFF. There was even a rack that said NEW ARRIVALS with the 50% OFF sign. Toward the back of the department there was a red sign with the words KLEARANCE $9.99 over a large round rack stuffed with clothes. I rifled through the racks and pulled out a leopard V-neck dress with skinny straps that was mini in the front and dipped down to floor length in the back. The print looked rubber-stamped on, and the fabric was full of static and thinner than a negligee; it had the quality of a cheap Halloween costume. The original price of this—under a sticker—appeared to be $32.99. I looked around the rest of the department and saw a $72.99 black spencer-style jacket with leopard trim in that same ugly fabric. I tried it on in my size and it hung pitifully. Even if it *had been* for a Halloween costume, I would have rejected it as too tacky. Even the $19.99 pleather leggings were so shapeless, they just sagged on the hanger.

I walked across the aisle to where the Lands' End merchandise was displayed—only a couple of racks were marked 30% OFF. Everything else in the area retained the original price. I struck up a conversation with a saleswoman who remembered the Kardashian styles I had seen a year earlier. There appeared to be more merchandise, including tights and more tops and bottoms, but the overall quality had clearly gone downhill—with paper-thin fabrics, washed-out colors, shapeless silhouettes. Why did the Kardashian styles look so cheap and flimsy compared to what I had seen in the same department a year ago?

The saleswoman explained that the Kardashian Kollection was a brand that typically arrived on the sales floor marked down 50 percent—except for the jeans. "It's always on sale," she said. When I commented that the "sale" price reflected the true value of the shoddy collection, even the saleswoman couldn't disagree.

"Who buy these?" I asked. She shook her head and sighed. "Yeah, it's just there."

It wasn't just the Yonkers store either. I was astounded a week later on September 23, 2013, when I ran across a UK *Daily Mail* article online pointing out the same hideous merchandise I had seen at Sears—at a branch store in Los Angeles. The headline read: "Has the Kardashian's bubble burst? Sisters' fashion Kollection slashed to as low as $9.99 at Sears—but no shoppers care." The article included photos with the same 50% OFF signs I had seen on new arrivals in the Kardashian section in Yonkers. It was more than just an eerie coincidence.

As customary, Sears declined to comment on the performance of any of the brands the store carries. But the *Daily Mail* also quoted a Sears spokesman as saying the Kardashian Kollection was the top-selling women's apparel brand on Sears.com.

Chris Raih, managing director of Los Angeles creative agency Zambezi, told *Adweek* that whether the Kardashians generated hundreds of millions in sales or far less, what really mattered was that Sears was the beneficiary of look-at-Sears publicity—which was important for a middling retailer struggling to establish a cool identity. "Whatever your personal feelings about the Kardashians, they play broadly," Raih said. "They have a celebrity that's self-propelling and an army of social media fans. So if you're Sears, you can count on—at minimum—awareness."

In any event, Kim Kardashian kept getting her name, face, and booty in front of millions through her relationship with fiancé rapper Kanye West and the baby daughter they had together. Now with North West, born June 15, 2013, joining Kourtney's two toddlers, it was only a matter of time before Kardashian Kids would appear. On January 24, 2014, the Kardashians confirmed to E! that they were cooking up a new line for children for Babies "R" Us. Their fashionista followers chimed in on Twitter with comments underlining how consumers will always react to whatever their favorite celebrities dish out, which is a mixture of slavish obedience and wannabe fervor.

"Yay!! My daughter is already a diva can NOT wait to have her in these clothes!!! Yay yay yayyyyyyy!" tweeted crystalann3.

Added kayladawn23, "I wish you all had casting calls for babies to model the clothing! My baby would be perfecttttt!"

Chapter Thirteen

. . . .

PARIS WHEN IT FIZZLES

Lindsay Lohan and "Tragiqueistan"

By the mid-2000s, with reality-show personalities elbowing their way onto the front row in New York's Fashion Week, big-time American celebrities from stage and screen began to flock to Paris for their fashion-show fix, to see and be seen on the front row at Givenchy, Chanel, Louis Vuitton, and Balenciaga without any desperate Housewives mucking up the photo ops.

Four times a year, Serious Fashion People converged in Paris in droves for the women's ready-to-wear collections and the haute couture shows—still relatively untainted by D-listers. The avant-garde designs and unbridled creativity that were the signature of many French labels still created fashion's loudest, heard-round-the-world buzz.

Mounir Moufarrige, the chief executive officer of the rapidly fading house of Emanuel Ungaro, badly needed some buzz. Moved by what had now become an immutable law—it took celebrities to create splash in fashion, the edgier the better—Moufarrige set his sights on the edgiest celeb he could think of, the controversial actress Lindsay Lohan, shamelessly naming her to be "artistic advisor" of the fashion house in 2009.

At twenty-three, Lohan was a tabloid personality of the Paris Hilton school—strawberry blonde, freckle-faced, and not as good-looking, but she could act. Her infamy for boozing and drugging didn't seem to hurt her across the Atlantic, as it smeared her stateside. Europeans saw her as just another wild-child American who had the ability to connect with young fashionistas. "I like the way [Lohan] dresses. . . . She changes her outfits five times a day," Moufarrige told *WWD*.

Lohan's contribution to Ungaro would largely be window dressing. The star of *Mean Girls* and *Freaky Friday* would get her picture taken in the clothes and impart some youthful sizzle to the brand as she "worked" alongside Ungaro's chief designer, Estrella Archs, an unknown Spanish designer who was the sixth person to occupy the hot seat after founder Emanuel Ungaro retired in 2005.

Moufarrige was up-front about his calculations. "Designer-led fashion is likely not to be enough. It's a slow process going the traditional route," he told *WWD*. With Lohan, he said, "Odds are it could work. [All the attention] we're going to get is going to be a plus. I think the noise level around Lindsay will be very, very big." He called his new strategy with Lohan "electric shock treatment."

Indeed, the beleaguered Ungaro fashion brand—available in only seventy-five stores around the world by 2009—had been on the decline for years, ever since 1996, when the then sixty-two-year-old couturier had begun winding down his thirty-one-year solo career. That year, the famous Italian footwear maker Salvatore Ferragamo SpA paid about $40 million for controlling interest in Ungaro. The game plan was to put the French fashion house on an aggressive marketing track, reviving it with handbags, accessories, and a youthful image, while taking full advantage of the skills of Emanuel Ungaro, the last great couturier of the 1960s—a contemporary of Yves Saint Laurent and Hubert de Givenchy—who was still vibrant and working. "It is an easy idea," Ferruccio Ferragamo, the executive overseeing Ungaro, told me back then.

Yet even from the start, I knew that reviving Ungaro was going to be a long shot—especially since Ferragamo wasn't a dynamic marketer itself. Ferragamo—whose founder, Salvatore Ferragamo, invented stiletto pumps in the 1950s—had itself missed riding the crest of fashion's upscale "shoe moment," upstaged by both Manolo Blahnik and Christian Louboutin, who were credited with redefining high heels.

Over the course of 1997 and 1998, I shuttled five times to Paris to spend time with Mr. Ungaro as he attempted his business's first makeover. We talked at his atelier at 1 Avenue Montaigne, where I watched the early stages of Ungaro's transition—as the couturier struggled to catch the wave of status handbags. An incredulous Ungaro admitted to me that he didn't consider handbags as a stand-alone trinket to stamp out by the thousands; he created a particular handbag to accessorize an ensemble.

That naïve revelation alone underscored to me that the makeover of Ungaro as a fashion business that caught and capitalized the latest trends was not such an "easy idea."

Ungaro was the archetype of the tortured artist, uniformed in his white lab coat, who sketched, draped, and painstakingly pinned—in perfectly spaced, perpendicular rows—muslin toile fabric in twelve-hour stretches of solitary confinement in his atelier, while the chamber music of Beethoven and Wagner played in the background. He said the creative process was exhilarating but "full of suffering." He was as old-school as it gets, having apprenticed for six years under Cristóbal Balenciaga, who everybody in fashion agreed was the most celebrated couturier of the twentieth century. Ungaro had one foot in the ivory tower of elite haute couture—made-to-measure handmade clothes for the world's richest socialites—with his other foot firmly planted in the commerce that paid the bills: the merchandise Ungaro marketed through licensing contracts with manufacturers. Nearly all of Ungaro's $280 million in annual revenue came from twenty-five licensees in America and Japan that he had nothing to do with.

Most American women were familiar with the Ungaro brand only because of Emanuel by Emanuel Ungaro, a successful, midpriced line of women's apparel designed by GFT, an Italian licensee for American department stores that generated about $170 million in annual wholesale revenue at its peak in the mid-1990s. Meanwhile, what Ungaro created inside the labor-intensive workrooms of his atelier, where well-paid seamstresses turned out handmade garments one by one, amounted to selling a paltry three hundred couture outfits a year, at a loss of $3 million.

But the GFT-driven Emanuel gravy train eventually dried up, and the house of Ungaro was left sputtering in the first years of the new millennium. The frustrated Ferragamo family owners gave up on Ungaro, finally finding a buyer in 2005, and the septuagenarian Emanuel Ungaro retired.

A Marriage Made Somewhere South of Heaven

The new owner of Ungaro was Asim Abdullah, a wealthy forty-something Pakistani computer engineer who made his fortune in technology. Abdullah was on a business trip in Paris when he fell under the spell of the luxury goods boom that turned Vuitton, Prada, and Gucci into multibillion-dollar empires—and the glossiest brands in business. Abdullah was drawn to the fashion flame and wanted to be involved in reviving a couture legend. He was prepared to invest many millions, to hire the best management, and he had the patience that it took for a turnaround.

He chose Moufarrige, a seasoned fashion CEO, who was best known for hiring the inexperienced Stella McCartney at twenty-five, appointing the Beatles legend's daughter as the designer at Chloé in 1997 to replace the famously busy Karl Lagerfeld, who also designed Chanel and Fendi.

Stella was a graduate of London's prestigious fashion school Central Saint Martins, but Lagerfeld wasn't impressed. He told *WWD* back then, "I think [Chloé] should have taken a big name. They did, but in music, not fashion. Let's hope she's as gifted as her father."

It turned out that Stella was indeed a good hire. She had genuine fashion chops—and performed even better after she was paired with a talented codesigner, Phoebe Philo, and managed skillfully by Chloé's CEO, Ralph Toledano. And by being the daughter of the famed Sir Paul

McCartney, Stella came with built-in celebrity cachet, ensuring she would get noticed in a way that other designers didn't—especially when her dad sat in the front row at Chloé shows, applauding his daughter and drawing huge media attention.

Now Moufarrige hoped for another celebrity-fashion marriage made in heaven between Ungaro and Lohan. He brimmed with confidence when he spoke to *WWD* shortly after Labor Day in 2009, intent on impressing the fashion industry readers who closely followed the influential trade newspaper. He called Lohan "the ultimate fashion girl" who would lend a "'consumer' voice to the mix that is vital today." Lohan had been on the September cover of British *Elle* and on Spanish *Vogue*'s August cover.

What's more, Lohan was already on the fashion track. In 2008 she began her collaboration with Kristi Kaylor, a Beverly Hills entrepreneur specializing in celebrity marketing. They founded 6126, a leggings-based line—named for the June 1, 1926, birth date of Marilyn Monroe, Lohan's favorite movie idol. At 6126, Lohan was involved in choosing fabrics and colors and approving the designs—and modeling in the look books.

Lohan told *WWD* in the same article that she wanted to take Ungaro to a "younger place" with edgier fashion: "When I'm involved in a project I give my all to it. I feel like there's a correlation between everything I do, whether it's pop music or film. I've always played a big part in what I wear, the costumes. Clothing is something that's so expressive in so many ways. It really interests me. To be in a position where I'm working with a fashion house in Paris sets it apart from every other celebrity brand."

As expected, the news about Lohan's fashion gig in Paris shocked the hell out of everybody. Fashion industry people collectively shook their heads in skepticism that the unstable actress could pull it off. Lohan was the quintessential tabloid party girl, whose most remarkable fashion accessory in 2007 was an alcohol-detection ankle bracelet mandated by a court after she was booked for driving under the influence and possession of cocaine, according to *People*. She had also been in and out of drug rehab.

Moufarrige shrugged off her reputation, claiming "the fashion industry thrives on controversy anyway." Stretching to make his point, he made a weak attempt to throw Emanuel Ungaro under the bus, reminding people of the couturier's younger years in the 1960s: "Emanuel Ungaro himself was very controversial. He always felt women had to dress to seduce. His first perfume he called Diva."

Meanwhile, Archs, Ungaro's chief designer, who was forced to play second fiddle to Lohan at Ungaro's October 2009 fashion show, was candid about the potential conflict she might have by collaborating with the actress: "Have you ever met two women who agree completely about fashion?" she asked *WWD* a month before their show.

So Bad It's Terrible

The day before the highly anticipated Ungaro show, fashion reporter Eric Wilson stopped by Ungaro's studio to check out Lohan in action. He wrote in *The New York Times*:

> She picked up a black and white scarf and tied it around her head, then replaced it with a black one, and then clumsily stuck a red sequin-covered heart to the side of her head while a team of designers watched her.
>
> "This is just so cool," Ms. Lohan said, turning her attention to a white minidress splattered with sequins. "It needs more rhinestones, just so it pops." Off to the seamstress it went. Pointing to another white dress, she said: "I call it Michelle Pfeiffer in *Scarface*. I was just in my office sketching for next season. I was here until, like, one o'clock last night."

Expectations for Lohan's fashion-show debut at Ungaro to be a study in Schadenfreude ran high. And as it turned out—from the photos and eyewitnesses—it went beyond the realm of "so bad it's good into the realm of "I-can't-believe-what-I'm-seeing" horror, an unfortunate place one of my colleagues referred to as "Tragiqueistan."

The Ungaro collection was a parade of cheesy sequins and hearts galore, including models wearing heart-shaped pasties over their bare breasts and heart appliqués stuck to their foreheads. *WWD* called it "embarrassing," while fashion editor Fabien Baron told the *Times*'s Wilson, "Call the fashion police."

Designer Estrella Archs (left) and Lindsay Lohan (right) taking their runway bow at the Ungaro show in Paris in October 2009.

As for the venerable Emanuel Ungaro, now seventy-six, he felt the blasphemy of his namesake label brand, calling the collection "a disaster." According to *Agence France-Presse*, Ungaro expounded further on the show in front of an audience at the Estoril Film Festival in Lisbon, Portugal. He said: "I'm furious but there isn't a thing I can do. I have absolutely no link with that house."

Lindsay Lohan's brief lamented tenure at the house of Ungaro ended abruptly. Moufarrige resigned a few months later. The Ungaro meltdown was the joke of 2009 Paris Fashion Week as fashion insiders clucked about how celebrity designers had no place in high fashion—and never in Paris, of all places. Lohan's was the worst performance on a Paris runway that anyone could remember.

That was true—at least until rapper Kanye West came to town a couple of years later.

Chapter Fourteen

. . . .

WHEN KANYE COULDN'T
Kanye West and the Failure of Attitude

This is basically my third presentation to the world. . . . I basically had to learn clothes through Style.com, through [fashion bloggers] Scott the Sartorialist, through Tommy Ton, and luckily I was rich enough to make mistakes and learn . . . and that's what I'm in the process of doing. So I just want everyone to be patient with me.

—Kanye West, January 2014

Late one afternoon in July 2011, Kanye West was riding through SoHo New York, fretting about his big performance in Paris, slated for early October. Before getting out of the car, he made a quick phone call to make sure it was okay to drop by. Then he headed inside a building on Broadway near Prince Street to pay an impromptu visit to Ralph Rucci, the venerable New York couturier to wealthy fashion connoisseurs. It would be a meeting that no one would ever hear about.

At thirty-two, Kanye West was preparing for his first official fashion moment. He'd already become rich and famous, acclaimed as a highly creative and gifted record producer, writer, and rap artist with a cache of more than one hundred music awards, including fourteen Grammys at that point. Kanye was best known as the master of the art form known as sampling, which emanated from the dark ages of vinyl, when nightclub DJs scratched records on multiple turntables to layer, distort, and reconfigure pop sounds.

Sampling evolved into its own sophisticated, computer-driven discipline fueled by innovators like Kanye. He jumped way out front, grafting his original raps over his cut-and-paste samples, brilliantly showcasing his music scholarship, as well as the connections and deep pockets it took to pay royalties to all those original artists he sampled. His albums highlighted the stable of all-star performers he collaborated with, including Jay Z, Pharrell, Lil Wayne, and Estelle. "Kanye musically can't be touched, he's one of the few geniuses we have in hip-hop," said Kazeem Famuyide, senior editor at *Hip-Hop Wired*, in a 2012 Bio.com video.

"By manipulating tempo, chopping and stretching, samples are putty in his hands," wrote Lucy Jones in a 2013 blog post on NME.com.

But fame and riches and acclaim in the music world weren't enough for Kanye, a lifelong clotheshorse and sneakerhead. Relying on his pluck, connections, and deep pockets—as well as fashion sampling—he was about to introduce himself to the world as a fashion designer on the biggest stage of the world of style: Paris Fashion Week.

Kanye West is not your stereotypical rapper—he's no angry brother from the hood composing rhymes on a street corner. Born in 1977 in Atlanta and raised in Chicago, he was solidly middle-class, the only child of loving parents who exposed him to international travel and sent him to art school. He was three when his parents divorced. During the school year, he lived with his mother, a college English professor. He spent the summers with his father, an award-winning news photographer and church counselor.

What he lacked in inner-city street cred, he made up for with an outrageous, cocky, and loudmouthed persona, impulsively spewing on camera whatever popped into his mind—such as "George Bush doesn't care about black people," a sentiment he blurted out during a live TV fund-raiser after Hurricane Katrina in 2005. This spotlight-grabbing behavior could backfire, as when Kanye embarrassed himself by storming the stage at the 2009 MTV Video Music Awards, grabbing the microphone from winner Taylor Swift as she was making her acceptance speech and declaring that Beyoncé should have won the category instead. Even President Obama didn't mince words about his antic, telling a CNBC interviewer after the incident, "She's getting her award. What's he doing up there? He's a jackass."

But if anything, the bad-boy infamy only burnished his celebrity. And it certainly did nothing to diminish his ego, which, as October rolled around and the fashion world converged on Paris, was propelling him to put himself out there as a designer for all the world to see.

Sample This!

Kanye—a fast study and multitasker who got by on as little as two to three hours' sleep a night—had worked hard at becoming a fashion insider. He was a front-row runway fixture at dozens of shows in New York and Paris. I sat next to him once under the Bryant Park tents at Zac Posen's runway show. The wide-eyed rapper was quietly charming, appearing awed by the whole gestalt. No texting or idle chatter from him— he stared at the runway with rapt attention, soaking it all in.

As a hot celebrity, he got big points from fashion insiders for turning the tables and becoming a student to designers like Karl Lagerfeld, Phoebe Philo at Céline, Ricardo Tisci at Givenchy, Azzedine Alaia, and Giuseppe Zanotti—and the result was a win-win, each side basking in the reflected glory of the other. In New York, Kanye got to talking with Gap designer Patrick Robinson at a dinner at Anna Wintour's house in 2008, and soon Kanye was welcomed inside Robinson's professional lair at Gap's design studios. Robinson told me that he put the earnest and hardworking Kanye together with a group of design assistants. They labored on ideas for a possible merchandise collaboration, but it fizzled when cost-conscious Gap executives shut down the experiment after a few months, Robinson said. Still, the experience kept Kanye's fashion juices flowing.

In 2009, Robinson handicapped Kanye's chances of making it for *The Cut*, a *New York* magazine blog: "I tell him, if he wants people to take him seriously in fashion, they have to see blood first! They have to see the blood and the sweat, to see that he really wants it—but he definitely has the capability." But Robinson, who had designed Giorgio Armani's women's collections at the tender age of twenty-three and then spent twenty fitful years bouncing from one high-profile job to another, said he didn't want Kanye to underestimate the difficulties he faced: "I keep telling him he should stick to music."

That was one piece of advice Kanye would ignore. He was starting to see fashion as a way for him to monetize his fame beyond the limitations of pop music. "The *Titanic* has already hit the iceberg in the music business because of the Internet," he reflected in a HOT 97 radio interview in 2013. "That means us as musicians have got to position ourselves as celebrities to still be able to make the same amount of money that we were making off of just focusing on the records."

But Kanye wasn't in the position to do that by accident. He'd been knocking at fashion's door for years before he had Anna Wintour on speed dial. Way back in 2004, he set himself up as the fashion-press darling of *Complex*, a fast-and-happening multicultural urban-style magazine founded by graffiti artist and street-wear designer Marc Eckō. *Complex* put Kanye on the cover five times, commissioned him to do a few style columns, and made him guest editor for the first time for the August/ September 2007 issue (a stint in which he drove staffers crazy with his obsessive last-minute changes, I heard at the time from the publicist).

The gigs did a lot to position Kanye as a fashion influencer, imparting his wisdom on sneakers even as he leveraged his obsession with urban footwear for his first venture into the world of design. In 2009, Kanye scored a publicity bonanza by collaborating with Louis Vuitton on $800 men's sneakers called Don, after the nickname "Louis Vuitton Don," which Kanye gave himself on his 2004 debut album *The College Dropout*.

Kanye worked with Vuitton's shoe designers to create distinctive-looking space-age sneakers, with a sci-fi winged flap up the back that came in all white or red or blue. Sneakerhead collectors coveted them, but big sales were hardly the point. The very existence of a "Kanye sneaker" delivered an urban-cool vibe worth marketing millions to the LV trademark.

In Paris in January 2009 at Vuitton's menswear runway show, Kanye sat on the front-row bleacher next to Vuitton executives as male models wearing Dons passed by. Afterward, the beaming rapper told the Associated Press on camera: "This is the biggest moment in my life because I was designing stuff from like fourth grade and in art school. . . . That's the best thing about the position that I'm in . . . that I can do something with Louis Vuitton and create something from scratch. It's just overwhelming."

Air Kanye

Kanye would get another chance to delight sneakerheads in a collaboration with mighty Nike Inc., also in 2009. But Kanye's association with Nike was nowhere in the neighborhood of Michael Jordan's multimillion-dollar Air Jordan franchise. Nike was looking to expand its cool beyond pro athletes, and Kanye presented a golden opportunity to generate a viral blast of hip-hop cred. For Kanye, Nike gave him commercial design credentials, as he could proudly claim responsibility for "creating" a hot-selling shoe.

Of course, Nike's Air Yeezy sneakers (Yeezy was Kanye's nickname) were "hot-selling" only in a sense—there were only three thousand pairs available, selling at $275 a pair. Such intentional scarcity ignited the hype—and the resale market, as Air Yeezys popped up on eBay, soaring to ten times the list price, to $2,750—not to mention a "pre-owned" pair that went for an astonishing $90,000, fueling rumors that Kanye financed the purchase himself. Air Yeezys worked well enough that Nike didn't pass on the chance for an encore, Air Yeezy 2, which came out in 2012.

But by 2013, Nike was done with Kanye and didn't introduce the third Yeezy shoe that was originally planned. In November 2013, Kanye announced that he now had a sneaker contract with Adidas, with terms undisclosed.

Beyond the Hoodie

A couple of marketing moments in the celebrity-driven sneaker world were flimsy credentials next to designers who created women's fashion collections and red-carpet gowns. But Kanye nevertheless had pulled off his hat trick, anointing himself as a designer as well as a leading fashion arbiter.

The prestigious Accessories Council trade group even saw fit to award Kanye as stylemaker of the year for 2010. Everywhere he went, paparazzi obliged by photographing Kanye for all to see; his casual style was tailored and edgy—minus the typical hip-hop props: the logos, the baseball caps, and the bling. Kanye had graduated from his youthful Ivy League neatness into a vision of Euro swagger in straight-leg ripped jeans, tricked-out leather jackets, V-neck cashmere sweaters, thick scarves around his neck, wraparound shades, an LV satchel in tow—and always sporting the latest in fly sneakers. Alongside dapper athletes like Amar'e Stoudemire and Victor Cruz, "Kanye West is the biggest fashion role model out there," Jim Moore, the longtime creative director at *GQ*, told me in 2012.

Rap entrepreneur Sean Combs's Sean John label may have paved the way for Kanye's fashion crossover, but Kanye wasn't thinking of hooded snorkel jackets in the young men's department at Macy's. He set his sights far higher. He was going for the gold: high-fashion women's wear he would unveil in Paris. I remember thinking at the time that Kanye wasn't just rolling the dice, he was delusional.

For all his flitting through the designer salons in Paris, London, and Milan, Kanye was utterly naïve when it came to the ways of the Continentals. Europeans were largely old-school classic when it came to fashion—and had no interest in wearing clothes "designed" by a celebrity. It was true that Armani, Versace, and Chanel spent millions flying stars over to Europe for their runway shows and to fashion galas they sponsored all over the world—they relied on star power to impart edge and cool to their branding. But Europeans, rich and middle-class alike, were far more sophisticated when it came to what they wore—and that didn't include fashions or fragrances marketed by celebrities. That was an American phenomenon.

No one could have ever talked Kanye out of the notion that the Parisians would love him. Perhaps he was staking his luck on the tradition of Parisian acceptance for black American artists and writers like Josephine Baker, Richard Wright, and James Baldwin, who fled America starting in the 1920s to enthusiastic welcome in France. When I heard of Kanye's plans for a runway show in Paris, all I could think of was Kanye and Jay Z inside a suite at the five-star Hôtel Le Meurice on the Rue de Rivoli, recording their 2011 hit "Niggas in Paris."

Yet the fact was, the French would always resent a wealthy American celebrity, black or white, powerful enough to underwrite his own show and attract all the top fashion editors to pay homage to a collection that everybody knew was going to be cobbled together by ghost designers and highly paid stylists. It had been only a couple of years since Ungaro's Lindsay Lohan disaster had succeeded only in further eroding one of the most venerable couture names in Paris.

Maybe catching a whiff of Lohan's lingering stench in the dog days of July, inching closer to the October 1 date of his runway debut, the famous rapper began to panic—knowing damn well that even his best might not be good enough for the City of Light. Which is why he paid a call to Ralph Rucci.

Romancing Rucci

Of course, Rucci was intrigued when his office manager told him that Kanye West had called from his limo, hoping that he was in the office. Celebrities have that effect on people, who will always want to meet them.

Chado Ralph Rucci is located at 536 Broadway, inside a narrow office building, on the fourth floor. When the Philadelphia-born Rucci launched his fashion business in New York in 1994, the college philosophy major added the name "Chado," which is a centuries-old Japanese tea ceremony, known for its exactitude, integrity, and elegance, reflecting "the same principles I try to bring to my clothing design," he has said.

A lush orchid sits in the reception area leading into an empty beige parlor with mirrored walls—where there are no signs of fashion collections or mannequins. But go farther inside, and you'll see the action of a busy couture atelier, where Rucci's efficient team of highly skilled pattern makers, technicians, and sewers turn out exquisite, mostly hand-made creations, many of which are custom orders. The workrooms are pristine and orderly—very Chado—just as Rucci intended them to be. With estimated annual sales under $20 million, Chado Ralph Rucci has managed to stay profitable without fragrances, jeans, or midpriced clothes.

Given Kanye's penchant for Parisian fashion houses, he was instantly in awe of the erudite, mid-fiftyish Rucci, one of the last modern designers to uphold the refined and restrained couture tradition and beloved by the world's fashion elite. In 2002, Rucci became the first American since Mainbocher more than sixty years before to be invited by French fashion industry regulators to participate in the haute couture shows in Paris, and he showed there for three seasons to huge accolades.

Kanye stopped by that day to get to know Rucci—and to see where that might lead. It was the end of the workday, so Rucci suggested dinner nearby at Mr. Chow in Tribeca. (Kanye contacted his secretary to arrange for the check to be paid in advance, a smooth move that impressed Rucci.)

Kanye bared his soul to Rucci that evening. "He really wants to be a major designer. He told me he has already sunk a couple of million dollars in this workroom in London and he had hired a designer. He had his laptop with him, so he was showing me some of the silhouettes they were doing.

"I didn't want to say anything at first, then I said it was very Phoebe Philo [Céline designer], who is a friend of [Kanye's]. And I said it also looked like [Givenchy's] Riccardo Tisci. He said, 'Riccardo did prints for me.' Then I said, 'What do you want to do? You want to show a collection in Paris in October? It's July!'"

Kanye kept chatting about his design experiences so far, including interning at Fendi. He had been checking in with Wintour from time to time, for advice. He boasted that Azzedine Alaia, one of the most revered and reclusive designers in Paris, had even allowed him to come over to his atelier and watch him at work. Kanye loved having access to all those experts, but he was still perplexed. He had invested millions and he still didn't have a collection ready for Paris.

Kanye talked Rucci into meeting with him the next day, so Kanye could see some of the stunning examples of Rucci's past work. They met in the Bronx, where Rucci stores his archives of hundreds of couture garments in a large storage unit in the same location that the Costume Institute of the Metropolitan Museum of Art uses. "It is beautiful and clean and temperatures are set. Every garment is in a canvas bag, with a photograph attached to it, with the date and everything," Rucci said.

I know how privileged I felt the first time Rucci walked me through his collection so that I could examine his treasured originals up close. His luxurious masterpieces are crafted in the most sumptuous silks, wools, and cashmeres, with intricate seams, perforations, quilting, and embroidery. Like a proud papa, Rucci loves to show off his creative feats, explaining how he experimented with new techniques in order to get his desired result. He practiced fashion at a level of craftsmanship that few designers would ever experience.

Kanye's deference and deep appreciation had won Rucci over so far—until he got carried away on a cloud of chiffon. Rucci recalled: "Kanye was going crazy, salivating. 'Pull that out, pull that out!' he said. I finally said, 'Kanye, what do you need?'"

Kanye piped up: "Will you design the collection for me? Please? We can take techniques from this and this . . ."

Rucci half chuckled and told him, of course not! He had no time to work for others, especially now, with New York Fashion Week around the corner. But Kanye pressed harder. And then Rucci realized he was dead serious about helping himself—to Rucci's archives. "I said, 'No pictures.' He wanted to borrow pieces from the archives. No. Then he wanted to buy garments. I said we don't sell any of them, that's why they're archived. Then, I had to put the brakes on. Anyway, this goes on for the rest of the summer, he keeps calling. My birthday is July thirty-first, and he pops up and says he wanted to take me out. It was so mind-blowing to watch it unfold."

Pesky Kanye called again in August, followed by a desperate plea in late September—a week before his Paris show. But to no avail. He texted

Rucci's right-hand manager: "Please tell Ralph I will pay him to come over to London; I need him to pull everything together."

How confounding. "First I was insulted, then I realized I was dealing with a very unsophisticated, impressionable guy. It was just too sad," Rucci said.

Run-up to Runway

While Kanye's hounding of Rucci stayed below the radar, all throughout 2011 news items regarding Kanye's progress trickled out as fashion people gossiped and speculated just how the inexperienced rap celebrity would launch himself as a women's-wear designer during Paris Fashion Week. Intrepid reporters in London discovered where he had quietly set up his fashion workrooms: inside a building that was formerly a nightclub, where a team of Central Saint Martins fashion students worked under British designer Louise Goldin, with assistance from the fashion department head at the college and a menswear designer from Vuitton. It was starting to sound more like an internship program than a fashion business.

In a report in the London *Guardian*, an unnamed source close to the operation recounted: "Kanye was in fairly often; for all the fittings. [He] was very nice and polite and talked knowledgably [*sic*] about shape etc., but was prone to changing his mind a lot—in fact the whole process was slightly excruciating as there were *so* many opinions that it took forever to get anything done."

It sounded a lot like the obsessive music maker in his studio. Only there, the quest for excellence could be counted on to produce a stream of blockbuster hits.

October 1 in Paris was another packed day on the Fashion Week schedule, with runway shows from headliners like Jean Paul Gaultier right before the Kanye West show at nine thirty P.M. at the Lycée Henri-IV, a historic public high school in the Latin Quarter neighborhood. For the first time in Paris, Kanye would be backstage working—instead of in the front row watching. And speaking of front rows, waiting there for the Kanye show were the celebrity fashion designers of the moment, twin sisters Mary-Kate and Ashley Olsen of The Row, and, like a bad omen, the celebrity designer loser of 2009, Lindsay Lohan. It helped to have top models like Karlie Kloss and Chanel Iman on the runway—and Kanye had created a rocking music sound track, including a sampling of some of his own hits.

But the reminder of his stunning success as a musician played awkwardly against that strange spring collection of ill-fitting, often skimpy nightclub clothes that shouted hooker, with their plunging necklines, dangerous cutouts, mini hemlines, and pants that were either sagging or uncomfortably tight. The biggest disconnect of all in a *spring* lineup: long-haired fur on fingertip vests and fur-trimmed stiletto sandals. A lot of cooks had a hand in simmering this unseemly fashion soup, and it was, by all accounts, a hot mess.

At the end of the show, a sweaty and visibly nervous Kanye, in white T-shirt and jeans, gestured barely a bow, to tepid applause. The press scrambled to get reactions to the show, first from Wintour, who deadpanned: "Ask someone else."

Robin Givhan wrote on TheDailyBeast.com: "As often happens, this was not an auspicious debut. The collection lacked focus. The silhouettes were unflattering. And the whole project looked to be that of a beginner overreaching. In short, it was dreadful."

When real designers misfire on the runway—and it happens in every career—they suck it up and move on to the next season. But not the prickly Kanye, who couldn't stand the idea that he, as a rookie, was unfairly being ridiculed for his very first show. His ego shattered, he lashed out defensively, cursing and blaming the press "for not supporting me." As Paris Fashion Week carried on, folks quickly forgot about Kanye's sorry little show, but he still couldn't let it go as he rolled around town the rest of the week bitching loudly about all the bad reviews and making ridiculous excuses, claiming that the runway clothes weren't ill-fitting— they were *designed* to hang that way.

In this universe, Kanye's signature bluster didn't register, except as something to laugh at. But even the disaster of a show and the bad handling of the reviews would be forgotten. When you're a celebrity of Kanye's stature, you always get another chance—and the crowds will keep coming to see you. Even the high-handed French.

And so the next Paris fashion-show season in February 2012, six months later, Kanye staged his encore: a fall collection filled with black leather, fur, and more fur, in front of his girlfriend Kim Kardashian and his BFFs from music, Alicia Keys, Sean Combs, Mos Def, and Common—all of whom performed at the after-party Kanye threw that night, which was reported to be fabulous.

Kanye West, here in 2013, in one of the hoodies he designed for A.P.C. menswear in Paris.

And how about those clothes on the runway? Improved, for sure—but Kanye had no place to go but up. Even so, fashion sharpshooters in the audience and watching the video busted him for too much sampling from other designers. On YouTube, "Miuccia Pradaify" commented: "The boots are ripped off from Viktor & Rolf fall 2008, the beige capes are ripped off from Givenchy spring 2009, the rest is taken from Altuzarra fall 2010. Copy and paste does not make you a creative genius."

Kanye West (in white), here in 2014, designer of a capsule collection for A.P.C.

Meanwhile, Kanye stayed in Paris but shifted into somewhere he could shine—designing a group of fashions for an established sportswear label. A.P.C., a Gap-style brand. His first capsule collection was modest—a couple pair of jeans, hoodies, and some T-shirts priced from $120 to $280—but drew tons of traffic to A.P.C.'s website and was said to have sold out on the Sunday it debuted. He would come back in early 2014 with another capsule group for fall.

A Force of Nature

After 2012, Kanye took a break from the runways, launching another hit album, *Yeezus*, in 2013. The response to the album was the kind of blockbuster success and adulation he yearned for in fashion—which probably compelled him to try to goad the folks at Louis Vuitton into boosting his fashion profile, as in *How about going for another collaboration?* in the in-your-face manner that Kanye operates.

Mouthing off to NOW Radio 92.3 on November 29, 2013, Kanye fumed on-air, complaining that the "head of Louis Vuitton" refused to meet with him when he was in Paris recently. As the interviewer egged him on to tell all, Kanye, all puffed up, bloviated: "And [the head of Vuitton] said, 'I don't understand why we need to meet with you.' I said, 'Let me explain to you why you need to meet with me: Everybody in New York City right now, don't buy any Louis Vuitton until after January. Now do you want to meet with me?' Influence. They don't think that I don't realize my power."

He was showing off to radio listeners in this cryptic message in the cadence of a rapper. It wasn't quite a call for a boycott, but a veiled threat—a don't-mess-with-me warning that Kanye West was a player to be reckoned with! Winner of twenty-one Grammy Awards! Fashion taste-maker! A badass who could steer shoppers away from the Louis Vuitton brand anytime he felt like it! In his imagination, of course.

Kanye was full of himself as usual, but he wasn't wrong. Celebrities did indeed have real power in fashion, to lead throngs of people to dress a certain way and buy things they didn't really need at prices they couldn't really afford. In other words, they had the power to keep the industry afloat.

It was a truism that has never escaped Anna Wintour, who ignores the antics and concentrates on the energy that celebrities like Kanye bring to fashion. She told me in November 2013, "You can't believe the e-mails I get from Kanye about some sneaker he has seen in Japan—you know, the e-mails go on, like, this long"—she spread her hands wide—"because he is so passionate about it. . . . He and Sean [Combs] had the same love of fashion, and that is obviously something that I love to see.

"Kanye is a force of nature. He is not going to do anything under the radar. That's just not who he is, and that's why he is so much fun. He has good taste and he is very clever and I think that he will succeed. I think that he will not give up until he does. He has made it in the music world, and he now desperately wants to make it in the fashion world and he will find a way."

Chapter Fifteen

. . . .

JUST SAY NO TO THE FAME GAME
The Olsen Twins Make It the Old-Fashioned Way

> They know how to work with tailors; they can talk about inverted pleats;
> they know what a dart is, they know when the princess seam needs to be
> elongated. This is the designer education they have picked up over the
> years. This is what the Olsens have become.
>
> —Robert Verdi, Hollywood stylist and consultant, 2013

Mary-Kate and Ashley Olsen, the twin sisters who had been TV and movie stars from the age of nine months on, were just nineteen in 2006 when they stepped out during New York Fashion Week as high-fashion designers—and not celebrities. Their upscale women's fashion label, The Row, didn't ring of bling, but whispered with solid conviction.

Even the name was pointedly vanilla, as far from referencing their fame as it could get. Instead, it connoted old-world finery—as in Savile Row, London's storied "golden mile of tailoring," where the world's finest custom suit makers operated. The Row is a name that evoked art-istry and peerless craftsmanship, as "everything felt like it was tailored for your body," Mary-Kate once explained.

My recollection of The Row's first show is of a dimly lit downtown New York venue where there was no front-row-celebrity hoopla—only about one hundred or so fashion editors and retailers and a few photogra-phers were invited. It was a tightly edited show—no more than twenty looks—with long wrap skirts, loose sleeveless tops, cashmere, black silk crepe de chine pants. During this low-hum presentation, the models walked at a breezy pace, as we got a good look at these modern silhouettes in featherweight, draped materials. The low-key clothes looked sensational.

Fashion people were still buzzing with a mix of incredulity, skepticism—and the expected spitballs—about the auspicious debut of The Row weeks later, right through the Milan and Paris collections. The takeaway went something like this:

They're beginners who got lucky. Don't forget, they're actresses, not designers.

They were prodigies on TV as babies. Maybe that carried over into fashion.

No way they did it. I wonder who they paid to get it designed?

If there was a man (or woman) designer behind that particularly opaque curtain of The Row, nobody has ever flushed it out. So absent evidence to the contrary, it was now the Olsens' turn with The Row to be the latest in high-pitched, high-concept apparel—what fashion insiders call "dog-whistle fashion." Sophisticated. Intellectual. Expensive. Their style reminded me of the legendary masters of minimalism in their 1990s heyday—Zoran and Martin Margiela, and more recently the grittier, American-in-Paris Rick Owens. Their severe, simple, mostly black clothes oozed with snob appeal and cachet because, by design, only those in the know can fully appreciate them.

The Row purposely pitched to the golden-gated community of slender, affluent women who dreamed of owning the very best of the basics. Now, thanks to The Row, they could find them. These champion shoppers thought nothing of buying in multiples: $260 T-shirts and $750 white jersey blouses by The Row—staples that were perfectly cut and su-perb. Likewise, they snapped up The Row's sumptuous black turtleneck sweater in alpaca and silk ribbed knit for $1,150. The Row delivered luxurious leggings: in stretch lambskin leather, matte and inky black, justifying their $2,950 price tag simply because they didn't exist elsewhere in the marketplace. They were the unique find that became one of The Row's hardiest perennial hits.

These were among the wardrobe essentials worth buying again and again, for those in the know who could afford them. Such was the precious merchandise that had been the very definition of luxury fashion long before designers had to be validated by a movie star on a red carpet.

The Anti-Celebrities

The word spread fast among the cognoscenti. The Row evolved steadily, rolling out exquisite handbags (at an average price of $4,000) and $460 sunglasses, never disappointing its discerning clientele. The Olsen sisters—wise beyond their youth and celebrity—looked to be the real deal, the exception among designer start-ups who typically take several years to catch on, if ever. The Row clicked from the beginning, building a loyal, elite critical mass at retail.

"The Row has always been about great product, the manufacturing and the fit—it sold from day one," said Natalie Massenet, founder and chief executive officer at Net-a-Porter, the world's leading online luxury fashion retailer. She told me in 2013 that for her customers, The Row "is a go-to brand for key luxury pieces like leather stretch pants and jackets."

The fact that the Olsens' names weren't on the label took The Row out of the celebrity fashion sphere, which worked just fine, as the many chic women who love The Row just don't think about the association. Connoisseur fashion plates like Cindy Rachofsky, a fiftyish Dallas philanthropist and art collector—married to a former hedge fund manager—has been wearing The Row since about 2009. When I spoke to her in November 2013, she ticked off a long list of her closet favorites by The Row, namely: cashmere sweaters, a floor-length cape, leather leggings, a leather dress, blouses, and black pants. "What The Row satisfied for me was that higher-end-of-casual clothing element for my wardrobe," she said. Before The Row, she'd have to cherry-pick through other designer collections to locate such premium staples.

Of course, Rachofsky had always been aware of the famously stylish Olsen twins and their fashion brand from all the magazines. She says: "But not for a minute did my interest in The Row have any bearing on what I thought of them as actresses or fashionable women. No, not at all."

She says she has a lot of designers who are friends, but she didn't seek out the Olsens when they hosted a fashion-show reception at Neiman Marcus in Dallas: "I don't really care about meeting them. I'm not a designer celebrity stalker."

Who could even guesstimate the annual sales of this highly guarded, privately owned fashion concern that was believed to be self-financed and made no disclosures? Somewhere north of $50 million at retail in 2013 seemed plausible, given The Row's expanding product line and all the stores they were in, including Neiman Marcus, Bergdorf Goodman, and Net-a-Porter.com. And sales climbed far higher when you factored in two more midpriced hit fashion labels—Elizabeth and James, and Olsenboye for JCPenney—that the Olsens added since The Row, further evidence that they were players, outstanding among America's young fashion entrepreneurs.

Their success was all the more unusual, because in an age when so many fashion designers were angling to become tabloid famous in order to survive in the crowded mass market, here were genuine TV and film stars deliberately shedding their glittering personas to take on all the uncertainties and challenges faced by other noncelebrity young designers such as Phillip Lim or Jason Wu.

Growing Up Twin Actresses

Mary-Kate and Ashley Olsen had come by their arm's-length embrace of fame naturally. Though they had been thrust into the limelight as infant actors and maintained a rabidly active national fan club until they were fourteen, the Olsens grew up in the protective cocoon of handlers and chaperones who kept them safe—inside the gated velvet rope of the Hollywood elite among other rich and famous people. They had learned young to value privacy and keep a comfortable distance from all the interviews and tabloid voyeurism that had come to dominate the lives of so many celebrities. They saw their success not as an end in itself, but as a means to follow their passion, which happened to be fashion. They didn't need adoring masses. For affirmation, they relied squarely on each other.

Back Onstage at the CFDA

On the night of June 4, 2012, at the Alice Tully Hall at Lincoln Center, the Council of Fashion Designers of America awarded The Row by Mary-Kate and Ashley Olsen as the best women's-wear designer of the year.

Winning a major CFDA award just six years after they launched put the Olsens squarely in the major league among top international fashion players—mentioned in the same breath as Lanvin, Balenciaga, or Prada. Poised and measured, the Olsens still carried themselves with confidence on the red carpet—that deep self-assurance of lifelong fame is dyed into their fabric—but the still-powerful afterglow of their celebrity allure was overshadowed that night by their date to the gala, the actress and former Revlon supermodel Lauren Hutton.

Tanned and smiling, with a wavy, cropped coif, the sixty-seven-year-old Hutton stood out, spiffed and sporty in all-white: The Row's T-shirt, blazer, skinny pants, and matching linen $250 T sneakers, contrasting starkly against the plush red of the carpet. Standing between the beaming Mary-Kate and Ashley, in gowns, Hutton explained why she loved wearing The Row: "You feel *delicious* in them. Sort of just free—you don't have to think about [your clothes], you don't have to worry."

Barbie's Celebrity Friends

Mary-Kate and Ashley Olsen, born on June 13, 1986, in Los Angeles, were fraternal twins who looked enough alike to take turns playing the role of Michelle Tanner (complying with child-labor laws limiting how much time each could work) on *Full House*, the TV sitcom where viewers watched them grow up during the series's entire eight-year run.

The precocious blonde-and-blue-eyed youngsters, beloved by a wide swath of the TV-watching masses, continued to act together and separately into their teens—raking in millions that all flowed (wisely steered by their parents) into their joint business venture, Dualstar Entertainment Group, which worked in some fifty-two product categories, including more than fifty straight-to-video movies, pop albums, and toys, notably the bestselling Mary-Kate and Ashley twin dolls, promoted as "Barbie's celebrity friends."

At age twelve, the Olsens loved to draw outfits and make other suggestions for their namesake "tween" clothing line of items for under $20, featuring handkerchief tops, low-rise jeans, and blazers, promoted as "Real Fashion for Real Girls." Sold exclusively at Walmart stores, the collection steadily generated hundreds of millions in annual sales, buoying Dualstar into a Martha Stewart–like franchise, said to have generated as much as $970 million in 2003, as Robert Thorne, their manager, told CBS's *48 Hours* on TV.

In Los Angeles, the Olsens were mannerly and wholesome private-school kids who got modest weekly allowances for doing household chores while living in joint custody of their divorced parents. They just happened to be among America's most successful working actresses—among the youngest multimillionaires—who blossomed into adolescent businesswomen, actively participating in developing their own brand. "We worked so much that they wanted to make sure we knew exactly what was happening and why—and our opinions mattered," Mary-Kate recalled to the *Telegraph*.

Fashion became second nature to the twins, who spent their formative years in film wardrobe departments, where they liked to rifle through all the colorful clothes of the grown-up actresses. Their own frequent costume changes in front of cameras required countless hours in fittings with designers, tailors, and their assistants. The young fashionistas got used to wearing designer clothes by Chanel and Marc Jacobs that had to be resized to fit them. "When you cut something down small, it has to be precise," Ashley once explained.

Under the microscope of camera close-ups from every angle, actors' on-screen wardrobes must fit perfectly and more. Movie costumes were typically built to the exacting standards of haute couture ensembles in Paris. They were tweaked and retweaked to accommodate dance movements, to accentuate curves, or to hide figure flaws that are negligible in real life but magnified on-screen. Every skirt slit, every pocket, every crooked seam was considered. Experienced leading ladies like Joan Crawford grew so knowledgeable she became like a collaborator to Adrian, the fabled costume designer who created her broad-shouldered look.

Hollywood stylist Robert Verdi told me that some of his longtime movie-star clients "have moved past needing me, as they have figured out [on their own] what to wear to the party."

Having a creative eye and the confidence to trust your own instincts is invaluable too. Ashley once wrote about how Mary-Kate decided to redesign a kimono-style dress she planned to wear to a prom. "She grabbed a stapler, totally reconfigured the whole thing, and made it her own—visible staples and all."

Dumpster Chic

When the Olsens turned eighteen in 2004, they took full control of Dualstar from their parents and headed east to enroll as freshmen at New York University. They took some acting classes, and Mary-Kate did a few TV and movie roles as they both explored other interests, tapping into the experts to whom celebrities like them would always have access. Mary-Kate became an intern for Annie Leibovitz, the celebrity photographer for *Vanity Fair*, while Ashley landed a fashion internship with women's designer Zac Posen.

Simply by being themselves at NYU, Mary-Kate and Ashley unwittingly carved out new personas—as fashion role models around Manhattan. Young women began to copy their edgy way of dressing, an unkempt, downtown look known as "Dumpster chic." The waifish, pint-size (just around five feet tall) Olsens wore messy, long blonde hair with dark roots and smoky eye makeup. They got dressed by piling on grungy layers of stretched-out sweaters, lacy vintage tops, maxi skirts, floppy hats, and bug-eye sunglasses—a bag-lady effect, documented by all the paparazzi candids of them published in the tabloids. Mary-Kate's look "became dottier and dottier, until it morphed into a kind of homeless masquerade, one that was accented by subtle luxuries like a cashmere muffler, a Balenciaga lariat bag and of course her signature carryout latte from Starbucks," wrote Ruth La Ferla in *The New York Times* in 2005.

This dressed-from-granny's-attic motif of Mary-Kate and Ashley had a quirky appeal all of its own. "They were unimpeachably groovy and cool," Simon Doonan, longtime executive at Barneys New York, told me.

It was a widely shared opinion. Their innate chic caught the eye of red-carpet gown creators Badgley Mischka, who enlisted the Olsens to appear in a full-page print ad in April 2006, in a year when Badgley Mischka needed to raise their profile and hip quotient. The brand was now marketing a midpriced collection of party dresses and its first perfume.

The Badgley Mischka ad was very Diane Arbus: a tightly framed shot of the Olsen sisters standing in a white hallway, staring blankly, straight ahead. They seemed like little girls playing dress-up in grown-up evening gowns. It was a quirky fashion image that stood out from the pages of *Vogue*, *Elle*, *InStyle*, and *Vanity Fair*, but only because it featured the famous TV twins. It was the first and only time that the Olsens would model for a fashion label other than their own teen Walmart brand.

For more than a year after arriving in New York, Ashley devoted herself to her own special project: confecting the perfect T-shirt. She started from scratch, experimenting with fabrics and silhouettes; she even enlisted an apparel factory in Los Angeles to help her work it out. The resulting scoop-neck T-shirt appeared ordinary enough but was full of subtle nuance. It was cut from a single piece of viscose jersey with a vertical satin seam running down the middle of the back. "It's all about the drape and the fabric and finding the balance between the two," Ashley would later explain.

Finding the balance proved so seductive the Olsens decided to launch themselves as fashion designers, abandoning Hollywood together. Ashley's couture T-shirt got them started, and they added a few other casual pieces they came up with and sold to friends and small boutiques.

In naming The Row, the Olsens were adamant about not wanting their own names to define the brand. Almost a decade of seeing their names and likenesses at Walmart had been more than enough. "We did it with our faces at the beginning, and we knew we didn't want to do that anymore," Ashley reminisced to the *Telegraph*. "It's far more fun this way."

Around the same time, the Olsens launched a second brand to cover the midtier—the $100 to $600 price range—called Elizabeth and James (named after their siblings). It was a young women's brand that included interpretations of the favorite vintage pieces that they wore themselves, as well as blazers with sleeves sewn to stay pushed up around the elbows. They would eventually add an even lower, third-tier teen label—priced from $20 to $50—exclusively for JCPenney called Olsenboye (their family's full surname in their native Norwegian). In every case, the twins' affiliation wasn't evident—unless you closely read fashion magazines or the trades.

The Olsens made use of their celebrity in launching their fashion businesses in only one sense: Their entertainment ventures had made them rich enough to underwrite the start-up themselves, and to do it right. (Among the richest young stars in Hollywood, each twin had an estimated net worth of about $137 million in 2009.) They would build their new brands' business by hiring the top people—The Row's president and chief operating officer since 2012 was Francois Kress, formerly the president of Prada USA, for example. They could also afford to produce The Row in the best factories—mostly in New York and in Italy.

So Very Barneys New York

In 2007, The Row rolled out in that capital of dog-whistle fashion, specialty retailer Barneys New York, whose executives were more interested in the clothes than the celebrity of the Olsens. "I immediately sensed something different," remembered Julie Gilhart, Barneys senior vice president and women's fashion director at the time. She loved that The Row covered such a narrow niche—well-tailored basics—that was so promising because it was largely untapped. "They were so smart and open—and they hadn't even turned twenty. The customer needed knits, and they had this great collection of knits. They had really thought this whole thing through."

What's more, The Row was so very Barneys, with its emphasis on black and neutrals. Gilhart said: "The Row started out as a collection of underpinnings: a T-shirt, a tank sweater, a lot of tops, and leggings. That's where we started to do business with them. And then it became denim and leather and wool. Then it just expanded, everybody had to have The Row pull-on pants."

The Olsens were big believers that their job didn't stop at the design studio; they took the time to go to Barneys to do in-house clinics with sales associates. During such sessions, the former actresses became animated as they talked up the latest novelties and how they coordinated with staples from previous seasons. Like coaches in a huddle with Barneys associates, the Olsens use these clinics to "get people fired up," says Gilhart. "For that, they get an A-plus."

The Olsens' version of a runway show is always intimate and austere, like the tearoom presentations that I attended at The Carlyle—a fittingly swanky, low-key, very Upper East Side hotel—where models walked around tables of small groups of fashion editors and retail buyers while a guitarist or pianist played. The Olsens briefly greeted guests on their way out, but gave no backstage interviews.

The Olsens may have kept their name off the label, but they were hardly shrinking violets when it came to promoting the brand. The former actresses knew that being mysterious and elusive carried its own allure and mystique. The less people really knew, the more intrigued they were. All access was fiercely controlled by their publicists. Yet the Olsens had learned from childhood that once in a while they needed to play ball, so they gave a handful of strategic interviews to the top fashion magazines or made an occasional drive-by TV appearance on *Good Morning America* or *The Ellen DeGeneres Show*, where they stuck closely to the fashion script, ignoring questions about their social lives, which included dating famous men. In 2014, Mary-Kate got engaged to Olivier Sarkozy, a global financier and half brother to the former president of France. Ashley had been linked in the past to Lance Armstrong and Justin Timberlake. They didn't brag about their celebrity clients either, but famous women were photographed wearing The Row, including Jessica Biel, Julianne Moore, Angie Harmon, and First Lady Michelle Obama, as well as Hutton, who modeled in The Row look books distributed to clients.

The Guessing Game

When the sisters spoke together they left the impression that they were doing everything by themselves. They never talked about the highs or setbacks, or any of the mechanics or personnel. (Through their publicist, the Olsens and their executives repeatedly declined to be interviewed for this book.)

The big mystery at every fashion house is who does the heavy lifting, especially when the designers are celebrities who didn't go to fashion school, had never worked in fashion or retailing. Yes, the Olsens were astute fashionistas—collectors of fine vintage clothing and antique jewelry, they had worn their share of couture labels. They claimed in their 2008 coffee table scrapbook, *Influence*, to have gotten close to designers like Karl Lagerfeld, Diane von Furstenberg, and Christian Louboutin.

But the more successful The Row became, the more some people started to poke. The most frequent rap on The Row was that the Olsens were wealthy celebrities who had bought their way in, using ghost designers to design their collections. It was certainly not implausible given that, for many celebrities, fashion was a side business that they worked at only sporadically. Even though the Olsens were full-time designers, people still wanted to believe that they had outside help.

I loved how candid singer Gwen Stefani was about her use of seasoned fashion pros—designer Zaldy Goco and stylist Andrea Lieberman—to help her turn out L.A.M.B., her women's fashion line, which enjoyed its own fashion moment that began in 2003, and claimed retail sales as high as $40 million a year later. The platinum-blonde Stefani, a hip, lifelong clotheshorse who grew up sewing her own dresses and even made some of her early stage costumes, was pretty matter-of-fact about it. "Everybody out there has a team of people behind them. That's just the way it is," Stefani admitted to *The New York Times*. "Before, I thought I actually had to do all the drawing. Now I know that what you really are is a producer. Not every single idea has to be mine."

And the fact was that most consumers just weren't *that* particular. They didn't care what was in the sausage, or who made it, any more than those excited shoppers I'd interviewed at the Kardashian event at Sears cared that the leopard bustier dresses, skinny jeans, and hobo handbags they were buying had little more of Kardashian in them than the name on the label and a glossy picture in a magazine.

But given that the Olsens were playing in fashion's couture big leagues, a certain amount of connoisseurship was expected from them. Stylish, affluent women weren't groupies in search of $50 souvenir

T-shirts. They expected the real deal. Some people whispered about the Olsens—and Lysa Cooper, a celebrity stylist who had dressed Beyoncé and Rihanna, just came out and stated her suspicions to *Vogue Italia* in July 2013. The Row was "the only celebrity line that's any good [because] they hired designers to do the work for them. [The Olsens] 'yay' or 'nay' [the concepts]."

Cooper added, "They are the best at ripping off other lines that I have ever seen." She cited as examples the work of Paris-based designers Rick Owens and Ann Demeulemeester, purveyors of luxe layering pieces—cashmere T-shirts and tanks, and edgy leather jackets—that resemble those of The Row. The Olsens and all the other celebrity designers should "go to school," she sniped. "If you go to school, then maybe you can talk some shit."

The guessing game of "who is a real designer" has been aimed at many successful fashion businesses over the years, especially in the United States. In Paris, the birthplace of couture, where the government used to rule on which fashion houses could carry the name of haute couture, it was something of a blood sport to diss the top American fashion businesses for being merely "sportswear houses," as unsubstantial as fast food, lacking creative artistry and true craftsmanship.

The French pooh-poohed Calvin Klein for the billions he raked in on designer jeans, fragrance, and underwear; they sneered at Ralph Lauren for being an Anglophile imposter who mined billions on repurposed preppy style. The house of Yves Saint Laurent went so far in 1994 as to sue—and win a French commercial court decision against—Ralph Lauren. YSL cofounder Pierre Bergé charged in *WWD* that Lauren's $1,000 sleeveless tuxedo gown copied "line for line, cut for cut" YSL's $15,000 haute couture sleeveless tuxedo gown—a creation that was protected under French law.

The Best Revenge

It was a dubious charge at best, given that sleeveless tuxedo gowns had been ubiquitous in the marketplace for years. But nevertheless, the lawsuit was designed to shame the American, to put him in his place—behind the French. (After the court ruled against Lauren, he was slapped with a $411,000 fine. What Ralph Lauren Corporation eventually paid, after it was reduced on appeal, wasn't publicly disclosed.)

In any event, growing bigger and better was the best revenge. Lauren would enjoy the last laugh: annual sales of $7 billion in 2013 and a sumptuous eighteenth-century mansion of a store on the stylish Left Bank of Paris, whose elegant and bustling adjacent restaurant, Ralph's—featuring 27-euro ($37) hamburgers, made from imported beef from Lauren's own Colorado ranch—was the hardest reservation to get in town.

Such were the dramas, jealousies, and contretemps that flared up across the greater fashion industry. More than commerce was at stake. The aggrieved believed they were striking in defense of artistry, creativity, and connoisseurship, which continued to erode in the wake of fast-fashion and celebrity-fashion brands that had been threatening traditional designers since the dawn of the twenty-first century.

The celebrity designers were now at the bottom of the fashion hierarchy, reviled by purists even more than fast-fashion knockoff artists, because celebrities were phonies who had brazenly hoodwinked consumers—taking all of the credit for work they had little or nothing to do with. At least that was the tenor of the bitching coming from the purists.

But those assumptions oversimplified and caricaturized the state of an industry where no designer—creative artist or celebrity—goes it alone inside the studio. Fashion design is more than ever a collaborative endeavor, a complex process that involves many skilled and creative people at every level.

In the end, whether the Olsens ever put pencil to paper or not, there is no question that they actively run their business, hire the key people, and yay and nay their way to an enduring and fabulously appealing line of fashions that outdo the competition. And they do it all while never having to play the celebrity card.

Well, maybe not *never.*

When it came time for The Row to introduce handbags in 2011, the company chose to go for over-the-top luxury. Barneys put out a dozen or so $39,000 alligator backpacks, and shoppers not only oohed and aahed, they bought every one, Mark Lee, Barneys chief executive, confirmed to me.

The typical woman who carries an alligator handbag is likely to be wearing it across her wrist to accessorize some elegant outfit. She isn't likely to knock around in faded jeans with an alligator backpack hanging off a shoulder, not unless she has some vision of somebody way cool—perhaps a celebrity—wearing it that way.

And that's when Ashley Olsen stepped in to do her part. Brent Cox, a columnist on TheAwl.com, called the photos that circulated "Ashley's Handbag Perpwalk." They were all over the Internet, candids showing Ashley Olsen in aviator sunglasses, walking with her head down in jeans and flip-flops with a $39,000 alligator backpack in full view slung over her shoulder. The Row's handbags hadn't even hit Barneys yet, where they were soon to be launched exclusively. But that didn't stop all those fashion gossip sites from posting this candid shot of Ashley Olsen and giving their readers the 411.

Ashley Olsen, in 2012, wearing The Row's $39,000 alligator backpack designed by her and her twin sister, Mary-Kate Olsen.

On TomAndLorenzo.com: "Call us lazy whores if you want, you won't be the first ones, but we took a good long look at these pictures and realized that it doesn't really matter what we say here because the conversation's only going to go in one direction. Ashley Olsen out and about with her new backpack. The bag is from her new handbag line in collaboration with amnio-mate Mary-Kate, called The Row. The crocodile backpack is priced at $39,000."

And on the *Daily Mail* site: "The highlight of [The Row's] new accessories range is a backpack, set to retail for an eye-watering $39,000. And though no images of the pricey bag were released by the label, the former child stars, twenty-five, have no issues with carrying one themselves."

Blogger Brent Cox concluded that this blitz of free advertising was a classic case of product placement by a publicist who contacted lots of influential fashion sites "and alerted them that the bag carried by Ashley in that photo that just hit the wires is in fact an exclusive new handbag that is manufactured by Ashley's own line and retails for an awful lot of money!

"It is a shrewd move. The first [The Row] bags to be released [actually] cost more like $4,000. That's still a lot of money, but much closer to the amount that a young fashionista could afford. And how better to participate in the casual, meticulous style of the Olsens, as evinced by the Ashley Handbag Perpwalk, then [sic] by purchasing one that's an eighth the cost?"

Chapter Sixteen

. . . .

DESIGNER BRAND OF THE YEAR
Victoria Beckham aka Posh Spice

Victoria knew she had to prove herself [as a creative designer] in the fashion industry. She did it in the right way, starting very small . . . surrounding herself with the right people . . . an excellent design team, who helped her turn that passion into a successful business.

—Glenda Bailey, editor in chief of *Harper's Bazaar*

The Olsens' combination of celebrity, fashion marketing success, and respect from the industry was a vanishingly rare accomplishment. But they weren't the only certifiable celebrities to voluntarily drop the fame thing to pursue the route into high fashion and really succeed. Across the Atlantic, there was Victoria Beckham, formerly known as "Posh" of the famed pop-singing Spice Girls.

On November 28, 2011, at the Savoy Theater in London, Victoria Beckham won top honors at the British Fashion Awards, where she was named best designer brand of the year, beating two nominees who were among the top names in fashion in the UK: Tom Ford and Stella McCartney.

It was a heady moment onstage when designer-presenter Marc Jacobs called her name. Victoria, looking splendid in a backless black halter gown, made a tearful acceptance speech.

It was all hers to savor. Victoria was now starring as a fashion designer—a new profession she had worked so hard for, one that so neatly dovetailed with her personal brand as a stylish pop celebrity. Driven women like Beckham were masters of studied, exacting calculation—and all was going according to plan.

The celebrity-as–fashion designer had become a cliché in America, a rite of passage for actors and pop singers, a box to check on their to-do list next to the one marked "fragrance." It was a sideline gig that kept them au courant in the headlines, while imparting a stylish cool factor, as well as a revenue stream, at least while it lasted. But that wasn't enough for Victoria Beckham.

Like the Olsens, Victoria aimed to be adopted into the world of fashion. She was determined to be regarded as one of the best in the hardest space to conquer in fashion: the high-end couture level, where the real designers roamed.

It was far easier for Mary-Kate and Ashley to make the transition, as they could maintain two identities—actresses as children who grew up to become designers as adults. But Victoria, who was thoroughly tied to her singer/famous spouse identity, would have to do more. She would have to establish credibility and gravitas. The upper echelons of the fashion establishment wanted to see her creating—not just taking a runway bow. She would have to give it her all, to use her best self-effacing charm on retailers and customers—not to mention the skeptical fashion press. Being voted by her fashion peers as best designer brand of 2011 went a long way to underscore that she belonged in the club.

A Posh Life

Formerly known as "Posh" of the famed pop-singing Spice Girls, Victoria Beckham jumped into the rag-trade hustle around the same time as the Olsens, in 2007. As if her storybook life with soccer heartthrob David Beckham and their growing brood wasn't stimulating enough, Victoria set aside her singing career to chase her creative obsession. She became the high-fashion designer for her namesake collection of $3,500 body-con dresses, which had been her go-to look for years.

Skinny, angular, and tough-girl pretty, with chopped-off hair, Victoria Beckham loved being a style icon. It wasn't a coincidence that her stage name had been "Posh." Her concert getups were rock-star-edgy costumes, and in real life she turned out in her movie-star shades, tight dresses, stilettos, and Hermès Birkin handbags. (She was rumored to own more than one hundred Birkin bags, worth more than $2 million, including the limited-edition "Himalayan Birkin," a $100,000 model made of exotic skins, reported the *Telegraph* in 2006.)

Even before the launch of her apparel line, Victoria became ubiquitous in the fashion world. The glamorous Beckhams—the tabloids dubbed them "Posh and Becks"—bowed at Macy's with his-and-her fragrances in 2005. She was a coveted front-row "get" at every Fashion Week, and she cut a mean runway strut in Milan as a guest model for both Roberto Cavalli and Dolce & Gabbana. She rocked a downtown vibe, modeling *R* logo tank tops and hot pants in ads for Rocawear, the street-wear fashion label that was part of Roc-A-Fella Records, the urban music label founded by Jay Z and Damon Dash.

By 2007, she published a bestselling fashion book, *That Extra Half an Inch: Hair, Heels and Everything in Between*—and formally launched her career as a creative designer, vying to be a peer alongside her celebrated fellow Brits Stella McCartney and Phoebe Philo of Céline.

And like the Olsens, Victoria Beckham courted her posh audience— wealthy women who wanted to dress like her, including celebrities willing to pay retail, like Sarah Jessica Parker, who had the ideal body for Beckham's narrow silhouettes. SJP loved Beckham's frocks, and she bought hers, just like everybody else, she told me.

London-based Net-a-Porter called Victoria Beckham "one of our most popular brands." "The demand for her collection keeps increasing," Massenet also told me in 2013. "As soon as [Beckham's collections] go down the runway, we get calls for preorders immediately. . . . The sweet spot is dresses, in particular, and women keep coming back."

Leave Macy's, Kohl's, and Sears to Jessica Simpson, Madonna, and the Kardashians. Victoria Beckham and the Olsens had made it to the top the old-fashioned way, by selling millions of dollars' worth of top-drawer couture merchandise to customers who weren't impressed with their celebrity credentials. Their merchandise moved consistently because it was perceived to be as good as or better than what other top designers were selling, earning them not only profits, but also respect from their working peers.

Growing Up Victoria

For every girl, it's the fantasy worth wishing for: to be rich, to be famous, and to catch her Prince Charming. The dream came true for Victoria Adams, born April 17, 1974, in Essex, England, to a well-off British family who afforded her the singing and dancing lessons and the advanced drama studies that put her on the show business track. She was a little girl with a singular laser focus—to be famous—and she kept telling everybody that's where she was headed. She said she was duly inspired by the ambitious characters in the 1980 movie *Fame*: "I had all the garb. My tracksuit, leg warmers, the bag—that is when I started to take my dancing really seriously."

And so fame was to be—first coming to her in 1994 after she won a spot to become a member of the Spice Girls, the prefab pop group that electrified teenyboppers around the world with their feel-good mantra of "girl power."

She learned the ways of showmanship. The Spice Girls were shallow singers and dancers whose bubblegum groove depended on the visuals, the midriff tops, and the individual moxie of each nicknamed player: Ginger, Posh, Sporty, Baby, and Scary. The pre–Britney Spears, G-rated Spice Girls dazzled with their catchy megahits like "Wannabe" and their lilting English accents. Like the second British invasion, they stormed the world on concert tours, with screaming mobs trailing them everywhere as they sold more than thirty-eight million records, surpassing all kinds of pop music benchmarks. The Svengali of the Spice rack was Simon Fuller, the visionary producer who, years later, created *American Idol*, the reality-show blockbuster of a lifetime. By 2001, the Spice Girls broke up and went their separate ways.

Victoria's Posh was destined to be the breakout star of the group, as she proceeded with a solo singing career and her own TV talk show. Victoria, with the squint-eyed pout, was the badass fashionista whom legions of Spice Girl fans worshipped. She could *wear* those trendy clothes and *work* that attitude—a "blend of cold insouciance and smoldering wouldn't-you-like-to-know glamour," as *Elle* once put it.

Bending Beckham

Falling under her spell was the UK's most famous "footballer," David Beckham, who said he was a goner at his first sighting of Victoria in a leopard catsuit in a Spice Girls video. Fuller, who also served as David's manager, introduced them to each other, and love struck hard, beginning the era of the good-looking, world-famous "Posh and Becks." The tabloids chased the couple incessantly, and *OK!* magazine wrote them a check for 1 million pounds ($1.6 million)—for the rights to publish the photos of their lavish wedding ceremony inside a castle in Ireland in 1999.

Mr. and Mrs. Beckham took their fashion notoriety to the bank. Blond, chiseled, and stamped all over with tattoos, David Beckham modeled Giorgio Armani underwear and stripped down again to advertise a men's "body wear" collection—featuring $14.95 cotton briefs—developed for him by fast-fashion giant H&M.

Meanwhile, his perennially tanned whippet of a wife became known in the British tabloids as queen of the WAGs—the nickname for the wives and girlfriends of British footballers—often photographed on shopping sprees together, who were typecast as shallow and acquisitive Real Housewives. Victoria—a pop-star force in her own right—was far from your average WAG, but she still had to fight hard to shake the image. She set out to prove that she didn't just wear the designer labels—she was becoming one herself.

Victoria relentlessly branded herself with her signature tight-dress look. For Elton John's annual White Tie and Tiara ball in London in 2005, she chose a head-turner—a one-of-a-kind strapless sheath gown embellished with intricate blue-and-white patterns from a rare Ming vase that belonged to its designer, Roberto Cavalli. The stunning gown had won kudos when Cavalli created it expressly for his show during Milan

Fashion Week—and Victoria, skinny enough to slip into that runway garment, asked him to let her take it on another spin in public. But only if he modified it to give it a more pronounced silhouette. "She insisted that I take the dress in at the bottom so tightly that she wouldn't be able to sit down," Cavalli remembered to fashion author Hal Rubenstein in *100 Unforgettable Dresses*. "She wouldn't wear the dress otherwise. I do exactly what she asked me to do and so she stood the whole night."

Always on her toes, that was fashion queen Victoria. The belle of the ball was as conspicuous as she wanted to be—and she got what she came for: a trove of party pictures that circulated around the Internet.

With the solid financial and managerial backing of Simon Fuller, Victoria shifted into fashion around 2005. Her high-profile celebrity—including her *Being Victoria Beckham* reality show, then airing in the UK, and two bestselling books: her autobiography, *Learning to Fly*, and *That Extra Half an Inch* style guide—kept her on the map, in Europe in particular. But the Beckhams, with their three sons, moved to Los Angeles, where David had signed on to play soccer with the Los Angeles Galaxy team. For Victoria, the fashion designer "career mum," it was a relief to be away from the dogged British tabloids as she settled into her new career.

Designer jeans, a seemingly straightforward point of entry for the fledgling Victoria Beckham fashion brand, would be part of her learning curve. In the twenty-first century, in the wake of Dress-Down Nation, the jeans with the most status were "premium denim," which were all about fit rather than a designer label. Upscale denims were usually priced from $85 and higher, infused with a smidgen (1 to 3 percent) of stretch, with a medium- to low-rise cut—skinny jeans in dark indigo. They were skintight wrappers. When worn with high platform pumps, they translated to a big-city look—steaming hot on stick-thin fashion plates like Victoria. No wonder she had the confidence to launch in 2007 her "dVb" collection of jeans priced from $250 to about $375, among the most expensive on the market.

At those prices, the premium denims were thus a niche product with limited distribution to upscale stores. I remember seeing dVb jeans at Saks Fifth Avenue, and in Los Angeles, where Fred Segal or Kitson sold them. But despite reports that they were selling well in the UK, the general feedback circulating in New York and LA was disappointment in the quality and the fit of the jeans. Kitson owner Fraser Ross was frustrated that Victoria wasn't doing her part to market the jeans to women who identified with her. He told *People* in 2010, "In a tough economy, you need to be in partnership with the people that are selling your line to your fans. That's the bottom line. . . . Victoria lives fifteen minutes from the store. That's just bad business."

In the Wrong Neighborhood

What was going on? Victoria had been counting on having it both ways—using her Victoria identity to sell but doing it on the sophisticated high end of the market. She miscalculated. A woman looking for a hot pair of high-end jeans had to try on a dozen or so to find a style that made her butt look shapelier. The cool factor resided in the fit—not in the label. It was a purely pragmatic test—hot or not.

Which meant she'd placed her jeans in the wrong neighborhood. They belonged more in stores of the likes of Macy's, where her $55 Victoria Beckham fragrance was sold. By trying to sell them to haute couture customers, Victoria was effectively steering her jeans away from her fans. Victoria would end up revamping her jeans team—according to press reports—and going back to the drawing board to retool the jeans, which she continued to market, but which never caught fire in the United States as stores like Saks Fifth Avenue stopped carrying them.

At the same time, Victoria had been working on a fashion project that was near and dear to her personal tastes—a high-end dress collection. Her fitful start with jeans clearly made her wary of making a false move when she introduced her dresses. She knew that as a celebrity-turned-designer—on the couture floor, no less—she had no margin for error. Fashion editors would cut her no slack and be quick to write her off as another famous, well-dressed wannabe. So in 2008, she began gingerly with her fashion collection, centered on fitted sheath dresses priced from $1,500 to about $3,800, which were made in the UK but shown during New York Fashion Week, where the publicity machine roared compared to London. And, wary of jumping onstage too soon, Victoria stayed underground for two years, holding small presentations with a handful of top fashion magazine editors and a few retailers. Ironically, such private presentations, usually thrown by struggling young designers who couldn't afford to do a show, carried a cool exclusivity in their own right because not everybody was invited—or even knew they were happening.

Victoria, who could afford to do whatever she wanted to, had her own motives. She could quietly work out the kinks of her collections without being on a big stage, and she could reintroduce herself to individual members of the press, dialing back her outsize personality. More than anything, she wanted to be taken seriously. She wanted people to know that she knew she had a lot to learn.

What Would Victoria Wear?

She debuted her first collection for spring 2009 in a suite at the Waldorf-Astoria, where she hired three models to try her dresses on for editors who dropped by for appointments. Victoria was described as dressed in one of her very own sheath dresses, perched on a settee, providing a running commentary, including exposing the innards of an unzipped dress so editors and retailers could see the boning and corsetry that was designed to mold a woman's body into a svelte silhouette after the zipper went up. Beckham talked her head off in those little meetings. And the buzz began and so did the sales to the tune of about $7 million in that first year, the fashion house told *WWD*.

A typical Victoria Beckham dress in her popular Icon silhouette was a couture interpretation of a figure-molding body-con dress, which by design was suitable for an exclusive, very narrow subset: slender women with fit figures, good arms, and narrow hips—in other words, clones of Victoria herself. One sleeveless style with contouring seams was made of dense ribbed jersey ($1,795), while the Icon polo dress ($2,685) in double crepe wool, silk, and cotton, resembled a tight polo shirt, with its button placket, tiny collar, and sleeves that stopped right before the elbow. On hangers, the dresses held a stiff outline as if they were clinging to an invisible cardboard backing. In addition to the usual neutrals, Victoria's palette included blue, orange, hunter-green, yellow, and color-block combinations. These were revealing, look-at-me dresses—what I call a "Hey, baby!" dress, in honor of the ogling construction workers on the street.

In 2010, I attended one of the little presentations Victoria gave at a vacant town house on East Sixty-Third Street during Fashion Week for about twenty editors at a time. Waiters circulated with hot tea in cups and saucers before we went into the salon to sit in an elongated semicircle. Victoria played the gracious hostess, commenting on the fifteen or so outfits the models wore. Before the show started, Victoria walked over to greet each guest individually. She stood right in front of me with steady eye contact, bending over to introduce herself, asked my name, and welcomed me to her presentation with a smile and a firm handshake. It all felt a little staged and hokey. *This woman is earnestly trying*, I remember thinking.

As the show began she spoke softly and authoritatively, pointing to the exposed back zippers, calling out the fabrics and other garment details. She could be jokey or downright self-deprecating in describing the elements of design. For example, she told Ruth La Ferla of *The New York Times* in 2010: "I might get a piece of fabric and tie it around me, then ask an assistant to pin it for me. I'm not claiming to be a master draper. The bottom line is: Would I wear this?"

Coming from the celebrity who had great taste and fashion instincts, who wasn't a trained designer, her honest revelations came across as charming.

Despite such admissions, all her people took pains to explain how much in control she was, working every day, running her fashion house. Every story about her talked about how she was a control freak, a workaholic perfectionist who set her alarm to be up at three A.M. so she could be on Skype to meet with her London office and steer the ship.

"She's incredibly involved in pricing, wanting to know where we're at in terms of turnover and how costs are being managed," Zach Duane, the company's senior vice president for business development, told *The New York Times* in 2010—the second consecutive year that the brand generated sales "in excess of $7 million."

Losing the Spice

The growing sales didn't stop everybody from sniping. As with the Olsens, the fashion world circulated criticisms, calling Victoria unoriginal at best and dependent on ghost designers at worst. Cathy Horyn, the fashion critic at *The New York Times*, called her couture "ladylike vamp dresses straight from the movies. I could see them on TCM [Turner Classic Movies channel] any old time."

Fashion's high-end ranks were full of derivative styles that traditional designers got away with recycling all the time. But for Victoria Beckham—who lacked design credentials and had a closetful of fitted couture dresses from Roland Mouret, L'Wren Scott, and Narciso Rodriguez—the bar seemed to get raised, much to the annoyance of supporters, who responded: *What's wrong with a little cutting and pasting to create a hybrid dress that feels new?*

The quality and workmanship, everybody agreed, were excellent.

From the start, fashion sharpshooters pointed to Roland Mouret—whose fitted sheaths Victoria had worn for years and whose fashion house Simon Fuller had also invested in—as a possible collaborator who helped design her collections. "All I've got to say is those dresses looked like they were Roland Mouret's children," Hollywood stylist Robert Verdi told me.

Addressing the rumors, Mouret told *WWD* in 2012: "Yes she is a friend and yes she asks for advice and yes I told her the name of a pattern cutter, but she has lots of friends she asks for advice."

The sniping and cattiness would eventually die down because, after all, retail buyers were ordering whatever the fashion house shipped. The company grew at a deliberate pace, rigorously controlling distribution, avoiding overproduction—all to maintain high quality, the stores were told. It was a common luxury-goods strategy to hold back and deny stores everything they wanted to order. The result was that demand would always outstrip supply, creating waiting lists and frenzied, buy-it-now buzz.

I spoke with Natalie Massenet, Net-a-Porter.com founder, who is American. Despite Victoria's celebrity, she told me, "We made our initial decision to carry her because of the fashion. Her clothes are flattering and feminine, with an elegance. We bought as much as we possibly could; we would have bought more. As soon as the clothes went [online], they sold out immediately. There is huge demand for the dresses," she said, "whether it was a denim skirt or an evening dress."

With every passing year, people's references to Victoria Beckham as a Spice Girl become rarer, especially from women under thirty, who were too young to even know about the group. "I'm proud of my past, but these women are not Spice Girl fans. These are women who love fashion. They appreciate quality," she told *WWD*.

Kari Schlegel Kloewer, a Dallas real estate broker, gravitated to the Victoria Beckham label, which fit right in with the other sheath dresses she's been wearing by Roland Mouret and Dolce & Gabbana. Kloewer, who is twenty-nine and a willowy size two, and her mom both ended up buying Victoria Beckham dresses when they went shopping for dresses to wear for the festivities before her May 2011 wedding. As soon as she saw this white dress with a tight fitted bodice, which was "white but not too overly innocent," she had to have it to wear for her rehearsal luncheon. The personal shopper at Neiman Marcus rang all the branch stores to locate the dress in her size. She recalled: "We had to fight to get that dress. That's the beauty of it. There's such limited distribution of Victoria Beckham that you don't have to worry about seeing others in your dress."

And how about the cachet of wearing dresses designed by one of the famous Spice Girls? Kloewer was in grade school when the Spice Girls were hot. "Everybody was aware of them. But I wasn't a follower of them, nor did I know the names of each girl, I had no clue. I knew Victoria as the wife of David, and that's when she became more on my radar. And then as a designer. It was like, 'Oh, isn't he married to this really cute gal?' And then it was like, 'Wasn't she a Spice Girl? Oh, really?' It was just one of those kind of things."

Chapter Seventeen

. . . .

BEYOND THE BLING

Can Fashion Survive Celebrity?

It was a two-minute, black-and-white video by director Martin Scorsese that reeked of *La Dolce Vita*. Driving a vintage Alfa Romeo convertible, Matthew McConaughey, in a suit and loosened skinny black tie, pulled up in front of a hotel to fetch Scarlett Johansson, so luminous and lovely in her black lace cocktail dress. As the couple rode through the empty streets, they flirted: "I like your dress," he tells her. "It likes you back," she says. Finally, they stood outside on a balcony, with the Manhattan skyline framing the shot. The music soared on cue as the couple leaned in closer. But instead of a kiss, there were perfume bottles in Technicolor, with a voice-over: "Dolce and Gabbana. The One."

The medium was Hollywood, and the message was movie stars. But where were Domenico Dolce and Stefano Gabbana, the famous Italian fashion designers who paid the hefty, A-list freight for all this? Nowhere to be seen, save for that two-second stamp, intruding at the end of all this orchestrated glamour.

That fall 2013 commercial running on YouTube was a perfect window into the state of contemporary fashion. Celebrities are starring, front and center in the frame, so that the actual fashion, and the designers who create it, are crowded almost completely out, reduced to a mere footnote.

When you see so many celebrities penetrating fashion brands—as well as celebrities becoming fashion labels themselves—you wonder, is there anybody left to carry on the tradition of creating real clothes?

"Hell yes!" asserts a chorus of fashion designers, defenders of the art of making true fashion, many of whom are frankly fed up with the fashion industry's obsessive celebrity chase. As these creators tirelessly experiment with techno fabrics and unique silhouettes, they're driven to discover something new that will capture the world's imagination and move fashion forward. They steadfastly believe that their quality-will-out determination will save the day, as they aspire to uphold fashion's time-honored traditions of originality and innovation.

These artists haven't disappeared. In fact, today there is an abundance of them, like Phillip Lim, born in 1973, arguably the most efficient designer in American fashion. He's probably the only fashion creator who pulled off a near-impossible feat—profitability—in the first year of his business in 2005. I interviewed him in 2009 for *Vogue* and marveled at his talent and confidence in his own taste. He designed sporty, thoroughly modern collections for women, men, and children—under his 3.1 Phillip Lim label—with only three assistants and no stylists to second-guess his original ideas. Lim dreamed up smart novelties that nobody had ever done, such as an exquisite $650 shadow-stripe black wool blazer—which was two jackets in one: Zip on its sequin lapels and the daytime blazer became a cocktail tuxedo jacket. His signature flourish on coats and jackets: removable underarm shields to absorb sweat.

Overexperimentation is the big time waster and money drain in every design studio. But Lim's genius is that his batting average is damn near perfect in most seasons. He told me: "I am designing and merchandising at the same time," painstakingly mapping out what's needed to satisfy retailers each season, which is a mix of styles: half new and half repeats—those bankable bestsellers. Lim created a total of 240 garments and wound up manufacturing *all of them* for his fall 2009 collection because the stores ordered them, which "is pretty much the way he does it every season," his business partner Wen Zhou said. Lim's consumer fans are legion, including rapper Kanye West, who tapped Lim to create a distinctive white dinner jacket for his groundbreaking thirty-four-minute "Runaway" music video in 2010. So what? The cerebral and reserved Lim couldn't care less about a photo op with Kanye or anybody else.

"I didn't go into fashion to become a celebrity," Lim told me in 2013.

Rediscovering Design

"Everyone talks about branding, branding, branding," designer Derek Lam told me, clearly irked at how fashion has become a celebrity marketing exercise. The winner of two CFDA awards who founded his fashion house in 2003, Lam lives for good design, putting "quality and aesthetics in the forefront" of his agenda. Celebrities don't even get invited to Lam's runway shows anymore. "We really don't want celebrities at our shows. They are detracting from the clothes," Lam's CEO and partner Jan Schlottmann told me.

Lam said: "I want to be known for my work more than for the fact that I can do a clever sound bite." He says he means no offense to his predecessors Michael Kors, Isaac Mizrahi, or Marc Jacobs—all of whom turned themselves into media personalities—"but [celebrity] is not relevant to me."

Lam gets juiced not from glimmers of fame, but when experts who really know fashion get what he's doing, like *New York Times* fashion critic Cathy Horyn, who wrote this review of Lam's New York Fashion Week showing in 2012:

> That confidence, expressed in a mere 27 outfits, all of them as thoughtful as they were tempting, was exhilarating. Mr. Lam dealt with many classics, like the clean-cut camel coat or poncho, but he didn't try to manipulate them into novel shapes. If anything, he sought to simplify things as if to make us rediscover them. . . . In both fit and attitude, the outfits were relaxed. Indeed, you had to remind yourself that there was very little tailoring in the collection, and in part that's why the clothes looked so right.

But despite bright lights like Lim and Lam, among a number of others (Alexander Wang, Proenza Schouler, Jason Wu, Thom Browne, etc.), serious fashionistas have a growing and justifiable concern over which designers will be able to take over the reins in the American fashion industry when aging lions like Oscar de la Renta and Ralph Lauren reach the end of their careers and the accelerating addiction to celebrity crowds out young talent.

And there was plenty of that. Oddly, the fashion celebrity obsession had created a bumper crop of actual designers. As the lure of celebrity promotions pumped countless millions into the industry, fashion had become a viable profession for more people who excelled in art and business—who were clamoring to attain the fame and fortune of Michael Kors, Tom Ford, or Marc Jacobs, artistic designers who have managed to have it both ways, designing fine fashion while stoking their own celebrity and brilliantly tapping into the fame zeitgeist.

All around the United States, record numbers of fashion wannabes have enthusiastically chosen to major in fashion design; they're so creative and ambitious and in a hurry to make their mark, inspired by the designer contestants on *Project Runway*. At the Art Institutes, a coalition of college-accredited art programs in major US cities, fashion-related majors are up 45 percent since the reality show premiered in 2004. And at one of the top-ranked schools, Parsons The New School for Design in New York, the School of Fashion is the biggest department, with more than one thousand students in 2013, up from 220 students in 2000.

Egging on every fashion-student hopeful was the knowledge that in the age of reality TV, celebrity was actually within reach for a handful of lucky designer nobodies. For inspiration they needed look no further than the TV reality-show poster boy who proved what's possible: Christian Siriano, the twenty-one-year-old winner of season four on *Project Runway* in 2008. Cheeky, with an edgy, asymmetrical haircut, Siriano became famous for his sassy lexicon: "fierce" for ultracool, and "you're a hot tranny mess" when your look isn't working. Siriano became the youngest winner and the biggest breakout star of *Project Runway* since the show's inception in 2004. Actress Amy Poehler played him in a *Project Runway* parody called "Fierce: The Hot Mess Makeover Show" on *Saturday Night Live*, while

Siriano, as a guest star on the sitcom *Ugly Betty*, hammed it up playing himself, making his entrance with three dolled-up models, declaring, "The house of Siriano has arrived. Worship me, bitches!"

Siriano's fame emanated from his mass-market relatability—that was out of reach to new designers too bland or anonymous to be well known. Siriano's sparkling persona gained instant traction. "He's a WASPish gay with a witty one-liner who can also design and get on TV," as one fashion insider sized him up to me. Siriano became catnip to sponsors who chased the up-and-comer—allowing him to amass capital to underwrite his fledgling fashion house. Starbucks paid Siriano to appear on a limited-edition gift card, and he even did a line of fashionable kitchen sponges—think leopard print—for O-Cel-O, which featured him in a "Clean with Style" sweepstakes in 2010.

At the same time, Payless ShoeSource came calling, knowing that its mainstream shoppers would rush in to meet the celebrity designer—which they did. Christian Siriano for Payless succeeded because it delivered a lot of bang for the buck, with embellished pumps and trendy booties priced from about $34.99 to $39.99. As sales surged, Payless added stylish $29.99 faux-leather Christian Siriano handbags.

Siriano—the one-season wunderkind of *Project Runway*—stuck in the hearts and minds of his fans well beyond the end of his TV run. In 2012, Siriano launched his own line of wedding gowns exclusively for Nordstrom. His annual business in 2013 was believed to be in the low millions—too early to declare victory but absolutely holding his own, which was more than could be said for many fledgling designers who'd been in business a lot longer and were still anonymous.

Transcending the Tadpoles

Traditionally, freshly minted young designers would have been thrilled to settle for a lowly assistant position with established houses like Oscar de la Renta or Marc Jacobs. But nowadays, more graduates were ready to strike out on their own, confident that they were ready and had something new to say—and could somehow get themselves noticed.

It always astounded me how many starry-eyed young designers truly believed that they were entitled to have a successful fashion career—with their name on the label and their own boutiques, despite the realities of the marketplace.

Dress-Down Nation continued to dampen the demand for expensive dress-up clothes—which was the very niche new designers counted on for establishing their reputations and connecting with women. Sure, there would be a few, like Jason Wu and Proenza Schouler, who could push through into the elite level of fancy clothes on the basis of obvious talent and the ability to find solid financial backing as they built their following. But most new fashion businesses are upended in their first five years—simply because they can't weather that steep incline: the money-losing start-up stretch that can extend for years and years of anonymity, leaving the shoppers they want to reach unaware that they even exist. And even those who manage to tough it out, scraping together the resources to throw seasonal runway shows and picking up piecemeal, here-and-there retail orders that they are often forced to sell on consignment, most would remain inconsequential tadpoles flailing around, barely making ripples in a big pond.

Today's retail turf was unlike anything Calvin Klein and Ralph Lauren faced in the early 1970s, when their priority was selling to American department stores like Saks Fifth Avenue, Neiman Marcus, Macy's, and Bloomingdale's—who were then the retail locomotives that fueled the greater industry. Back then, before fast-fashion knockoffs blanketed the malls and the Internet, designers could actually claim ownership of their original ideas, the innovations that gave them an identifiable signature and won them exposure at retail, cementing the designer in the minds of shoppers. The tail end of the era of designers being able to claim ownership of a particular style happened in the early 1990s, when Calvin Klein introduced bias-cut slip dresses, establishing an infectious trend that Klein managed to own for a moment—a solid season, maybe—before slip dresses became a runaway fad, with cheaper versions engulfing every retail floor, from Macy's to Walmart.

When's the last time I've been able to attach a trend or silhouette to a particular designer? It's hard to say because designer originators are being drowned by a tsunami of knockoffs from the fast-fashion chains almost the moment the originals hit the runway—just one more impediment to keep designers from making their mark. Zara—the world's biggest apparel brand—can create a new style from scratch, manufacture it, and ship it to thousands of its Zara shops around the world in about sixteen days—compared to slowpoke conventional designers, who show their fall collections on the runway in February and start delivering those goods to stores in mid-July, at the earliest. Today's multibillion-dollar fashion circus is a lightning-fast, high-stakes game played on multiple platforms across the global marketplace, a 3-D chessboard where the competition is fiercer and more dauntingly complex than ever.

The Angel Wears Prada

It was against that intimidating backdrop, in 2003, that the CFDA/Vogue Fashion Fund was born—an initiative started by the prestigious fashion designers' trade group and *Vogue* to help develop the next generation of creative talents for American fashion despite the market headwinds raging against them.

No less than *Vogue* editrix Anna Wintour has enthusiastically put her weight behind the effort, which awarded generous working capital grants—up to $300,000 for the winner and $100,000 for two finalists—as well as a year's worth of free counseling from some of the industry's most experienced executives. "They are at a point in their career where they are getting attention," Wintour said of the annual winners when the award was initiated. "They need business advice."

Given the strides that a decade's worth of winners have made so far, "you will agree that we've done that," she said, noting names such as Proenza Schouler, Rag and Bone, Thom Browne, and Derek Lam, among others—all of whom have had a measure of financial as well as critical success.

But even the fashion purists behind industry awards can't deny the missing element from this design-first orientation. As Wintour admitted to me: "At the same time, part of today's success—and this is part of what we think about when we are voting for the winners—do they have the personality? Do they understand how they can use social media, how they can use television, how they can deal with the press to promote their talent and also themselves?"

In other words, can they become celebrities?

"Today's designers coming up . . . [self-promotion] comes natural to them," Wintour said. "We don't have to tell them they need to use social media or they need to be comfortable with the press. That's how they are. This is today's way of communicating. There are some who are better than others, and that has to do with their own personalities.

"You look at people like, say, Karl Lagerfeld, who certainly comes from a different generation, but he has brilliantly understood how important it is to have credible talent today but also be comfortable with being a public persona. There are those who are deeply talented, like Narciso [Rodriguez], but they just don't want to play in the public arena, and I'm not saying that is wrong, it's just there's a level that they are going to just stop at. They won't be able to rise any further because: A) they don't have the money [corporate financing behind them] and B) they don't have the kind of public persona or personality."

The career of Rodriguez began with a major celebrity moment: He designed the distinctive bias-cut gown that his friend Carolyn Bessette wore for her wedding to John F. Kennedy Jr. in 1996. Rodriguez also worked under corporate umbrellas for LVMH (as the women's designer for Loewe leather goods), and for Liz Claiborne Inc. from 2007 to 2009, when it controlled the Narciso Rodriguez brand and became its financial backer. But alas, Narciso—shy and stubbornly independent—never had the temperament for thrusting himself into the spotlight—which he disdains. "It feels like fashion has become about branding and being famous," he told *New York* magazine in 2013, with an air of resignation. His ideal fashion house wasn't necessarily big—but always independent, exquisite, and profitable, like Azzedine Alaia, the beloved luxury designer based in Paris, a nonconformist who played by his own rules.

So while Rodriguez would turn out one-time, mass-market capsule collections for Kohl's and eBay, he would have to count on his existing fans—especially his celebrity mascots like First Lady Michelle Obama, Julianna Margulies, and Claire Danes—to keep him on the radar. "I'm not interested in how things are packaged or branded, or more about the styling than the design of the product itself," he told *New York.*

It makes you wonder, with all the talented designers all over the map, which ones will manage to translate into today's real world, where the opportunities for creative designers to break through to the big-time—always limited to begin with—are even smaller. The world has changed so much—and Dress-Down Nation ain't going away.

It's not just that the marketplace is more crowded than ever. It's also more chaotic. Blame a lot of that on women's increasingly idiosyncratic fashion habits, which have thrown a wrench into the system. Beginning with the 1980s designer boom, the likes of Yves Saint Laurent, Chanel, and Christian Dior built empires by winning over women who remained loyal to their labels, conditioned to buying across the price spectrum from casual to dressier ensembles, shoes, and handbags—not to mention designer perfumes.

Fashion houses built themselves into mega-brands by collecting millions of aspirational customers who would buy in at moderate price points, then over the years, trade up among their tiered labels—often color coded—such as Ralph Lauren's blue label, black label, and top-drawer purple label.

But now, as celebrity noise in the marketplace drowns out designers, formidable competition from fast-fashion multibillion-dollar brands Zara, H&M, Forever 21, Topshop, and Uniqlo steals all the oxygen. Together, these giants successfully appeal to women and men who want to look stylish as cheaply as they can get away with. Such marketers deliver real fashion designed to fit in everybody's budgets. Which means that the resourceful $40,000-a-year teacher with a knack for fashion can easily be up-to-the-moment chic without dressing in expensive, head-to-toe designer looks.

Finding the Edge

Even affluent customers have gone rogue—as they proudly proclaim that they prefer to dress in a wide patchwork of brands, with a smattering of J.Crew and fast-fashion brands mixed in. The bragging rights now go to the well-dressed woman who is such a confident individualist that she invents her own original style by cherry-picking the best components across the wide world of fashion retailing. And she's no longer the exception. There's a wide swath of spiffy dressers out there—not just on the streets of Paris or Manhattan, but in cities everywhere, as evidenced from all the candid pictures on YouTube, Instagram, and the hundreds of style sites like TheSartorialist.com and KeepItChic.com.

This is the steep, slippery slope that new designers must contend with, making it harder for them to get noticed, harder to stand out, and harder to break away from the pack when they do. It makes it all the more important for designers to have an edge that has nothing to do with fashion, an edge that raises their premium high above the din.

And like it or not, that edge is celebrity.

It's a self-reinforcing pattern. Celebrities crowding into fashion make it harder to get noticed, and the fact that it's harder to get noticed makes using celebrities all that much more necessary.

As Anna Wintour pointed out, this doesn't mean that traditional designers are obsolete. Phoebe Philo, the celebrated minimalist designer at Céline, is an admirable exception—a working mom who carried herself far below the radar as she climbed through the design ranks in a traditional way, yet manages to make tidal waves in fashion and at retail—backed all the way by her mighty LVMH corporate parent.

Still, it does mean that more fashion designers will have to embrace the new glittery reality if they want to make it to the top. As Michael Kors, Karl Lagerfeld, and Tom Ford have illustrated, designers who turn themselves into celebrities can become just as relatable to consumers as movie stars.

A Ford in Our Future

Tom Ford, the handsome, talented, and self-possessed fashion designer, has experienced a dream career that few will ever know. Born in Austin, Texas, in 1961, Ford moved to New York after high school—where he acted in TV commercials and studied architecture and fashion at Parsons School of Design. After graduation, he spent the next four years as a design assistant on Seventh Avenue for women's-wear designer Cathy Hardwick and then at the celebrated sportswear house Perry Ellis, under Marc Jacobs, when he was head designer in the late 1980s. Ford relocated to Milan in 1990 to take on a challenge that nobody wanted: chief women's designer at Gucci—a storied, has-been brand that was undergoing a dubious turnaround.

Gucci proved to be a high-risk, high-reward gamble that paid off. By 1992, Ford had become Gucci's design director—overseeing all its products and the design of its stores, when the reborn Gucci label was heating up again. During his fourteen-year reign at Gucci, Ford personified Gucci's sex appeal—recasting the Italian brand once prized for its GG-logoed men's loafers in his own image as it became known as Tom Ford for Gucci, featuring sexy, colorful fashions worn by stars like Madonna, Gwyneth Paltrow, and Mary J. Blige. Every jaded fashion journalist melted under the hot star-wattage of the affable dreamboat designer who was Tom Ford. I loved arriving to that surprise inside my hotel room in Milan for Fashion Week. There would be a small crystal vase of white roses and a handwritten card on Gucci stationery: "Teri, Welcome to Milan! Tom."

Ford and Gucci Group CEO Domenico De Sole became legendary as high fashion's dynamic duo who together led the makeover of Gucci. Their success became the cornerstone of Gucci Group, the publicly traded luxury fashion empire they built by acquiring brands such as Yves Saint Laurent, Bottega Veneta, Alexander McQueen, and Stella McCartney (who Ford personally championed).

In fact, it was Gucci's initial public offering in 1995 that began the practice of attaching the word "luxury" to practically every upscale fashion brand. Gucci Group's annual revenues soared into the billions, but Ford would eventually lock horns with PPR, the French holding company that took control of Gucci Group in 2002. PPR vetoed Ford's expanded duties as creative director at Yves Saint Laurent—allowing him only to continue his longtime leadership of the Gucci brand. Ford and De Sole both resigned abruptly in 2004. Amid a shower of confetti, Ford took his final runway bow at Gucci in Milan, in an emotional farewell.

Such a high-stakes corporate tantrum might have been catastrophic for a designer of lesser public persona. But because of the power of Ford's burgeoning celebrity, he could walk away proud and unsullied, confident that Gucci wouldn't be his last stand on fashion's big stage. The fact remained that Tom Ford was not only a talented designer and creative marketer, he was also a bona fide, megawatt celebrity—with a stature to rival the GG trademark itself.

We fashion insiders never doubted for a moment that there would be another Ford in our future. Meanwhile, the intrepid designer fearlessly took a detour to make his mark in the movie business first—and then got busy kicking some butts across the established luxury fashion players in business.

Designer Tom Ford (right), director of *A Single Man*, with the film's leading man, Colin Firth (left), at the 2010 Golden Globe Awards.

During his hiatus from the runways, Ford did what he knew best: He polished his personal brand to a high gloss, starting with his oversize, 416-page, ten-pound, $89, slipcovered, Tom Ford coffee table book chronicling his years at Gucci, which became a collector's item. Then, as guest art director at *Vanity Fair* for a single issue in April 2006, he put himself on the most memorable *VF* cover of the year: There he was in a tuxedo in his best Bond-ian pose, leaning between two naked movie stars, Keira Knightley and Scarlett Johansson.

And to most everyone's surprise, in 2009, Tom Ford, rookie director and co-screenwriter, nailed it. He conquered Hollywood in his stylish debut movie, *A Single Man*, starring Colin Firth—who won a Golden Globe for his role and an Oscar nomination—and Julianne Moore.

For a designer icon with a Q rating any Hollywood A-lister would envy, a fashion comeback was a cinch. Ford took no time at all to catapult himself back into the Gucci leagues, with the introduction of Tom Ford menswear in 2006 and then women's wear in 2009. He proved luxury and eye-popping prices could still be done, making high-end deluxe cool: men's suits from $3,700 to around $7,100, $400 sunglasses, and $150 fragrances.

He wore his own sharp tailoring as splendidly as did all Hollywood's leading men: Firth, Brad Pitt, Justin Timberlake, and Daniel Craig in his role as James Bond. Jay Z, who has a closetful of Tom Ford suits, "name-checked" Tom Ford in many rap lyrics and even wrote a song titled "Tom Ford" in 2013.

"Who would not be flattered to have an entire Jay Z track named after them?" Ford asked *WWD*. "I mean, come on, it's pretty rare that something like that happens. . . . It's a kind of validation of one's work, as it means that one has really penetrated and made an impact on popular culture."

Ford epitomized the celebrity designer whose clothes were worn by celebrities—drawing millions to his eighty-one Tom Ford stores around the world, all before the brand turned ten years old.

Ford has no hesitation in attributing his success to his high visibility. "What I do publicly is a performance. It's part of my job, and I'm good at it," he said. "We have customers—a lot of them—who spend more than a million dollars a year with us because they come in and just order: suit, suit, suit, suit, suit, suit," he continued, snapping his fingers, to *The Wall Street Journal* in 2013.

The Music of the Stars—John Varvatos

A Tom Ford comes along only once in a generation. But there would be other designers who instinctively cracked the code of celebrity and made it work for them, as well. Like menswear designer John Varvatos.

Born in 1954 in Detroit, John Varvatos was steeped in rock-and-roll bands and the music of Motown—he went to all the concerts and club gigs. Starting in high school, "I really wanted to look cool, so I was always trying to dress like a rock star," he recalled to *New York* magazine. So it was beat-up leather jackets, weathered jeans, boots, T-shirts, and downtown swagger. He took the time to master the look of effortless chic—what the Italians call *sprezzatura*—which depends so much on the knack of the wearer to mix unexpected patterns and colors together in a mélange that can range from quirky to elegant, to sensational effect.

Majoring in science and education at Eastern Michigan University, and living off his job at a local menswear boutique, Varvatos got his degree—and veered off into pursuing a fashion career instead. Throughout the 1980s and 1990s he climbed rungs in the men's divisions at America's most notable brands: Ralph Lauren and Calvin Klein. By the time he got around to launching his own label in 2000, he was the consummate insider and inevitably celebrated as America's top menswear designer, winning back-to-back CFDA awards in 2000 and 2001.

The John Varvatos esthetic is without logo or gimmicks: It's the aspirational, grown-up, manly designer label. His customers are affluent guys over thirty who have outgrown Banana Republic and live in sportswear that's a tad rebellious but finely crafted—like a John Varvatos $2,700 double-breasted leather shirt jacket.

Varvatos is good-looking and trim—personifying the grown-up cool of his brand. During my interview with Varvatos at his showroom in July 2012, he was wearing tight jeans with an interesting wrinkled white cotton jacket with articulated elbows and laced-up sleeves. When I asked him about it he explained: "This is from our spring collection. As a designer you get bits of inspiration from a lot of things: jackets from waiters, fencing, and bits of it come from—I hate to say it—from a straitjacket."

The John Varvatos brand possesses a sophisticated, hip identity, which is hard to achieve in the narrow idiom of menswear. And that identity

Print ad from 2013 for John Varvatos menswear, featuring Willie Nelson and his sons.

was cemented by celebrities—namely musicians.

There's an authenticity here that isn't contrived. Varvatos, the rabid music fan, has always been inspired by rock bands—their improvised rhythms, their bodacious insouciance—and he always made music men the heart and soul of his brand. It's not that Iggy Pop, Alice Cooper, Dave Matthews, or even Willie Nelson with his long braids—all of whom have appeared in Varvatos ads—dress the way most regular guys would. There's no need for hard-sell marketing. As music legends, they are powerful and evocative symbols whose association with Varvatos imparts an ineffable quality of cool to his designs.

Varvatos couldn't believe his good luck in 2009 when he learned that a run-down building on the Lower East Side of Manhattan at 315 Bowery was vacant and available for rent. To music aficionados, that real estate was hallowed ground; it was the former location for CBGB—the famed punk-rock club that opened in 1973. Varvatos knew the locale firsthand—he'd made a pilgrimage from Detroit to CBGB in 1979 to see the Ramones in concert.

So he was determined to turn the space into a John Varvatos boutique, despite the fact that it was only ten blocks from his SoHo store, and that the once-seedy Bowery neighborhood hadn't completely gentrified. "There's a lot of history there, and I could feel it," he told me. "This wasn't about marketing or being strategic. It was an organic emotional thing. I'm just a fan of artists."

Varvatos recaptured CBGB on the first Thursday of every month when the Bowery boutique staged free-of-charge jam sessions featuring the likes of Guns N' Roses, Dave Matthews, Ringo Starr, Eric Burdon— even Paul McCartney has shown up to jam on the stage in the store. The Bowery store "has been the biggest game changer in our brand," Varvatos told me. "It satisfied our passion for music and respect for it. We are the go-to brand for jazz or blues or rock. We get these artists who want to be associated with our brand and wear it. At the time of the Grammys, we are besieged with artists who want to wear our clothes, soul, blues, jazz, rock, and pop." And that's drawn even more artists to appear in Varvatos ads. He ticked off more names to me: Lenny Kravitz, Steven Tyler from Aerosmith, Robert Plant and Jimmy Page from Led Zeppelin, The Roots, and Roger Daltrey from The Who. "We've had all these amazing artists in our ads, and we don't pay them any kind of money. They do it as a favor."

Such was the grounding that kept the Varvatos niche profitable—if not growing into the hundreds of millions, progressing steadily and staying relevant. Varvatos was content to let his clothes and his music men do the talking, while he concentrated on designing fashion in his studio. "I never thought when I started my brand that I would ever be the face of it," he told me. "Maybe I was shy about it. I never wanted to—I never gave it a thought."

That was until Varvatos started having his own celebrity moment.

Automaker Chrysler tapped Varvatos—its famous native son in the fashion world—to impart some stylish buzz into its bestselling Chrysler 300 luxury sedan. The campaign began with a 2012 special John Varvatos

Designer John Varvatos with his Chrysler 300C John Varvatos Limited Edition 2012.

limited-edition Chrysler 300: a numbered run of two thousand automobiles that started around $41,000, sold in an online auction. Then a "luxury edition" of the Varvatos Chrysler came out in 2013.

Varvatos was meticulous. He flew several times to Detroit to work closely with the Chrysler design team on every aspect of the car, such as customizing the interiors with metallic-wrapped leather seats and titanium trimming. But his biggest change was structural: lowering the car's chassis by a full three inches to make it sleeker and less bulbous.

On Chrysler's website the headline reads: "John Varvatos returns to the Motor City to remake an icon." Varvatos appeared in the commercials with another Detroit native, his rocker pal Iggy Pop. In one thirty-second spot, a shiny black Varvatos Chrysler is parked in front of his Bowery boutique, where the designer opens the door and lovingly rubs the back of the leather driver's seat. The announcer says:

To perfect every detail, work with a perfectionist who sweats every detail. If you want to refine a luxury car you're proud to put your name on, work with a guy whose name is his reputation. The 300C John Varvatos Limited Edition.

The camera closes as both Varvatos and Iggy Pop—his long hair blowing—enter the car from opposite sides.

After Chrysler, Varvatos got a call from NBC asking him to do *Fashion Star*, a reality competition show that searched for "the next big brand in fashion." NBC had already gotten Jessica Simpson on board and was also speaking with Nicole Richie, who "said she didn't want to do it unless I was," Varvatos recalled.

Initially, he turned *Fashion Star* down—just like he had turned down *Project Runway* at its inception. He was wary of the TV hype: "I was concerned all along about my credibility as a real designer."

But upon further reflection—with other friends in the media and business reminding him of the power that his own celebrity could garner for his brand—he finally said yes. After the first season of *Fashion Star*, he felt that "the show needed improvement." Even so, he couldn't help but notice the impact in name recognition and brand awareness: "Our website traffic was up eighty percent." He signed up for the second season, convinced that turning himself into a celebrity was a win-win.

"Listen, the world has changed," he told me. "I really thought that those [fashion] insider people would think it was cheesy. . . . They put it to me this way: 'You came off very funny, really credible on the show, and that's all you need to think about.'"

The most measurable impact on the Varvatos brand after the first season was boosting sales of John Varvatos fragrance at stores like Macy's, he said. The overall brand awareness came at a key time—when Varvatos was opening its first store in London, as well as other stores across America.

"The big question is, is there a payoff for all of this? Brand awareness and monetizing it are two different things," he said. Varvatos is aware that the cachet of his brand—which has estimated sales of more than $100 million a year—comes from its limited distribution. "We aren't looking to do a collection for Macy's. Our strategy is to stay the course, with twenty to twenty-five stores. But what I love about it [the celebrity factor—his and the famous music men's] is that if we try to do something bigger at another time, the brand awareness is always there."

The Common Good

Varvatos was an establishment designer whose validation by fashion's inner circle could take him only so far in the twenty-first century. The way for him to stand out had been through his celebrity associations, first with the famous rockers, then with Chrysler, and then his own reality-show TV branding. Each phase increasingly forced him into the mass marketplace, where a high profile would allow him to stay on the radar and not be engulfed by more commercial brands like Calvin Klein and Giorgio Armani—all of whom had their own athletes and movie-star surrogates to keep them in full view.

For designers of women's apparel, the biggest squeeze of late has come from the mega-market punch of fast-fashion brands along with the noise created by mass-marketed women's celebrity brands (Jessica Simpson, Selena Gomez, Lauren Conrad, Nicole Richie, Jennifer Lopez, and the Kardashians, at Macy's, Kohl's, and Kmart) that collectively have made business far more difficult for any contemporary women's designers trying to make a breakthrough into the greater mainstream. Together they've thwarted the opportunities for a new high-end fashion design business to create a cash cow cushion of lower-priced mainstream basics the way Ralph Lauren did with his polo shirts and khakis.

But celebrity—like fast fashion—has been a powerful force that has changed the landscape in ways that are new but not necessarily bad.

Celebrities as billboards for fashion have a long history and a potency that is here to stay. As Anna Wintour notes, "I think some of the celebrities wearing [designer] clothes have been good for fashion. . . . I think that anything that raises the profile of fashion is wonderful . . . on the red carpets all over the world, whether it is the Met [the annual gala hosted by the Costume Institute at the Metropolitan Museum of Art] or the Oscars or whatever, it maybe helps all of us."

And celebrities who jump into the ring as designers—partnering with experienced manufacturers as Jessica Simpson did, or seriously tackling fashion design the way the Olsen sisters and Victoria Beckham have—are showing how the best creators of fashion at every level can win. Says Wintour, "Even if you are looking at Target, they are going after really good designers [Missoni, Phillip Lim, Jason Wu, Prabal Gurung, Proenza

Schouler] to make their collections. They're not going after the desperate housewives of Alabama or bad fashion just because they are celebrities. They are going after the really good brand names, and that I applaud. The more we can bring good fashion at whatever price point, that is fabulous."

Thus marks the further democratization of fashion—in a world where elite consumers are buying fewer expensive clothes than they have in the past, and middle-class people now enjoy unprecedented access to get a taste of high fashion at affordable prices. The fashion playing field, while still uneven at the ultra-luxury end, has nonetheless become dramatically flatter.

Designers' zeal to compete with celebrities and build their own name recognition has forced them into doing capsule collections for Target and H&M—spreading little pieces of their genius around retail. The net result: More people get to have a piece of real fashion than ever before.

And how can that possibly not be a good thing?

Appendix

Selected List of Celebrity Fashion Lines

Celebrity	Fashion Line
50 Cent	G-Unit Clothing
Adam Levine	Adam Levine (Kmart)
Alexa Chung	Alexa Chung for Madewell
Alyssa Milano	Alyssa Milano
Amelia Earhart	Amelia Earhart Fashions
André 3000	Benjamin Bixby
Arnold Palmer	Arnold Palmer
Avril Lavigne	Abbey Dawn
Beyoncé and Tina Knowles	House of Deréon
Bono and Ali Hewson	EDUN
Carl Banks	Carl Banks
Carlos Santana	Carlos by Carlos Santana
Carson Kressley	PERFECT by Carson Kressley

Celebrity	Fashion Line
Chloë Sevigny	Chloë Sevigny for Opening Ceremony
Chris Kirkpatrick	FuMan Skeeto
Daisy Fuentes	daisy fuentes (Kohl's)
David Beckham	David Beckham Bodywear (H&M)
David Hasselhoff	Malibu Dave
Donald Trump	Donald J. Trump for Men (Macy's)
Elizabeth Hurley	Beach
Elle Macpherson	Elle Macpherson Intimates
Erin Wasson	Erin Wasson x RVCA
Eve	Fetish by Eve
Fat Joe	FJ560
Giuliana Rancic	G by Giuliana Rancic (HSN)
Greta Garbo	The Greta Garbo Collection (Nordstrom)
Gwen Stefani	Harajuku Lovers
Gwen Stefani	Harajuku Mini (Target)
Gwen Stefani	L.A.M.B.
Heidi Montag	Heidi Montag
Helena Bonham Carter	Pantaloonies
Hilary Duff	Stuff by Hilary Duff
Iman	IMAN (HSN)
Ivanka Trump	Ivanka Trump
Jack Nicklaus	Jack Nicklaus (JCPenney)
Jaclyn Smith	Jaclyn Smith (Kmart)
Jay Z and Damon Dash	Rocawear
Jenni "JWOWW" Farley	Filthy Couture
Jennifer Hudson	Jennifer Hudson Collection (QVC)
Jennifer Lopez	Jennifer Lopez (Kohl's)
Jennifer Lopez	J.Lo by Jennifer Lopez

Celebrity	Fashion Line
Jennifer Lopez	JustSweet
Jennifer Lopez	Sweetface
Jessica Simpson	Jessica Simpson
Joan Rivers	Joan Rivers (QVC)
John Cena	Never Give Up by John Cena (Kmart)
Johnny Carson	Johnny Carson Apparel
Justin Timberlake and Trace Ayala	William Rast
Kanye West	Kanye West
Kanye West	A.P.C. Kanye
Kate Moss	Kate Moss for Topshop
Katherine Heigl	The Katherine Heigl Collection (scrubs for Peaches Uniforms)
Kathie Lee Gifford	Kathie Lee Gifford (Walmart)
Katie Holmes and Jeanne Yang	Holmes & Yang
Kim Gordon and Daisy von Furth	X-Girl
Kimora Lee Simmons	Baby Phat
Kimora Lee Simmons	KLS by Kimora Lee Simmons
Kourtney, Kim, and Khloé Kardashian	K-DASH by Kardashian (QVC)
Kourtney, Kim, and Khloé Kardashian	The Kardashian Kollection (Sears)
Kourtney, Kim, and Khloé Kardashian	Kardashian by Bebe
Kris Jenner	Kris Jenner Kollection (QVC)
Lamar Odom	Rich Soil
Lance Armstrong	Livestrong (Nike)
Lauren Conrad	LC Lauren Conrad (Kohl's)
Liam Gallagher	Pretty Green
Lil' Romeo and Master P	No Limit Clothing
Lindsay Lohan	Emanuel Ungaro (Creative Director)
Lindsay Lohan and Kristi Kaylor	6126
LL Cool J	Todd Smith collection (Sears)

Celebrity	Fashion Line
Madonna	Material Girl (Macy's)
Mandy Moore	Mblem
Marc Anthony	Marc Anthony (Kohl's)
Maria Sharapova	Maria Sharapova for Cole Haan
Mario Lopez	MALO by Mario Lopez (Kmart)
Mary-Kate and Ashley Olsen	Elizabeth and James
Mary-Kate and Ashley Olsen	Olsenboye (JCPenney)
Mary-Kate and Ashley Olsen	The Row
Matthew McConaughey	JKL
Michael Jordan	Jordan (Nike)
Miley Cyrus	Miley Cyrus & Max Azria (Walmart)
Milla Jovovich and Carmen Hawk	Jovovich-Hawk
Natalie Portman	Natalie Portman for Te Casan
Nelly	Apple Bottoms
Nelly	Vokal
Nicki Minaj	Nicki Minaj Collection (Kmart)
Nicole Richie	House of Harlow 1960
Nicole Richie	The Nicole Richie Collection (QVC)
Nicole Richie	Winter Kate
Paris Hilton	Dollhouse
Penélope and Mónica Cruz	L'Agent by Agent Provocateur
Pharrell Williams and Nigo	Billionaire Boys Club
Pharrell Williams and Nigo	ICECREAM
Queen Latifah	Queen Collection (HSN)
Rachel Bilson	Edie Rose for DKNY
Rachel Zoe	Rachel Zoe
Rachel Zoe	Luxe Rachel Zoe (QVC)
Reba McEntire	Reba (Dillard's)

Celebrity	Fashion Line
Regis Philbin	Regis by Van Heusen
Rihanna	Rihanna for River Island
Russell Simmons	Phat Farm
Russell Simmons	Russell Simmons Argyleculture
Ryan Seacrest	Ryan Seacrest Distinction (Macy's)
Sarah Jessica Parker	Bitten (Steve & Barry's)
Sarah Jessica Parker	Halston Heritage (president)
Savannah and Sienna Miller	Twenty8Twelve
Sean Combs	Sean John
Selena Gomez	Dream Out Loud (Kmart)
Serena Williams	Aneres
Serena Williams	Serena Williams Signature Statement Collection (HSN)
Shaquille O'Neal	Shaquille O'Neal (Macy's)
Snoop Dogg	Rich and Infamous
Sofía Vergara	Sofia by Sofía Vergara (Kmart)
Star Jones	Status by Star Jones (QVC)
Steve Harvey	Steve Harvey
Thalia Sodi	Thalia Sodi Collection (Kmart)
The Game	The Frank Pace Collection
Mike "The Situation" Sorrentino	DILLIGAF
Tina Knowles	Miss Tina
Tony Hawk	Tony Hawk (Kohl's)
Twiggy	Twiggy London (HSN)
Venus Williams	EleVen (Steve & Barry's)
Victoria Beckham	Victoria Beckham
Victoria Beckham	dVb Jeans
Will.i.am	i.am Clothing
Yoko Ono	Yoko Ono Fashions for Men (Opening Ceremony)

Selected List of Celebrity Fragrances

Celebrity	Scent	Year
50 Cent	Power by 50 Cent for Men	2009
Adam Levine	Adam Levine for Men	2013
Adam Levine	Adam Levine for Women	2013
Alan Cumming	Cumming	2004
Alan Cumming	2nd (Alan) Cumming	2011
Amanda Lepore	Amanda	2009
Antonio Banderas	Diavolo for Men	1997
Antonio Banderas	Mediterráneo for Men	2001
Antonio Banderas	Spirit for Men	2004
Antonio Banderas	Spirit for Women	2005
Antonio Banderas	Antonio for Men	2006
Antonio Banderas	Blue Seduction for Men	2007
Antonio Banderas	Blue Seduction for Women	2008
Antonio Banderas	Seduction in Black for Men	2009
Antonio Banderas	The Secret for Men	2010
Antonio Banderas	The Golden Secret for Men	2011
Antonio Banderas	Her Secret for Women	2012
Antonio Banderas	Her Golden Secret for Women	2013
Avril Lavigne	Black Star	2009
Avril Lavigne	Forbidden Rose	2010
Avril Lavigne	Wild Rose	2011
Beyoncé	Heat	2010
Beyoncé	Heat Rush	2010
Beyoncé	Heat Ultimate Elixir	2010
Beyoncé	Pulse	2011
Beyoncé	Pulse Summer Edition	2012

Celebrity	Scent	Year
Beyoncé	Midnight Heat	2012
Beyoncé	Pulse NYC	2013
Beyoncé	Heat The Mrs. Carter Show World Tour Limited Edition	2013
Beyoncé	Rise	2014
Billy Dee Williams	Avon Undeniable	1990
Bret Michaels	Roses & Thorns	2014
Britney Spears	Curious	2004
Britney Spears	Fantasy	2005
Britney Spears	In Control Curious	2006
Britney Spears	Midnight Fantasy	2007
Britney Spears	Believe	2007
Britney Spears	Curious Heart	2008
Britney Spears	Hidden Fantasy	2009
Britney Spears	Circus Fantasy	2009
Britney Spears	Radiance	2010
Britney Spears	Cosmic Radiance	2011
Britney Spears	Fantasy Twist	2012
Britney Spears	Island Fantasy	2013
Britney Spears	Fantasy Anniversary Edition	2013
Britney Spears	Fantasy The Naughty Remix	2014
Britney Spears	Fantasy The Nice Remix	2014
Bruce Willis	Bruce Willis Eau de Parfum	2010
Bruce Willis	Bruce Willis Personal Edition	2014
Carmen Electra	Carmen Electra	2007
Carlos Santana	Carlos Santana for Men	2005
Carlos Santana	Carlos Santana for Women	2005
Catherine Deneuve	Deneuve	1986

Celebrity	Scent	Year
Céline Dion	Céline Dion	2003
Céline Dion	Notes	2004
Céline Dion	Belong	2005
Céline Dion	Always Belong	2006
Céline Dion	Enchanting	2006
Céline Dion	Paris Nights	2007
Céline Dion	Spring in Paris	2007
Céline Dion	Sensational	2008
Céline Dion	Sensational Moment	2008
Céline Dion	Spring in Provence	2009
Céline Dion	Chic	2009
Céline Dion	Simply Chic	2010
Céline Dion	Pure Brilliance	2010
Céline Dion	Signature	2011
Céline Dion	Sensational Luxe Blossom	2013
Cher	Uninhibited	1987
Cher Lloyd	Pink Diamond	2012
Christina Aguilera	Christina Aguilera	2007
Christina Aguilera	Inspire	2008
Christina Aguilera	By Night	2009
Christina Aguilera	Royal Desire	2010
Christina Aguilera	Secret Potion	2011
Christina Aguilera	Red Sin	2012
Christina Aguilera	Unforgettable	2013
Cindy Crawford	Cindy Crawford	2002
Cindy Crawford	Waterfalls	2005
Cindy Crawford	Summer Day	2006
Daddy Yankee	Daddy Yankee for Men	2008

Celebrity	Scent	Year
Daddy Yankee	Dyamante	2010
Daisy Fuentes	Dianoche	2006
Daisy Fuentes	So Luxurious	2007
Daisy Fuentes	Dianoche Ocean	2008
Daisy Fuentes	Dianoche Love	2009
Daisy Fuentes	Dianoche Passion	2010
Daisy Fuentes	Mysterio	2011
Danielle Steel	Danielle	2006
David Beckham	Instinct	2005
David Beckham	Intimately Beckham Women	2006
David Beckham	Intimately Beckham Men	2006
David Beckham	Intimately Beckham Night Women	2007
David Beckham	Intimately Beckham Night Men	2007
David Beckham	Intense Instinct	2007
David Beckham	Instinct After Dark	2008
David Beckham	Signature Women	2008
David Beckham	Signature Men	2008
David Beckham	Signature Women	2009
David Beckham	Signature Men	2009
David Beckham	Pure Instinct	2009
David Beckham	Instinct Ice	2010
David Beckham	Homme	2011
David Beckham	The Essence	2012
David Beckham	Instinct Sport	2012
David Beckham	Urban Homme	2013
David Beckham	Classic	2013
David Beckham	Classic Summer	2014
Denise Richards	Denise Richards	2012

Celebrity	Scent	Year
Derek Jeter	Avon Driven	2006
Dionne Warwick	Dionne	1986
Dita Von Teese	Dita Von Teese	2011
Dita Von Teese	Rouge	2012
Dita Von Teese	Erotique	2013
Dita Von Teese	FleurTeese	2013
Donald Trump	Donald Trump The Fragrance	2004
Donald Trump	Success	2012
Elizabeth Taylor	Passion	1987
Elizabeth Taylor	Passion for Men	1989
Elizabeth Taylor	White Diamonds	1991
Elizabeth Taylor	Diamonds and Emeralds	1993
Elizabeth Taylor	Diamonds and Rubies	1993
Elizabeth Taylor	Diamonds and Sapphires	1993
Elizabeth Taylor	Black Pearls	1996
Elizabeth Taylor	Forever Elizabeth	2002
Elizabeth Taylor	Gardenia	2003
Elizabeth Taylor	Violet Eyes	2010
Elizabeth Taylor	White Diamonds Lustre	2014
Elvis Presley	Teddy Bear	1957
Eva Longoria	Eva	2010
Eva Longoria	EVAmour	2012
Faith Hill	Faith Hill	2009
Faith Hill	True	2010
Faith Hill	Soul2Soul	2012
Faith Hill	Soul2Soul Vintage	2013
Fergie	Avon Outspoken	2010
Fergie	Avon Outspoken Intense	2011

Celebrity	Scent	Year
Fergie	Viva by Fergie for Avon	2012
Gabriela Sabatini	Gabriela Sabatini	1989
Gabriela Sabatini	Magnetic	1992
Gabriela Sabatini	Bolero	1997
Giorgio	Giorgio Beverly Hills	1981
Gloria Vanderbilt	Vanderbilt	1982
Gwen Stefani	L.A.M.B.	2007
Gwen Stefani (Harajuku Lovers)	Harajuku Lovers Baby	2008
Gwen Stefani (Harajuku Lovers)	Harajuku Lovers G	2008
Gwen Stefani (Harajuku Lovers)	Harajuku Lovers Lil' Angel	2008
Gwen Stefani (Harajuku Lovers)	Harajuku Lovers Love	2008
Gwen Stefani (Harajuku Lovers)	Harajuku Lovers Music	2008
Halle Berry	Halle	2009
Halle Berry	Pure Orchid	2010
Halle Berry	Reveal	2010
Halle Berry	Reveal The Passion	2011
Halle Berry	Closer	2012
Halle Berry	Exotic Jasmine	2013
Heidi Klum	Shine	2011
Heidi Klum	Shine Rose	2012
Heidi Klum	Surprise	2013
Herb Alpert	Listen	1989
Hilary Duff	With Love . . . Hilary Duff	2006
Ivanka Trump	Ivanka Trump	2012
Jack Black	Jack Black Signature Silver Mark	2001
Jack Black	Jack Black Signature Black Mark	2005

Celebrity	Scent	Year
Jack Black	Jack Black Signature Blue Mark	2005
Jack Black	JB	2010
Jaclyn Smith	California	1989
Jay Z	Gold	2013
Jenna Jameson	Heartbreaker by Jenna	2009
Jenni "JWOWW" Farley	JWOWW	2011
Jennifer Aniston	Lolavie	2010
Jennifer Lopez	Glow by J.Lo	2002
Jennifer Lopez	Still	2003
Jennifer Lopez	Live	2005
Jennifer Lopez	Live Luxe	2006
Jennifer Lopez	Live Platinum	2008
Jennifer Lopez	Deseo	2008
Jennifer Lopez	Blue Glow by J.Lo	2010
Jennifer Lopez	L.A. Glow	2010
Jennifer Lopez	Love and Glamour	2010
Jennifer Lopez	Love and Light	2011
Jennifer Lopez	Glowing by J.Lo	2012
Jennifer Lopez	Rio Glow by J.Lo	2013
Jennifer Lopez	Forever Glowing by J.Lo	2013
Jennifer Lopez	JLove	2013
Jesse McCartney	Wanted	2011
Jessica Simpson	Fancy	2008
Jessica Simpson	Fancy Love	2009
Jessica Simpson	Fancy Nights	2010
Jessica Simpson	I Fancy You	2011
Jessica Simpson	Vintage Bloom	2012

Celebrity	Scent	Year
Joan Collins	Spectacular	1989
Joan Rivers	Joan Rivers Now & Forever Private Reserve	2013
Jon Bon Jovi	Avon Unplugged	2012
Jordin Sparks	Because of You	2010
Jordin Sparks	Ambition	2012
Julio Iglesias	Only	1989
Julio Iglesias	Only Crazy	1994
Justin Bieber	Someday	2011
Justin Bieber	Someday Limited Edition	2012
Justin Bieber	Girlfriend	2012
Justin Bieber	Someday Summer Edition	2013
Justin Bieber	The Key	2013
Justin Bieber	Next Girlfriend	2014
Karolina Kurkova	Karolina Kurkova	2013
Kat Von D	Saint	2009
Kat Von D	Sinner	2009
Kat Von D	Adora	2010
Kat Von D	Poetica	2011
Kate Moss	Kate Moss	2007
Kate Moss	Vintage	2009
Kate Moss	Vintage Muse	2010
Kate Moss	Lilabelle	2011
Kate Walsh	Boyfriend	2010
Kate Walsh	Billionaire Boyfriend	2012
Katy Perry	Purr	2010
Katy Perry	Meow	2011
Katy Perry	Killer Queen	2013

Celebrity	Scent	Year
Katy Perry	Killer Queen Oh So Sheer	2014
Keith Urban	Phoenix	2011
Khloé and Lamar	Unbreakable	2011
Khloé and Lamar	Unbreakable Joy	2012
Khloé and Lamar	Unbreakable Love	2013
Kim Kardashian	Kim Kardashian	2009
Kim Kardashian	Gold	2011
Kim Kardashian	Love	2011
Kim Kardashian	True Reflection	2012
Kim Kardashian	Glam	2012
Kim Kardashian	Pure Honey	2013
Kylie Minogue	Darling	2006
Kylie Minogue	Inverse for Men	2009
Kylie Minogue	Pink Sparkle	2010
Kylie Minogue	Dazzling Darling	2011
Kylie Minogue	Music Box	2012
Lady Gaga	Fame	2012
Luciano Pavarotti	Luciano Pavarotti for Men	1994
Luciano Pavarotti	Pavarotti Donna	1995
Madonna	Truth or Dare	2012
Madonna	Truth or Dare Naked	2012
Manny Pacquiao	MP8 Scent of the Champion for Men	2011
Maria Sharapova	Maria Sharapova	2005
Mariah Carey	M	2007
Mariah Carey	Luscious Pink	2008
Mariah Carey	Forever	2009
Mariah Carey	M Ultra Pink	2009

Celebrity	Scent	Year
Mariah Carey	Lollipop Bling Ribbon	2010
Mariah Carey	Lollipop Bling Honey	2010
Mariah Carey	Lollipop Bling Mine Again	2010
Mariah Carey	Lollipop Bling That Chick	2011
Mariah Carey	Lollipop Splash Inseparable	2011
Mariah Carey	Lollipop Splash Never Forget You	2011
Mariah Carey	Lollipop Splash Vision of Love	2011
Mariah Carey	Dreams	2013
Mary J. Blige	My Life	2010
Mary J. Blige	My Life Blossom	2011
Mary-Kate and Ashley Olsen (Elizabeth and James)	Elizabeth and James Nirvana White	2013
Mary-Kate and Ashley Olsen (Elizabeth and James)	Elizabeth and James Nirvana Black	2013
Michael Jordan	Michael Jordan	1996
Michael Jordan	Legend	1997
Michael Jordan	23	2005
Michael Jordan	Flight	2011
Mikhail Baryshnikov	Misha	1989
Naomi Campbell	Cat Deluxe	2006
Naomi Campbell	Cat Deluxe at Night	2007
Naomi Campbell	Seductive Elixir	2008
Naomi Campbell	Cat Deluxe with Kisses	2009
Naomi Campbell	Naomi	2010
Naomi Campbell	Wild Pearl	2011
Naomi Campbell	At Night	2012
Naomi Campbell	Queen of Gold	2013

Celebrity	Scent	Year
Nicki Minaj	Pink Friday	2012
Nicki Minaj	Pink Friday Deluxe Edition	2013
Nicki Minaj	Pink Friday Special Edition	2013
Nicki Minaj	Minajesty	2013
Nicole "Snooki" Polizzi	Snooki	2011
Nicole "Snooki" Polizzi	Snooki Couture	2012
Nicole Richie	Nicole	2012
One Direction	Our Moment	2013
One Direction	That Moment	2014
Pamela Anderson	Malibu Day	2009
Pamela Anderson	Malibu Night	2009
Paris Hilton	Paris Hilton	2004
Paris Hilton	Just Me	2005
Paris Hilton	Heiress	2006
Paris Hilton	Can Can	2007
Paris Hilton	Fairy Dust	2008
Paris Hilton	Siren	2009
Paris Hilton	Tease	2010
Paris Hilton	Dazzle	2012
Patti LaBelle	Patti LaBelle	1996
Patti LaBelle	Patti LaBelle Girlfriend	1998
Paulina Rubio	Oro	2009
Pitbull	Pitbull Woman	2013
Pitbull	Pitbull Men	2013
Prince	3121	2007
Priscilla Presley	Moments	1990
Priscilla Presley	Experiences	1993

Celebrity	Scent	Year
Queen Latifah	Queen	2009
Queen Latifah	Queen of Hearts	2010
Reese Witherspoon	Avon In Bloom	2009
Régine	Régine's	1989
Régine	Zoa	1992
Rihanna	Reb'l Fleur	2010
Rihanna	Rebelle	2012
Rihanna	Nude	2012
Rihanna	Rogue	2013
Rihanna	777 Nude by Rihanna "Diamonds"	2013
Salvador Dalí	Salvador Dalí	1983
Samantha "Sammi Sweetheart" Giancola	Dangerous	2011
Samantha "Sammi Sweetheart" Giancola	Dangerous Desires	2012
Sarah Jessica Parker	Lovely	2005
Sarah Jessica Parker	Lovely Liquid Satin	2006
Sarah Jessica Parker	Covet	2007
Sarah Jessica Parker	Endless	2009
Sarah Jessica Parker	Dawn	2009
Sarah Jessica Parker	Twilight	2009
Sarah Jessica Parker	SJP NYC	2010
Sean "Diddy" Combs	Unforgivable	2005
Sean "Diddy" Combs	Unforgivable Woman	2007
Sean "Diddy" Combs	Unforgivable Multi Platinum	2007
Sean "Diddy" Combs	Unforgivable Black	2008
Sean "Diddy" Combs	Unforgivable Woman Black	2008
Sean "Diddy" Combs	I Am King	2008

APPENDIX

Celebrity	Scent	Year
Sean "Diddy" Combs	I Am King of the Night	2009
Sean "Diddy" Combs	Unforgivable Night	2009
Sean "Diddy" Combs	Empress	2011
Selena Gomez	Selena Gomez Eau de Parfum	2012
Shakira	S by Shakira	2010
Shakira	S by Shakira Eau Florale	2011
Shakira	Elixir	2012
Shakira	S by Shakira Aquamarine	2013
Shakira	Wild Elixir	2013
Shakira	Aphrodisiac Elixir	2014
Shania Twain	Shania by Stetson	2005
Shania Twain	Shania Starlight	2007
Sophia Loren	Sophia	1981
Princess Stéphanie of Monaco	Stéphanie	1989
Princess Stéphanie of Monaco	L'Insaisissable	1991
Taylor Swift	Wonderstruck	2011
Taylor Swift	Wonderstruck Enchanted	2012
Taylor Swift	Taylor	2013
Taylor Swift	Taylor by Taylor Swift Made of Starlight Musical Edition	2013
Tilda Swinton	Etat Libre d'Orange Like This	2010
Tim McGraw	McGraw	2008
Tim McGraw	Southern Blend	2009
Tim McGraw	Silver	2010
Tim McGraw	Soul2Soul for Him	2012
Tim McGraw	Soul2Soul Vintage for Him	2013
Twiggy	Twiggy Eau de Parfum	2012
Usher	Usher for Men	2007

Celebrity	Scent	Year
Usher	Usher for Women	2007
Usher	UR for Men	2008
Usher	UR for Women	2008
Usher	VIP	2009
Zsa Zsa Gabor	Zig Zag	1969

Acknowledgments

Fashion's seminal shift toward celebrities was bound to follow the democratization of the fashion industry, which I first explored in my 1999 book *The End of Fashion: The Mass Marketing of the Clothing Business*. As I watched *Project Runway* catch on as a prime-time TV hit, The Row by the Olsen twins become a coveted luxury label overnight, and stars like Nicole Kidman, George Clooney, and Cate Blanchett join Anna Wintour on the receiving line at the Costume Institute Ball every year, I felt it was high time for me to do another book.

My agent, Howard Yoon of the Ross Yoon Agency, loved hearing my ideas about celebrities and fashion when we first talked it over a lunch in New York in November 2011. I tapped out a book proposal, and then Howard made me think some more and refine it further. A huge thanks to Howard for his spot-on guidance and his stellar connections—namely, the excellent Tom Shroder, a former *Washington Post Magazine* editor and a four-time author in his own right. Tom is a journalist's dream: a hard wall to throw a ball against, and I can't thank him enough. Howard sent me to journalist Julia Livshin, who was invaluable in gathering and clearing all the photos. Ross Yoon's associate Anna Sproul-Latimer also worked on my proposal.

Thanks to editor Charles Flowers, my shepherd with *The End of Fashion*, who weighed in early when I needed him.

At Gotham Books, I am deeply indebted to editorial director Lauren Marino, who has been a rock-steady coach and who commissioned the arresting art for the cover. Her editorial assistant, Emily Wunderlich, was a huge help with the pictures and logistics. Bill Shinker was an early fan of my book, and I value his support.

Two savvy Fashion Institute of Technology students, Caroline Nelson and Olivia Grow, came to me via FIT professor Lynda Johnson. Caroline and Olivia tackled a grab bag of tasks, including compiling the lists of celebrity designers and celebrity fragrances in the appendix.

This is my thirtieth year affiliated with *The Wall Street Journal*—twenty-five years as a full-time staff writer, followed by the past five years as a contributor, continuing my weekly "Ask Teri" fashion Q & A column. My *WSJ* chums—past and present—are stellar, and they pitched in with suggestions, sources, and careful readings of chapters, especially the talented Johnnie Roberts. I am indebted to Deborah Ball, *WSJ* Rome bureau chief and author of *House of Versace*, and to my *WSJ* friends in the New York bureau: Rachel Dodes (who compiled some key stats), Ray Smith, Elizabeth Holmes, Dana Mattioli, Ellen Byron, Lisa Vickery, and Vanessa O'Connell. Regards to my "Ask Teri" editors Emily Nelson and Elizabeth Seay. Other *WSJ* alumni lent their moral support, including Maureen Kline, Ken Wells, Eileen Daspin, Bridget O'Brian, James B. Stewart, Jane Berentson, Ellen Joan Pollock, Alessandra Galloni, Alexandra Peers, Carolyn Phillips, Linda Williams, Doug Blackmon, Chuck Stevens, and Joe Davidson.

Every writer needs an Auntie Mame like *Allure*'s Joan Kron, a veteran book author who is eighty-six years young and still scooping reporters less than half her age. Joan doles out her famous "chocolate chips" (she coined it—I stole it!), juicy nuggets of advice that always lead me in the right direction. She and her *High-Tech* coauthor Suzy Slesin, founder of Pointed Leaf Press, shared so many smart ideas with me.

A hearty thanks to my BFFs (Best Friends in Fashion), journalists who unselfishly shared their keen insights and best sources, starting with Cathy Horyn, Robin Givhan, Constance White, Eric Wilson, Elizabeth Snead, Adam Glassman, and Lisa Marsh. Thank you to editors Susan Kaufman of *People StyleWatch* and Glenda Bailey of *Harper's Bazaar*. I love my longtime buddies at Hearst Magazines: Michael Clinton and Ellen Levine.

I am so grateful to *Vogue*'s Anna Wintour, fashion's champion angel, for her interview, in her latest act of camaraderie and kindness to me over the years.

Thanks to fashion historians: my dear friend in Paris, Pamela Golbin, chief curator of the Musée de la Mode et du Textile; Valerie Steele, FIT professor and author; Harold Koda, head of the Costume Institute at the Metropolitan Museum of Art; and my friend and author Caroline Rennolds Milbank.

The *Los Angeles Times*'s fashion writing couple, Booth Moore and Adam Tschorn, generously hosted me at their cozy "Hotel California" guest cottage, and thanks to my Kansas City mentee Anthony Walker, who drove me around the freeways. Also in Los Angeles I thank: Janice Min, Wanda McDaniel, Bob Mackie, Cameron Silver, Rachel Zoe, Rodger Berman, Marilyn Hester, and Frances Pennington.

A special thanks to the photographers of Patrick McMullan Company and Billy Farrell Agency.

For more than two years, I interviewed nearly 150 people, a number of whom asked to remain anonymous. I thank each one for their time and thoughtful reflections, allowing me to write the story with authority. Listed here in no special order, special thanks to: Vince Camuto, Alex Del Cielo, Sarah Goldstein, Tommy Hilfiger, Andy Hilfiger, John Varvatos, Robert Verdi, Natalie Massenet, Sarah Jessica Parker, Jennifer Hudson, Patrick Robinson, Alber Elbaz, Heather Thomson, Fern Mallis, Tory Burch, Brigitte Kleine, Ralph Rucci, Michael Kors, Anne Waterman Bassin, Diane von Furstenberg, Pharrell Williams, Catherine Walsh, Bernd Beetz, Ashley Barrett, Allan Mottus, Rachel Johnson, Keith Estabrook, Phillip Bloch, Jo Piazza, Lori Goldstein, Martine Reardon, Robin Reibel, Elina Kazan, Orlando Veras, John Demsey, Karen Khoury,

Karen Grant, Joe Spellman, Elizabeth Musmanno, Mark Lee, Hamilton South, Lynn Tesoro, Paul Wilmot, Hampton Carney, Tony Melillo, Elena Romero, Ted Marlow, Andrew Blecher, Mark Ellwood, Mark Locks, Jameel Spencer, Simon Doonan, Julie Gilhart, Robert Burke, Richard Jaffe, Emil Wilbekin, June Ambrose, Jaqui Lividini, Lori Rhodes, Mary Alice Stephenson, Kelly Cutrone, Theo Spilka, Rick Gelber, Lola Ogunnaike, Stephanie Solomon, and Robert Thompson.

I am grateful to my other fashion industry sources; I just hope I remembered you all: Linda Gaunt, Avery Baker, Steven Kolb, Lisa Smilor, Michael Gould, Katy Sweet, Dawn Brown, Audrey Smaltz, Bud and Colleen Konheim, Tracy Reese, Byron Lars, Maury Rogoff, Tom Julian, Kim Cihlar, Marylou Luther, Eric Rothfeld, Jeanne Beker, Larry Leeds, Stacy Berns, Deirdre Quinn, King Chong, Edward Wilkerson, Jim Fingeroth, Molly Morse, Jeffrey Banks, Mary Ann Wheaton, Terry Tinson, Mimi Plange, and Patrick O'Connell.

I send hugs to my inner tribe: my dear sister Genie Agins and her husband, Chris Nunes, and my nephew, Taylor Nunes Agins. E. Diane White, Jill Hudson Neal, and my Wellesley posse—Gay Young (who came up with "Hijacking" for my title), Marie Brooks, Zoe Bush, and Terry Gibralter. And: Christine Bates, Peter Greenough, Charlotte Greenough, Nick Greenough, Patrick O'Connell, Janice Blansit, Terry Kolich, Susan Fales-Hill, Wanda Dooley, Judy Byrd, Kevin Merida, Eric McKissack, Cheryl Mayberry McKissack, Gayle Townsend, Teresa Wiltz, Sharon Stangenes, Stanford Williams, Fatima Tomas, Idelcy Lando, and Hila Sabin.

Here's to you, dear, departed "PW"—Mommy—resting in peace, assured that I finished my second book.

Teri Agins

New York, May 2014

Notes on Sources

Hijacking the Runway is based on nearly 150 interviews, most of which were conducted between November 2011 and February 2014 in New York and Los Angeles. Individuals who I quoted directly are clearly depicted in the text, such as "he says," "said to me," "told me," or "remembered." I also used direct quotations from people I previously interviewed in my own published *Wall Street Journal* articles. I relied on verbatim quotations from some individuals when they had spoken on camera, which I transcribed from videos posted on websites such as YouTube.

My reporting includes secondary material from my own articles and from books, newspapers, magazines, court papers, blogs, and financial documents issued by publicly traded companies; such references and attributions are cited throughout the book where they occur. Publications such as *WWD, The Wall Street Journal, The New York Times, Vanity Fair, Vogue, Hollywood Reporter,* and *Forbes* were particularly important to me.

I developed the fashion beat at *The Wall Street Journal* starting around 1989, and for more than twenty years I was the lead fashion writer for the paper. I was an eyewitness to fashion history—the runway shows, parties, and assorted public and private events—some of which I describe in detail in *Hijacking the Runway*. I included anecdotes with reenacted dialogue drawn from my clear recollections or from the first-hand accounts of the people who were there. But I never depict such conversations as direct quotations in this book. There are a few instances where I used anonymous quotes in the text; I attempted to verify the account by cross-checking with at least one other source.

The selected lists of Celebrity Fashion Lines and Celebrity Fragrances were compiled by Caroline Nelson and Olivia Grow, under my supervision. We used various trade sources to locate and fact-check as many brands as we could. Any omissions or errors are unintentional and are my own.

Photography Credits

Interior

Page xiv: Bill Davila/Startraks Photo

Page xv: Seth Browarnik/WorldRedEye.com

Page 2: © Corbis

Page 5: © George Hurrell

Page 6: Popperfoto/Getty Images

Page 9: © David Seymour/Magnum Photos

Page 14: Fred Hayman Archives

Page 18: © Bill Nation

Page 23: AP Photo/Eric Draper

Page 24: Courtesy of Herkko Hietanen

Pages 34, 132, and 135: BFAnyc.com

Pages 40, 142, and 184: WENN.com

Page 43: © Dan & Corina Lecca

Page 48: Antony Jones/UK Press/Getty Images

Page 51: AP Photo/Charles Sykes

Page 59: Courtesy of Vincent Camuto from his personal collection. Photographer unknown.

Page 74: Courtesy of Tory Burch

Page 80: PatrickMcMullan.com

Page 87: AP Photo/Lynne Sladky

Page 100: Unimediaimages Inc./Paris

Page 113: AP Photo/Evan Agostini

Both images on page 114: Copyright © 2011 by Deborah Vankin/*Los Angeles Times*. Reprinted with permission.

Page 127: Macy's, Inc.

Page 137: Thomas Monaster/*New York Daily News* Archive/Getty Images

Page 147: Courtesy of Yakini Etheridge of RealityTVFashion.com

Page 158: Chris Polk/FilmMagic for Bragman Nyman Cafarelli/Getty Images

Page 161: AP Photo/Jason DeCrow

Page 172: Pierre Verdy/AFP/Getty Images

Page 184: Courtesy of A.P.C.

Page 200: © Splash News/Corbis

Page 224: *WWD*

Page 226: Courtesy of Danny Clinch and John Varvatos

Page 228: Courtesy of Chrysler Group LLC and John Varvatos

Insert

Jessica Simpson in Daisy Dukes: John Smith/Startraks Photo

Rachel Zoe in sunglasses: Bauer-Griffin

Jessica Simpson in sunglasses: Wayne Maser/Trunk Archive

Jessica Simpson with shoes and hangbag: Ruven Afanador

Julius Erving and Michael Jordan: Dick Raphael/NBAE/Getty Images

Fendi bags: *WWD*

Sketch of Armani gown: Courtesy of Giorgio Armani

Cate Blanchett: Wally Skalij/*Los Angeles Times*. Reprinted with permission

Tory Burch in her boutique: © Jeffrey Prehn

Tory Burch with the Camutos, and Sean Combs with Tommy Hilfiger and Calvin Klein: PatrickMcMullan.com

Jessica Alba, Tory Burch, and Ginnifer Goodwin at the Met Ball; Jennifer Lopez and Michael Kors at the Met Ball; and Anna Wintour, Tom Ford, and Julianne Moore at the Met Ball: BFAnyc.com

Sean John billboard: Scott Gries/Getty Images

Sean John invitation: Courtesy of the author

Lady Gaga: Timothy A. Clary/AFP/Getty Images

Jennifer Lopez with her perfume: Christopher Polk/Getty Images for Coty

The Kardashian sisters: © Annie Leibovitz/Contact Press Images

Kanye West: Nick Harvey/WireImage/Getty Images

Victoria and David Beckham: Kevin Mazur/WireImage for Chopard/Getty Images

Victoria Beckham in her design studio: Robert Fairer/*The New York Times*/Redux

Victoria Beckham modeling one of her designs: © Splash News/Corbis

Mary-Kate and Ashley Olsen with Lauren Hutton: Nancy Kaszerman/ZUMAPRESS.com

Index